What people are saying about …

TRANSFORMING CHURCH

"I found this thoughtful discussion to be a breath of fresh air. Intense, realistic research highlights our root problem: emphasizing church breadth instead of church health. Read and reflect on the probing questions of this book. When consistently applied with dependence on the Holy Spirit, watch for transformation in a church. One size does not fit all—every community demands unique leadership, seeking the vitality of each member in the pursuit of God's divine pattern. This book is outstanding—one of the best I've read in years. A real winner!"

Howard G. Hendricks, Center for Christian
Leadership, Dallas Theological Seminary

"Kevin Ford has given us a biblically grounded, well-researched, culturally incisive book. It will help professional and volunteer church leaders exercise leadership as our churches are transformed and, in turn, our communities are transformed; an important resource as the church navigates through challenging and often hostile waters."

Charles W. Colson, founder and chairman of Prison Fellowship

"If you want to know what makes churches vital for their members and agents of transformation for their communities, this book will answer your questions. This is a well-written compilation of case studies that anyone committed to growing healthy churches will want to read."

Tony Campolo, professor emeritus at Eastern University

"All too frequently the essential signs of a healthy church rely on anecdotes and biased selectivity. Kevin provides a solid research basis for the five indicators he explores in this book. Furthermore, he provides a balance between institutional and contextual factors, and offers valuable insights for leaders who are seeking to transition their churches from inertia to missional engagement within their ministry contexts."

Eddie Gibbs, professor of church growth at Fuller Theological Seminary

"Based on thorough research of the American church, *Transforming Church* offers no quick fixes. But it does offer tools for the hard work of nurturing genuine community, clear identity, focused mission, and hope for the future."

Grant Wacker, professor of Christian history at Duke University

"Why hasn't the American church transformed American culture; indeed, why hasn't it transformed the world? Kevin Ford offers some brutally honest answers to these questions and proposes some remedies that confront the status quo. *Transforming Church* may not provide easy answers for church leaders—but those with the courage to read it will find their reward."

Rich Stearns, president of World Vision United States

"This is the most savvy book I've read yet on leading change in the church. Change is often agonizingly slow. With solid research, remarkable wisdom, and the loving heart of a mentor, Kevin Graham Ford comes alongside church leaders and provides clear road signs for a fantastic journey of transformation. This is not a simple how-to book but rather a companion for the way."

Stephen A. Hayner, professor of evangelism and church growth at Columbia Theological Seminary

"*Transforming Church* is required reading for anyone serious about creating healthy, relational, biblically grounded, twenty-first-century communities. I'll warn you—there is nothing easy about this book, but it is definitely worth reading."

Walt Kallestad, senior pastor of Community Church of Joy

"For all who are like me and love the local church, please read and savor this book. The book diagnoses many of the maladies afflicting local congregations and then, through both prose and wonderful stories, tells us stories of beauty out of near ashes."

Lon Allison, director of the Billy Graham Center, Wheaton College

"I have read and reread *Transforming Church* because it touches the essence of what it is to be a biblical, Christ-centered, missional community of faith. Kevin Ford's five key indicators and their continuums will provoke healthy self-analysis for any sincere pastor and/or church board. This book, taken seriously, will shake us out of our complacency while encouraging us to be what we are meant to be, not a clone of some church-of-what's-happening-now consumer-oriented model."

John A. Huffman Jr., chairman, board of directors of Christianity Today International

"Nearly all organizations today face adaptive challenges that require new ways of practicing leadership. Churches are no exception. Thriving in a changing world demands ongoing renewal and adaptive work. Kevin Ford provides an outstanding resource, rooted in groundbreaking research, to the church community and beyond. This book is deeply insightful, comprehensive, and inspiringly practical. I highly commend it to anyone with the courage to lead adaptive change."

Ronald A. Heifetz, founding director of Harvard University's Center for Public Leadership

"I'm always on the hunt for books that get at the root issues of how churches can be more effective. I found one in *Transforming Church* and devoured it in a weekend read."

Alan Nelson, executive editor of *Rev! Magazine*

"Every so often, I'll come across a book that captures the essence of an issue so perfectly that it makes me want to stand up and say, 'That's it!' *Transforming Church* is one of those rare books. It gets to the heart of what hurts the church and what helps it to become everything that Jesus calls it to be. This essential book deserves a place on your bookshelf or night table."

Bob Coy, senior pastor of Calvary Chapel, Ft. Lauderdale

"Kevin Ford combines theological wisdom, on-the-ground experience, and insightful practical judgment in this terrific book that will transform your thinking and your leadership. I recommend it with great enthusiasm."

L. Gregory Jones, dean and professor of theology at Duke Divinity School

"I've been a pastor for twenty-nine years and the five indexes Kevin Ford looks at were the biggest gains in my pastoral life. They're like five rulers that help you measure where you're going and they light the path."

Greg Wenhold, senior pastor of Good Shepherd
Lutheran Church of Naperville

TRANSFORMING
CHURCH

TRANSFORMING
CHURCH

Bringing out the good to get to great

KEVIN G. FORD

David C Cook®
transforming lives together

TRANSFORMING CHURCH
Published by David C. Cook
4050 Lee Vance View
Colorado Springs, CO 80918 U.S.A.

David C. Cook Distribution Canada
55 Woodslee Avenue, Paris, Ontario, Canada N3L 3E5

David C. Cook U.K., Kingsway Communications
Eastbourne, East Sussex BN23 6NT, England

David C. Cook and the graphic circle C logo
are registered trademarks of Cook Communications Ministries.

The Web site addresses recommended throughout this book are offered as a resource to
you. These Web sites are not intended in any way to be or imply an endorsement on the
part of David C. Cook, nor do we vouch for their content.

Unless otherwise noted, all Scripture quotations are taken from the *Holy Bible, New
International Version®*. *NIV®*. Copyright © 1973, 1978, 1984 by International Bible
Society. Used by permission of Zondervan. All rights reserved. Scripture quotations
marked NLT are taken from the *Holy Bible, New Living Translation*, copyright © 1996.
Used by permission of Tyndale House Publishers, Inc., Wheaton, Illinois 60189. All rights
reserved; NKJV are taken from the New King James Version. Copyright © 1982 by Thomas
Nelson, Inc. Used by permission. All rights reserved; MSG are taken from *THE MESSAGE*.
Copyright © by Eugene H. Peterson 1993, 1994, 1995, 1996, 2000, 2001, 2002. Used
by permission of NavPress Publishing Group; NASB are taken from the *New American
Standard Bible*, © Copyright 1960, 1995 by The Lockman Foundation. Used by permission.

LCCN 2008935939
ISBN 978-1-4347-6704-2
eISBN 978-1-4347-6458-4

© 2008 Kevin Graham Ford

First edition published by SaltRiver/Tyndale
© 2007 Kevin Graham Ford, ISBN 978-1-4143-0893-7

The Team: Don Pape, Susan Tjaden, Amy Kiechlin, Jack Campbell, and Karen Athen
Cover Design: Julie Chen
Cover Photo: © Corbis Images

Printed in the United States of America
Second Edition 2008

3 4 5 6 7 8 9 10 11 12

102909

To Caroline, with love and gratitude

CONTENTS

ACKNOWLEDGMENTS

This book represents the collaborative effort of many people to whom I am indebted. I thank God for the love of my life, Caroline, my best friend, and a wonderful mother to our daughters, Anabel and Leighton, who endured too many nights apart while I wrote this book from hotel rooms or on airplanes. I am also grateful for the people who have made this book possible. Rob Wilkins, an outstanding journalist, did a fantastic job interviewing pastors and church members throughout North America. I credit Rob with the majority of initial drafting, on-site interviews, and narrative development for this book. Todd Hahn, a close friend and talented writer, was the closer. Over a short period of time, Todd gave life to this book.

I am also thankful for the intellectual capital that came from my colleagues at TAG Consulting, who supported the initial research efforts, continue to teach me a great deal about leadership, and help make me a better person. In addition, Beth Warden was extremely helpful in collecting trend data from churches. Don Smith of QED Consulting conducted the initial statistical analysis. Mark Brekke of Brekke Associates has been extremely helpful in the ongoing scientific research and statistical analysis for the Transforming Church Index. John Eames has been a terrific agent. Don Pape, Susan Tjaden, and the team at David C. Cook have been extremely helpful in supporting this project and partnering on future endeavors. Tom McCain, John Holm, Trevor Bron, and Scott Kronlund helped greatly in enhancing and revising the paperback manuscript. Karen Robbins, my administrative assistant, has helped keep my schedule manageable so that I had time to write. I also appreciate the relationships that I have developed with many of the pastors and leaders who are mentioned in this book. The pastors and churches in the Transforming Church Institute have become great sounding boards for the practical applications of these concepts.

My parents and extended family have been an inspiration and support to me in so many ways. Most important, I thank God for showing me grace, mercy, and unconditional love. Although I don't deserve it, I need it. I pray this book brings glory to Him.

FOREWORD

Since the beginning of our ministry, my team and I were convinced of the importance of the local church, and we committed ourselves to do all we could to work with the church. In fact, when Kevin Ford's father, Leighton Ford—my longtime associate and brother-in-law—joined our team, I asked him to be director of church relations for our first New York City crusade. He spent many months working with the churches to ensure that the crusade's results would last. This became a pattern for all our crusades.

And yet repeatedly over the years I have encountered discouraged pastors, dispirited church members, and ineffective churches. Only a transformed church can make an impact for Christ. But why do so many churches fail in this? And how can they change?

These are the questions Kevin Ford seeks to answer in this important and insightful book. Drawing on his intensive research and wide experience with churches, and with a clear vision of what the local church should be, Kevin delves into the deeper issues pastors and congregations must face. He promises no easy answers or quick fixes, but he does set forth a blueprint for church renewal that cannot help but transform our churches—and our lives. This book is "must reading" for every pastor and church leader, and I pray for its widest circulation.

—Billy Graham
Montreat, North Carolina

GETTING STARTED

If you're like me, you are always tempted to skip a book's introduction. I hope you don't. This is a book about the transforming church, and it describes a journey that takes years. Likewise, this book is not a quick read. It is best to take your time. Don't try to hurry ahead. Read and reread.

If you are looking for easy answers or seven steps, stop now. You will be disappointed. We live in a world of quick fixes, instant diets, thirty-minute delivery guarantees, and great abs in seven minutes a day. Yet we all know the best things in life take time. If you have the courage to begin the journey, I encourage you to keep reading.

Grass and Soil

When my family moved into a planned community in northern Virginia several years ago, I set my sights upon the perfect lawn. I didn't have a lot to work with; new construction left my lawn looking like it had endured an elephant stampede.

After clearing brush, barbed wire, and remnants of Civil War–era fences, I decided to plant grass seed. Somehow, it worked. My lawn became lush green, and I was impressed with myself. In my self-induced grandiosity, I imagined receiving a call from one of those home-makeover shows on the Home & Garden Television network. To keep the place looking like a fairway at Augusta National, I carefully followed a list of suggestions from a local nursery for proper fertilization, moisture, and weed control.

And then came our first summer. Within weeks, our yard was overrun with crabgrass and other ugly weeds. Splotches of brown replaced the lush green. By the time freezing temperatures had put it—and me—out of our misery, my lawn had become more spotted than a leopard, and I had a hard time looking my neighbors in the eye. But I refused to surrender.

I hired a lawn company to kill the weeds, and by early November things were starting to look better. Through the winter and spring my hopes rose, and by early June, the lawn was actually looking pretty good again. I imagined myself grilling brats and dispensing lawn-care advice to my admiring neighbors.

But then came the heat wave. Less than halfway through the summer, I was on a first-name basis with most of the workers from the lawn-care company. I put their numbers on my cell phone's speed dial. They treated the lawn again and again, but soon it looked worse than ever.

At the end of my rope and nearly broke, I asked a friend for advice. He recommended that I call a guy named Mark. Mark wasn't a flashy guy, but after twenty years of living and working in the area, he knew the lay of the land. When he came over to look at my lawn, I shared my sad story, with a few conspiracy theories about lawn-care companies sprinkled in.

When I finished, Mark looked at me and said, "Kevin, the problem is not the grass. The problem is the soil." Pointing to the brush and cedars behind my property, he continued, "Those ugly shrubs and trees grow best in bad soil. If you want a good lawn, you have to start with good soil. You've been applying chemicals to the grass. But the only way to prevent crabgrass and weeds is for your good grass to be thick and lush. You can't have thick, lush grass without good soil—and that will take at least five years to develop." His tips for me concerned improving the soil, not the grass: He told me to stop bagging the clippings, mulch the grass, apply a topdressing every two years, and make sure I aerated the soil at least once a year.

At first, I didn't like what Mark said. Surely in this age of advanced technology, there was a quick-fix chemical or a miracle treatment that would restore my grass to green splendor in a week or so. Waiting through a long process of growth and health didn't appeal to me. I had neighbors to impress, after all. And my dreams of being on the Home & Garden Television network were fading fast.

But Mark was right. Today, gazing at a mostly healthy lawn, I realize how much money, time, and energy I would have saved had I started with Mark's strategy. It takes years to grow a healthy lawn.

And it takes years to grow a healthy church. But too often, pastors and church leaders focus on the wrong issues: the grass rather than the soil. Their tendency is to focus on what Harvard leadership experts Ron Heifetz and Marty Linsky call "technical problems" as opposed to the more important and underlying "adaptive issues."[1]

Think of it this way. My lawn represented an adaptive issue. I needed to focus on the soil over a period of years. But my tactic was to focus on the sparse grass—the technical problem, or the symptom. No matter how many chemicals I applied, I couldn't make progress because I was trying to solve the wrong problem. In fact, the more I treated the symptom, the more problems I created: lost time, wasted money, irritated neighbors, and more chemicals in the environment.

Solving my lawn problems was a process. But if I hadn't committed to that process—started on that journey, if you will—I never would have made progress. My lawn wouldn't have changed.

Every church needs transformation. Those that don't change die. Don't get me wrong, I am not advocating change for the sake of change. The wrong kind of change can be toxic. Healthy change, however, is required for growth, maturity, and adaptation. Like any organization, churches can become stagnant, complacent, irrelevant, or ineffective without transformational change to keep them focused on their mission. But without a clear understanding of the nature of change, the chances of growing a healthy church are diminished.

This book is about churches that have the courage to embrace change and to confront adaptive issues head-on—what I call *transforming churches*. These courageous churches help transform people into God's image. They transform the communities in which they minister. And as organizations, they are continually transforming how they lead, operate, and minister.

The Journey of Change

Because change is a journey, our study of transforming churches will take the form of a journey. As part of the trip, I will introduce you to the Transforming Church Index, a congregational survey developed by our consulting firm, TAG Consulting. TAG Consulting has consulted with hundreds of businesses, organizations, government agencies, and churches across the years. We have worked with the largest employers in the nation and with family-owned businesses, but we have a unique passion for the local church. The Transforming Church Index is the centerpiece of the Transforming Church Institute, an ongoing forum where pastors receive professional coaching and strategic planning in a collaborative environment. This survey has taught us much about transforming churches and what it takes for a church to thrive, not only in our present culture but also for years to come. Based on this research, I will introduce you to the five key indicators of church health. Each indicator represents a fork in the road in the journey of change. They are not sequential, yet they cannot be separated. In fact, by concentrating on one, you will address them all.

Throughout our journey, I will tell stories of real churches in the real world. Some are small and some are large. Some are inner city, some suburban, and some rural. Some are traditional, and some are contemporary. Some are well known, but most are not household names. They represent, in many respects, the complexity of the church in America.

For the five primary narratives, I use the churches' real names and locations. For two or three of the shorter anecdotes, I mask the churches' identities out of respect for previous leaders and pastors.

Each of these churches is on a transforming journey, but each is at a different point in the process. We will hear the stories of these five congregations:

- Community Church of Joy, Glendale, Arizona (Evangelical Lutheran Church in America)
- Heritage Church, Moultrie, Georgia (nondenominational)
- Tenth Avenue Church, Vancouver, British Columbia (Christian and Missionary Alliance)
- The Garden, Indianapolis, Indiana (United Methodist Church)

- Fairfax Community Church, Fairfax, Virginia (Church of God, Anderson)

While this book is firmly rooted in solid research and tells the stories of real churches and real people, it also reflects the experiences of my own journey—the good, the bad, and the ugly. Context always impacts us, sometimes for the better and sometimes not. I press on, trusting that God is using the sum of my life experiences to transform me into His image. After all, a transforming church is one that, with God's help, transforms people. And I am one of those people.

It's clear that whether or not a church is effective has much to do with God and how He works through us. I acknowledge that and would never minimize God's role—but how that plays out is a bit of a mystery. We can't measure, predict, or control God's work, but we can measure, predict, and control (to a certain extent) human work. As a result, my focus throughout the book really is on what humans can and should be doing as we continually seek God's will. This book presents universal principles that could be used in any organization, but uniquely applies them to the church.

Navigating This Book

The book begins with an introductory chapter, followed by two chapters (a part 1 and a part 2) on each of the five key indicators of church health. Following each of the odd-numbered chapters, you'll find a "Speed Bump," which is intended to slow you down momentarily to reflect on the preceding material and how it applies to your own unique situation. Speed Bumps feature a "Transforming Church Checkup" section that includes questions to help you evaluate your church in light of the key indicators of church health. "Travel Tips" are provided to assist you in navigating the transforming church journey. And finally, before moving off the Speed Bump, you'll want to check your rearview mirror via the "Reflections" questions. These questions are intended to make you aware of what's going on around you before you travel on to the next chapter.

The journey to become a transforming church is not an easy one. Obstacles and challenges exist at each stage. However, whether you're a pastor, or a lay leader, or a church staff member, this is the most rewarding journey you will ever experience.

Are you ready to start?

1

THE JOURNEY OF CHANGE

Do not conform any longer to the pattern of this world,
but be transformed by the renewing of your mind.
Then you will be able to test and approve what God's
will is—his good, pleasing and perfect will.
—Romans 12:2

Rod Stafford looks out over the sparse congregation gathered in the high school auditorium and feels his spirits sink again. The people sit in quiet clumps, separated by a sea of chairs. This is not how Rod had envisioned things would be.

Rod became the pastor of Fairfax Community Church in 1986. He led the church through gradual yet consistent change to reach out to its community, develop internal leadership, and deploy its members in a wide variety of ministries. The church had adopted a more contemporary worship style and, in less than ten years, saw an increase in worship attendance from one hundred to three hundred.

For nearly fifty years, the congregation had met in an old building on a dead-end street. It faced a tough decision about managing its growth: stay or go. Instead of starting a third service in a cramped facility, they made the bold move to relocate to the auditorium at Fairfax High School. The leaders were fully confident that they would fill the auditorium in no time.

Now, less than two years later, Rod opens his Bible in front of a shrunken and dispirited congregation.

An hour later, Rod closes the service in prayer, knowing it will be another red-sweatshirt day. As he shakes hands with the departing congregation, he can picture himself repeating his Sunday-afternoon ritual: parking the car, unlocking and opening his front door, climbing slowly up the staircase of his house, opening his bedroom closet, selecting the red sweatshirt, putting it on and flipping up the hood, pulling the drawstring so tightly that only his eyes and nose are exposed, heading downstairs, turning on the television, and letting the afternoon stretch into evening, the evening into night, the night into morning. His family knows better than to intrude.

The Journey

I read J. R. R. Tolkien's trilogy, *The Lord of the Rings,* in high school and fell in love with it again through the film series in more recent years. At points in the book I will connect this story—about the epic journey of the hobbit Frodo and his companions—with the journey of becoming a transforming church. The trilogy, which Tolkien described as "fundamentally a religious work," tells the story of the quest to destroy a powerful magic Ring in the fires of Mount Doom to save the world from an evil lord. The destination is critical, but the power of *The Lord of the Rings* occurs in the transforming nature of the journey itself.[2]

A group made up of two men, four hobbits, a wizard, a dwarf, and an elf is named the Fellowship. Confronted with nearly hopeless odds, virtually resigned to defeat, and focused on a cause greater than self-fulfillment, the Fellowship commits itself to the journey together. They will be faithful to their calling, to their mission, and to their love for one another.

It is not just any kind of journey. Tolkien was careful to distinguish between *adventure* and *quest.* The great wizard Gandalf describes an adventure as a matter of choice. It's an undertaking designed primarily as a means to relieve boredom or satisfy a specific lust. Once the particular treasure is found, the adventure is over, and one returns home essentially unchanged by the experience—a "there and back again" affair. A quest, on the other hand, is primarily a response to a compelling call. This kind of journey is risky, uncomfortable, and sometimes simply dreadful. But it is also full of unexpected joy.

The apostle Paul, choosing a parallel metaphor, describes our lives on earth as a pilgrimage to our true home in heaven. The journey lasts from our births to our deaths and, at least on earth, carries no guarantee of "success" or even a final destination. What matters is the transformation in faith that happens along the way.

In my mind, the Fellowship can represent the church in transforming motion. We have no guarantee of success, but if we are faithful to our calling and mission, we will be changed through the journey.

Dead-end Churches

Why is it, then, that so many churches seem stuck at a dead end? As a consultant to hundreds of churches, I hear the same story over and over again. The names and circumstances change, but church leaders ask the same despairing questions: Why are we stuck? Why can't we change? Why aren't lives being changed? Why aren't we going anywhere?

I run into dead-end churches all the time.

It's not that churches deny the need to change—to move out into a transforming journey. Church members frequently invoke the need for transformation when they hire new pastors or ministry leaders. But these same leaders face a paradox: The churches resist the very change they claim to need.

The Age of Rapid Change

We live in an age where change has become the only certainty. Before the advent of the Internet, the amount of information in our world was doubling every two hundred years. Today, the amount of information doubles every eighteen months. While providing more choices, information overload also creates a cynical society. The average American receives 4,200 advertising messages per week—not counting spam or Internet advertising! The rapidly changing landscape has accelerated the breaking up of the modern era; so quickly, in fact, we haven't yet been able to name what will replace it. For the time being, "postmodern" is the best we can do. Boundaries are rapidly disappearing. We live in a global village; we can send e-mails to Thailand in a nanosecond.

In the rush of overwhelming information and new friends, old loyalties break down. Replacing the old geographical boundaries are new "virtual boundaries" for community, such as mission, values, common focus, and vision. In other words, some people feel more connected to an online group—made up of people they have never met and may live very far away from, but who share the same perspective, struggles, or interests—than they do to their family, neighbors, or local church.

In the world's new economy, the value of tangible assets is replaced by intangible assets—knowledge, information, name recognition (brand), market share, and innovation. A virtually unlimited number of consumers can purchase the same knowledge on a Web site at any one point in time, something that's impossible in one physical location. Imagine thousands of people walking into one Barnes & Noble store to purchase John Grisham's latest novel at the same time, and you get the picture. Concurrently, the rise of new generations, all of whom resist conformity, has created an increasing demand for products and services that are custom-tailored to individual needs. This demand has led to a mass-customized economy in which choices among options, sizes, shapes, and colors abound.

The New Economy

New leaps in technology are making it possible for unique products to be produced in response to individual tastes at lower costs. "Build to order" has become the new standard of production. Dell Computers, for example, allows you to "build" your new laptop online. The number of choices is almost mind-boggling. For their low-end home laptop alone, there are 33 different components that altogether have 162 different options to choose from. You can choose from 12 colors, 5 processors, 7 antivirus options, 10 colors of "mice," 4 environmental options, and the list goes on. My calculator cannot even compute the number of different combinations possible from the available options of just this base model! No longer do you have to drive to the local electronics store and purchase a basic gray computer.

Some forward-looking companies have even gone a step further than mass customization. The new trend is toward "cocreation." This means that, rather than inventing new products and services on their own, these innovative companies create them along with their customers in such a way that it provides a unique experience for each customer. As explained in a recent article in the *Washington Post*, whereas mass customization was about "a company offering customers many choices on a wide range of product or service attributes ... the company still had to decide which choices to offer and deliver them. In cocreation, the choices are infinite and the company neither imagines nor delivers them all."[3] One example of cocreation the *Post* presents is the iPod, where Apple created the equipment, but each consumer creates a unique experience by loading their own content, whether it's music, podcasts, or user-created material. Apple then helps distribute some of this material—which they didn't, and quite possibly couldn't, create on their own—through their iTunes online store. I have created numerous "playlists" on my iPod by clicking a few buttons. I have one for an outdoor party, featuring classic rock selections, beach music, Reggae, and other fun music. I have a dinner-party playlist with jazz and crooners. I have a worship playlist for times of meditation and praising God. And I have a seldom-played workout playlist. I'm even in the process of exploring how to upload some of my own original recordings for other people to download. Apple has allowed me to be a cocreator. This concept of cocreation has significant implications for how we do church, and is actually quite biblical. God created us to contribute, create, and actively participate. Why is it that we so often assume that our congregations just want to be spoon-fed?

The world has evolved from an agrarian economy (preindustrial) to a production economy (the Industrial Revolution) to a service economy (post–World War II) to the experience economy of today. In the twenty-first century, consumers look for the experience rather than the service. That is why companies such as Starbucks and Nordstrom offer not just products and services, but also a sensory experience. Take a cup of coffee, for example. In the production economy of the industrial age, coffee beans were a raw commodity, ground and packed in tin cans and sold on the grocery shelf for the equivalent of a few cents for a cup of coffee. In the service economy just after World War II, that same cup of coffee could be had at a diner for just a few cents more as customers paid for the production and the service. But today, in the experience economy, that same cup of coffee is now premium roasted, exotically flavored, converted into latte or espresso, and sold in fine-dining establishments and java hangouts for three dollars a cup.

The bottom line is that today's consumers don't buy a product; they buy an experience. Young consumers will scrimp on the staples of life to have more money to spend on a weekend snowboarding in Vail or mountain biking in the Andes. They crave the *experience*. Companies like Barnes & Noble and Borders have successfully reshaped the bookselling business—not just by discounting prices, but also by offering an enjoyable ambience with caffe latte and elegant lounges. In short, they have turned book browsing into an *experience*.

In the new economy, where people flow in and out of organizations according to changing conditions, hiring and pay are based on the ability to adapt, think, communicate, lead, flex, and innovate. When unemployment levels are low, employees can pick and choose jobs. If compensation and interest are basically the same, they will choose the better environment. Even if compensation and job interest are slightly lacking, they will choose the experiential environment. The old model of the paternalistic corporation offering lifelong jobs, guaranteed advances, and a testimonial dinner and gold watch at age sixty-five is a thing of the past. In the new model, companies are flexible, offering employees an opportunity for personal and professional growth in an environment that is open and honest and that treats them fairly. Today's employees no longer build loyalty, they build résumés—and employers accept this. After channel surfing and Web surfing, the next logical step was job surfing.

And this is the context in which the transforming church must thrive.

The church has the ability to influence the culture and shape the future. We have an important and life-changing message to share. But can we find a way to remain relevant, to change where needed yet still hold to our essential values? How can we "cocreate" church with God and with His people? How do healthy churches do that?

The Church's Primary Struggle

Our company, TAG Consulting, has consulted with hundreds of businesses and organizations, including several of the largest employers in the nation. While we see resistance to change in many industries, it seems somehow more pronounced in churches. Our company has done national research through the Transforming Church Index, a congregational survey. We discovered that the statement "Changes are readily embraced by our congregation" received the sixth-lowest affirmative score out of the 110 questions asked. In fact, nine of the ten lowest-scoring questions in the national database were somehow related to the process of change.

Leading change in a change-resistant subculture is a tough gig. It is made even tougher by the fact that most pastors, by their own admission, lack change-leadership skills.

A 2001 Barna study revealed that, while 63 percent of Protestant pastors believe they have the gift of teaching, only 11 percent believe they have the gift of leadership.[4] Another Barna study suggested that only 14 percent believe they are good at thinking and acting strategically. Other studies say that 80 percent of pastors feel frustrated in their roles and 95 percent have experienced significant conflict in their ministries. A poll by *Christianity Today* asked church leaders, "What's your strongest leadership trait?" Only 1 percent of pastors surveyed cited conflict management as their strongest trait while, at the same time, that skill ranked as the second most underrated.[5]

Strategic thinking, conflict-management skills, leadership savvy— these are all key ingredients in change-leadership and in transforming churches. Yet these are the very skills that pastors, by their own admission, are lacking.

The consequences are predictable. A Duke University study of major denominations discovered that 15 percent of pastors who were ordained in 1988 left the ministry within thirteen years. Those pastors cited lack of denominational support, burnout, discouragement, and conflict among the primary factors.

The recursive pattern of *desire change … resist change … desire change … resist change* becomes the formula for discouragement, burnout, and frustration among pastors, staff, leaders, and members.

Change is hard because change creates pain. But healthy churches—transforming churches—somehow manage to embrace change. Is there a magic pill?

The Transforming Church Index

During the first few years of our consulting work, members of TAG Consulting often operated like doctors forced to practice medicine with few diagnostic tools. In an effort to help churches identify the underlying causes of the problems they faced, we sorted through lists of symptoms. Mostly we were forced into calculated guesses about the deeper issues.

After awhile, we began to see some of the same problems resurface in predictable patterns. Slowly, we began to develop the ability to frame questions to uncover some critical issues, such as how well a church navigates change, resolves tough issues, defines and clarifies its identity and purpose, develops healthy community, equips members for ministry, mentors leaders, manages conflict, assimilates people, communicates with members, and impacts the local community.

The informal questions began to formalize over time, with input from management scholars, pastors, laypeople, and statisticians. We started collecting data, quantifying the results, running statistical reports, and analyzing the trends. Approximately 110 questions made the cut for the final survey, with about 50 providing the most significant information on church health. The survey is now called the Transforming Church Index, or TCIndex for short.

We have collected more than 25,000 surveys in our database, which includes data from churches of all sizes, models, denominations, and national locations. We found that the data initially "clustered" around five key indicators of church health. Each key indicator was a group of between ten and twenty questions from our survey. (More recent analysis has revealed fifteen clusters, subdivided under the initial five.) Based on those clusters, we were able to establish a norm for each key indicator.

We then queried the database for two types of churches: those that scored above the norm on at least four of the five key indicators and those that scored below the norm on four of the five key indicators. The national norm is not a perfect way of determining whether or not a church is healthy, since that would presume that 50 percent of American churches are healthy, but it was the most useful way that we could think of to establish a norm.

Once we had our two sets (healthier churches and not-so-healthy churches), we collected trend information related to membership, worship attendance, giving, and member involvement in ministry.

Many of our findings didn't surprise us. We had assumed healthy churches would be growing churches, and that assumption proved true—posting, on average, 21 percent membership and 28 percent attendance growth over a five-year span. In contrast, the not-so-healthy churches declined by 2.4 percent in membership and 5.7 percent in worship attendance over a five-year period.

Similarly, we were not surprised to see a significant increase in giving among the healthy churches, while the less-healthy churches barely kept up with inflation. This wasn't quantum physics. But it was important for us to demonstrate a basic correlation between core characteristics of health and positive growth trends.

So what did surprise us? For one, there were some very large and fast-growing churches that showed up on the list of not-so-healthy churches. Eventually, we came to the same conclusion as Jim Collins, author of *Good to*

Great. In a *Leadership* article titled "The Good to Great Pastor," Collins said, "Greatness does not always equal bigness. Big is not great and great is not big. In fact, the bigger you become the harder it may be to remain great."[6]

Healthy churches are usually growing churches, but growing churches are not always healthy churches.

Nothing could have prepared us for the biggest surprise from our data. We had expected a slight gap between the two sets in "members involved in ministry," but what we found more closely resembled a canyon: Among healthy churches, 93 percent of members considered themselves to be involved in some form of ministry (though not necessarily at their church), compared to only 11 percent of members in the less-healthy churches.

The picture was becoming a bit clearer. Church health, rather than church growth, was the primary indicator of a church's ability to transform its members, fulfill its mission, and reinvent itself.

The Five Key Indicators

As we continued to analyze the TCIndex results, we began to see the data organizing itself into patterns. We came to agree that each of the five key indicators of church health would have an underlying "problem" at one end of its dimension and a "solution" at the other end. The indicators have to do with the following:

1. How church members relate to one another. Unhealthy churches are a collection of people acting individually, while healthy churches relate as a community. We call this *consumerism vs. community.*
2. The church's "genetic code." Unhealthy churches lack a clear identity, while healthy churches have a clear sense of their DNA and take steps to align their ministries and culture with their code. We refer to this as *incongruence vs. code.*
3. The church's leadership. Unhealthy churches tend to be overly auto-cratic or bureaucratic, while healthy churches view leadership as a

shared function and as a ministry. The term we use for this is *autocracy vs. shared leadership.*

4. How the church relates to the local community. Unhealthy churches disengage from the world around them, while healthy churches are focused on their mission and have an outward orientation that starts with their own locale. We call this *cloister vs. missional.*

5. How church members think about the future. Unhealthy churches resist change and fear or deny the future, while healthy churches embrace change, even when it is painful. Our term for this is *inertia vs. reinvention.*

That's when it hit us: The problem side of each indicator correlates directly to a dysfunction in modern Western culture. Our culture is all too often characterized as a collection of individuals disconnected from one another, drifting without an overarching story or unifying values, expecting someone else to solve our problems, largely self-serving, and resistant to change. The parallels between these symptoms and the problem sides of unhealthy churches were too striking to ignore.

The church desires to change the surrounding culture. The truth, however, is that the church has been infected by the very culture it seeks to transform.

And this reality poses a question or three. How can we engage the culture without being co-opted? What would it actually look like to transform our culture rather than simply talking about it? And what exactly constitutes meaningful change anyway?

Five Movements

The Bible is clear that God has a hope and dream for the church to be a living community. For example, the early church is described as generous, caring, devoted to prayer and teaching, outwardly focused, and united in purpose (Acts 2:42–47). We were struck that each of the dysfunctions was in direct opposition to this description. The common thread running through all five dysfunctions is the overriding tendency to shift the focus from the biblical "we" to a cultural "me." The real work of the church—what I will refer to as *adaptive change*—is largely a movement along each of the key indicators, from cultural dysfunction to biblical dynamic.

1. Consumerism/Community

In our culture, the consumer is the center. This is perhaps the culmination of our nation's grand experiment with rampant individualism. Our economy and its attendant competition are designed to feed the ongoing cycle of consumption. Service industries have reached new heights in quality of service and attention, all with the goal of reaching more consumers and causing current consumers to consume more and more.

The church is not immune to the consumer mind-set. By focusing primarily on meeting "market" needs, the church often functions in production mode, looking to the endless creation of the best possible programs, products, and events. While such a search for excellence is, by itself, a positive—even biblical—pursuit, the machinery of endless production works against the development of community. Why is this? It's rather simple: A continual focus on feeding "me" rarely creates the more biblical and unifying "us."

2. Incongruence/Code

Who can forget the Enron scandal of the early twenty-first century? Whatever Enron's problems, the cause was not the company's stated core values: *Excellence. Integrity. Communication. Respect.* The problem was the stark incongruence between Enron's core values and its actual operating culture.

Incongruence—the disconnection between what we say and what we do—is commonplace, almost expected, in our culture. But transforming churches have a clear sense of identity, or what I call the *code*. A church's code gives it a sense of collective personality and uniqueness. The code represents the unique DNA that makes each church one of a kind.

Transforming churches work hard to bring their operating cultures into alignment with their codes.

Too many churches fall prey to formulaic approaches, becoming franchises of something else. If a Quarter Pounder, fries, and Diet Coke taste as good in Denver as they do in Dayton, then why can't a sermon, drama, or outreach from Charlotte always work in Tacoma? The tendency to import church models and styles in an attempt to reach the same results contrasts with God's desire for each church to be unique in its own cultural context—to have defining and aligning code.

3. Autocracy/Shared Leadership

In transforming churches, the task of leadership is a shared responsibility. This stands in contrast to much of American culture. Most American forms of leadership are based on the cultural notion that leadership equals power. The leader is the person with the most control. Sometimes power is rooted in position—the CEO, the president, the pastor, or the board. Sometimes power is the product of personal charisma or charm.

Leadership defined by power, through coercion and control, works against the biblical concept of *leadership defined as ministry*, through sacrifice and service. Jesus emptied Himself of His rights to power so that He could become one of us (Phil. 2:1–11). Similarly, the leader is one who, by using authority appropriately, invites others to share responsibility for ministry. She asks the right questions rather than providing all—or any—of the answers. Leadership, in a transforming church, is much less about who gets to make decisions and much more about how best to fulfill the church's mission in an ever-changing context. A transforming church develops a multiplying group of leaders who lead by serving in this way.

4. Cloister/Missional

Transforming churches exist for those on the outside. Reaching out to others is clearly one of God's primary purposes for the church. All organizations, however, tend to become inwardly focused and narcissistic over time. We all tend to take a great thing and institutionalize it. An unhealthy church is one that exists for those on the inside—a cloister. Like the culture it is called to transform, such a church devotes an unhealthy amount of attention to meeting individual needs. When the understood role of church members is to consume the best "products," the focus, whether intended or not, moves to excluding others.

Some churches "wall out" those who are unfamiliar with their traditions or dogma. Other churches offer programs and services to meet the consumer needs of people, without ever mobilizing them for outward ministry. Other churches are focused on creating a safe haven from the world.

By contrast, a transforming church is one that has a clear and focused sense of mission beyond its walls, regardless of its personality or worship style. Remember the most startling figure from the TCIndex results: 93 percent of members among healthy churches considered themselves to be involved in some form of ministry, compared to only 11 percent among unhealthy churches. In follow-up research, I discovered that the disparity was often the result of how churches defined ministry. Unhealthy churches tend to define ministry as what happens inside the church (ushers, committee members, Sunday-school teachers, and greeters). Healthy churches define ministry in broader terms—ministering and glorifying God in their neighborhoods, workplaces, social circles, and schools.[7]

5. Inertia/Reinvention

A consumer is not a creator. Disconnected from any greater purpose, isolated from meaningful relationships, expecting others to solve problems, and focused inwardly, the religious consumer is passive and largely unmotivated to make a difference in the lives of others. Church, for the most part, becomes a spectator sport. As long as the season ticket holders are satisfied, there is little reason to reinvent the event being offered.

On the other hand, transforming churches struggle through the process of reinvention to discover new ways of fulfilling their missions. Even the apostle Paul wrote that he was willing to change—or, as he put it, "become all things to all [people]"—to share the gospel with them (1 Cor. 9:22). Similarly, at times, transforming churches are forced to recognize that their current forms are no longer relevant to those who need the church the most. And, seeing this, they are willing to embrace change, even when this change involves painful sacrifice.

Sounds simple, right? Linear and logical—just move along the continuum.

Not so much. The process of becoming a transforming church is messier and often feels something like going days without food while fighting through a dense jungle at night … hoping to find bananas.

Monkey Business

Several years ago, I read about a university experiment. A group of laboratory scientists studying behavioral patterns put four monkeys together in a lab. After bringing in a tall pole with bananas on the top, they retreated to observe through a one-way mirror. Things went predictably at first. The monkeys competed against one another to reach the top of the pole and eat the bananas. The smartest and strongest retrieved the bananas, while the others had to wait for the right moment.

Then the scientists changed the environment by putting a pail of water at the top of the pole. Every time a monkey climbed the pole to reach the bananas, he got doused with water. After several repeated episodes, the monkeys learned to stop going after the bananas. The environment had forced the monkeys to change their behavior.

Eventually the scientists took the water away. There was no reason for the monkeys not to climb the pole, but the monkeys had already been conditioned. Even with the threat removed, they didn't attempt to climb the pole. The bananas were left untouched. The monkeys just stared longingly at them.

The third round of the experiment involved replacing one of the original monkeys. Not surprisingly, the new monkey scurried into the room, saw the bananas, and immediately started to climb the pole. What happened next shocked the scientists: The three original monkeys grabbed the newcomer by the tail, yanked his feet, and pulled him down. They were trying to protect him from being doused by water, which wasn't even there!

Over time, the scientists gradually replaced each of the original monkeys with new monkeys, which were eventually replaced with other monkeys, and so on through several generations. For a while, there was more tail pulling and leg yanking. Over a few generations, however, another interesting phenomenon occurred: The newest monkeys crawled into the room, stared at the bananas, but never even tried to climb the pole! No competing. No water. No tail pulling. No leg yanking. Just an unspoken norm understood among the monkeys: The bananas are to be seen but not eaten.

The story of the monkeys illustrates the real power of cultural dysfunctions: They operate largely on subconscious, and therefore largely unrecognized, levels. Part of what makes church or any other place where people come together so difficult is that it constitutes a living system. In truly mysterious ways, an organization is influenced by unseen interactions with its surroundings and previously developed norms. As we reflect on the monkey illustration, we can begin to see how the system:

- Forces individuals—in good ways and bad—to adapt
- Develops its unspoken norms outside of conscious awareness
- Shapes itself through unseen forces
- Tends to perpetuate itself, regardless of the specific individuals involved
- Creates results that cannot be blamed on any one person
- Resists change, creating an environment where individuals resist change as well

Further complicating matters is the fact that a living system always exists in the context of other systems. Each human being, for example, is a living system within the larger systems of nuclear and extended family, which in turn exist within the contexts of community, nation, hemisphere, and planet.

Because we are so deeply interconnected by living systems, it is critical to understand how they function. And it is important to recognize that systemic change of living systems normally comes slowly and at a price. There are no quick fixes on the way to becoming a transforming church.

No Quick Fixes

We are all suckers for the quick fix. If you have a headache, you take two aspirin. If you have a bad marriage, you file for divorce. If your computer crashes, you buy a new one. If you don't feel like cooking dinner, you call for delivery. If you hate your boss, you get a new job. Easy, right?

Let's face it: Change is difficult. According to the TCIndex and the experience of virtually every church leader in the country, churches resist change for one reason: It is painful. And most church leaders don't know what to do with that reality. If preaching about it doesn't work, the tendency is to preach about it more. If confronting the dissenters has not been effective, confront more. If people resist unilateral decisions, why not become more autocratic? More of the same never works.

In another *Christianity Today* poll, this question was posed to leaders: "What is the most important factor to consider when introducing change to a church?" Thirty-seven percent cited the internal culture of the church, 34 percent cited the leadership culture of the church, and only 7 percent pointed outside the church to the external culture.[8] Yet our research shows how powerful the outside culture is and how much it affects us. By failing to come to grips with how cultural dysfunctions deeply impact the health of the church, our leaders will continue to fail to discern an essential reality concerning the nature of change: *Culture shapes churches, and churches shape people—often through the power of what remains unspoken.*

Unaware of any deeper or underlying cause, leaders begin to deal with the symptoms. They attack them from every angle and perspective. They attend conferences looking for solutions. They examine different models.

They read the latest church-growth books. They bring in the latest guru. They use flip charts to brainstorm options. But no matter what they do, the problems don't go away. If they solve one problem, two new ones seem to crop up to take its place.

Adaptive change—the journey from cultural dysfunction to biblical health—is never accomplished through technical fixes.[9] An issue requiring adaptive change is much more complex, involving a set of interconnected problems, mutating over time, hidden within the human system of the church. The adaptive issue is usually outside of conscious awareness. It is the current state of unhealthy norms, behaviors, and attitudes. It resists adaptive change under the camouflage of the best of intentions.

Example: "If we change, we will lose some of our most significant members who are really invested in this church."

Translation: "If we change, we will lose our biggest donors [i.e., financial security is the unspoken operating value] who aren't supportive of our direction."

When the leaders of a church sense the presence of these issues hidden under the surface, they usually consider two options: deny the problem or hire a consultant. Sometimes, they call someone like me or one of my colleagues at TAG Consulting. They usually envision the deal as something like this: We will pay you to fix our problem.

When I tell them that I can't fix their problem, but I can help them work through it, many church leaders go back to option number one: deny there is a serious problem at all. But a surprising number of churches are willing to embrace and solve their own problems with some outside perspective, coaching, and guidance. They are committed to the journey. And those who commit to the journey are transforming churches.

Challenging the Norm

As I was writing this chapter, I was in Renton, Washington, consulting with St. Matthew's Lutheran Church. Together over the past year or so, we had conducted an on-site assessment of the church, facilitating a strategic planning session with the leadership and helping the staff redefine their organizational culture. I thought we had made good progress. I was surprised when Pastor Kirby Unti called and asked me to return. Conflict among the staff, he told me, had escalated out of control.

I was aware that the staff had historic issues around managing conflict. The players changed, but the problems tended to follow a similar pattern: Two people would get embroiled in a conflict, Kirby would try to mediate, and the other staff members would retreat. The conflict usually became personal but rarely fiery.

Recently, however, things had taken a turn for the worse. At a retreat, two staff members had gone for each other's jugular. Julie and Seth are both delightful, capable people, not the type to harm another or seek revenge. But they got into an argument over who should be involved in planning worship. The conflict escalated to name-calling, threats, and words not allowed on prime-time television.

Kirby asked if I could come back. I understood that we were dealing with adaptive issues, not a surface problem. How did I know? First, the intensity of the conflict was disproportionate to the stated issue (Who gets to plan worship?). This lack of proportion is always a sign of a lurking adaptive issue.

The second clue was that Julie and Seth were being blamed. We look for scapegoats when we are trying to solve the wrong problems. Scapegoats become convenient sacrifices so that groups don't have to deal with their adaptive issues. Sure, individuals always share some of the responsibility. But blaming individuals distracts the group from dealing with deeper issues. Think of it this way: Suppose the group focused on the problem between Julie and Seth until the "worship input" issue was worked out. It would then only be a matter of time before the same deeper problem would resurface with different players. Each time a new problem arises, it takes a different form and involves different players, but the underlying cause is always the same. The scapegoat problem invariably becomes a distraction from the deeper adaptive issues that need to be resolved.

I agreed to return. When I told the story about the monkeys, the staff seemed to get it. They knew they had some unspoken norms and patterns that were unhealthy. They knew they had to resolve the adaptive issues. But they didn't know exactly where to look. While we were discussing how the conflict emerged, what it was about, and how the system replicated the same patterns, Heather, the church's newest staff member, arrived. She apologized for being late and began to listen attentively. Feeling energized by having a safe environment to discuss conflict constructively, people began to open up. One staff member commented about how sad the recent conflict was. Julie and Seth had once been best friends, "almost like brother and sister."

In one of those rare "aha" moments of intuition, it hit me: The staff functioned too much like a family. The pastor, Kirby, was the father figure. The staff members related to one another like siblings.

As we discussed how a church should function differently from a family, some of the staff didn't buy it. They raised important questions:

"You mean we can't be friends anymore?"

"Can I still wear sweats to work on Friday?"

"If we're not a family, what makes us any different than if we were working at any other office?"

I was having a hard time articulating to them that a church staff could be warm and caring without functioning just like a family. Then for the first time, Heather spoke up. Having been on staff for about two months, she was the newest "monkey" in the room. "When I first came here," she said, "I expected this would be a place where I would share my gifts and talents—a place to grow and develop. I wanted to make a difference. But within a few days, I realized what I was really supposed to do was get to know each staff member at a very deep, personal level. I was uncomfortable sharing too much about my family and personal life, mainly because I'm more of an introvert. But I knew I had a lot to offer in my role with children's ministry. I guess I just assumed that at some point after I really became part of this family, I would then start using my gifts in ministry."

Everyone in the room was stunned. Even though Heather had missed the story about the monkeys, she had just shared why she did not feel free to go for the bananas. Before this meeting, she had never felt safe enough to raise the question. She assumed the unspoken norm was something that couldn't be challenged. Her observation, now spoken, launched an invaluable discussion on the ways members of a church staff should relate differently from a family.

The office was not a place for free counseling, playing cards, or going to movies. The mission of the church was its top priority. The church staff had made their relationships primary rather than allowing church to be a place to live out a vocation. Although friendly relationships were important, they should be expressed in the context of a highly productive and caring team, not a surrogate family.

Fake Bananas

Like it or not, we are largely shaped by adaptive issues, the forces and unspoken norms largely invisible to us. Just because something is unseen, however, does not mean that it lacks power. In fact, the opposite is often true: If a thing is hidden, its power is greater. The hidden nature of the adaptive issue is precisely why individuals often fail to question the unhealthy norms, or dysfunctions, that exist in the church.

Let me risk a diagnosis: I believe that in many churches, the bananas have become off-limits.

The fruit we desire and talk about the most—intimacy with God and others, relevance, connection to a purpose larger than self—for some strange reason seem the very things we are most unable to achieve. We resort to strategies that end up creating more frustration. We preach and teach about bananas. We cast a vision for eating bananas. We develop pole-climbing training programs. We go to conferences about bananas. We make models of plastic bananas. We read lots of books about bananas. We conduct twelve-step support groups for people who are starving for bananas. We argue over which side of the pole the bananas should be on. We elect people who represent our side of the pole. But no matter what we do, nobody ever seems to get around to eating the bananas.

We risk going bananas over the bananas.

The problem is, we never question the central concerns: What are the adaptive issues? Are the bananas really forbidden? What norms need to be challenged? What hidden values need to be surfaced? What attitudes or behaviors prevent us from fulfilling our mission?

The five key indicators we identified through our research represent critical transitions—potential forks in the journey of transformation. It's not always easy to know which way to go. In fact, the smoothly paved path heading straight ahead is often a dead end in disguise.

Our journey does not require us to know what the adaptive issues are up front. In fact, our initial assessments tend to point toward technical problems rather than adaptive issues. But the journey of change does require us to have the courage to seek out the adaptive issues. It requires the tenacity to wrestle with them once we discover them. It requires the humility to admit that perhaps we have been wrong. And it requires an honest acknowledgment that our churches may have been influenced by the very culture we are trying to transform.

When your church's health improves in the five key areas, you *will* improve in the way you deal with change. You will be on the way to becoming a transforming church—one that finds new ways to fulfill its mission and that sees people's lives being changed. Becoming a transforming church is not an easy journey, but it is one worth taking. It surely beats an endless succession of red-sweatshirt days.

THE JOURNEY OF CHANGE SPEED BUMP

Transforming Church Checkup

1. Are members at your church experiencing authentic life change?

2. Does your church have a clear sense of mission and a compelling vision for the future?

3. Does your church embrace change to fulfill its mission more effectively?

4. Are your leaders successfully mentoring and mobilizing your members for ministry?

5. Is your church effective in transforming your local community, town, or city?

Travel Tips

To prepare for the journey of becoming a transforming church, you will need to be well equipped. Bring the following:

1. Patience. The journey is long and hard. There are no shortcuts.

2. Servant attitude. Leadership requires self-sacrifice. It is rarely easy.

3. Humility. As you lead others on the journey, you must put self-interest aside.

4. Resolve. It is easy to take detours, but the journey requires you to move toward your mission without distraction.

5. Thick skin. Those who are on the journey will be attacked. You cannot take the attacks personally.

6. Fellowship. You cannot begin the journey alone. You need people who will be your friends and confidants along the way.

7. Openness. You may be surprised by what you find. A teachable spirit is one of the greatest tools a leader possesses.

8. Faith. There will be dark moments along the way. In these moments, know that God is with you.

9. Hope. While you may not know where this journey leads, you need to know that, for citizens of heaven, it will end well.

10. Love. You cannot be effective on the journey without motivation. Your ultimate incentive must be love for the church, the world, and God.

Reflections

1. How well do you personally embrace change? What
    excites you about it? What scares you?

2. What do you anticipate will be the greatest roadblocks
    to leading change in your own congregation? As a
    leader, what are your greatest fears in facing those
    roadblocks?

3. From the brief description so far of the five key
    indicators of church health, which one(s) do you
    anticipate will show health in your church? Which
    one(s) will indicate areas of struggle?

2

CONSUMERISM/COMMUNITY, PART 1

Individualism on Steroids

The body is a unit, though it is made up of many parts;
and though all its parts are many, they form
one body. So it is with Christ.
—1 Corinthians 12:12

It was a brutally hot day in the desert, but I was in a small, air-conditioned conference room at Community Church of Joy near Phoenix. Ten minutes after the meeting of pastors and ministry leaders was supposed to have started, nobody else was present. I waited alone, wondering if I was in the right room.

I didn't have a clue why I was there. Tim Wright—an acquaintance of mine and a key staff member at CCOJ—had issued a vague invitation: to give the church leadership advice on starting a consulting practice focused on developing leadership in corporate settings. And as an aside, he had said, "We also have a few internal issues about which we could use your input."

It was the summer of 1999. I had been working with TAG Consulting for only a year, and I was focused on developing our secular consulting practice. I hadn't really thought about consulting with churches.

I didn't know a thing about CCOJ, except that it was Lutheran. As I drove from the airport, I tried to picture what the church might look like. I had in my mind that most Lutherans were cut from the same mold—displaced Germans and Scandinavians. I pictured a congregation of mostly snowbirds who had left places like Minneapolis, Bismarck, and Fargo for unlimited sunshine and winter golf.

49

As I drove onto the campus, my preconceptions were shattered with every turn in the winding road. I saw children playing outside a building that looked like a Toys "R" Us. I saw a bell tower hanging in front of the entrance to the Memorial Gardens. I saw a worship facility that looked more like a convention center. I saw artistic directional signs pointing to Joy Memorial Gardens, Joy Leadership Center, Kids Country, Joy Bookstore, Oasis Counseling Center, Joy School, and Joy Youth Center.

Paul Sorensen, one of the pastors, was the first to arrive in the conference room. While we waited for the latecomers, I asked him to tell me about CCOJ's history, focus, and impact. Paul was more than happy to oblige.

"This was a very traditional Lutheran church, primarily a place for snowbirds and retirees. Walt Kallestad, our senior pastor, came here twenty-five years ago with a passion to reach those who had been turned off or turned away from church. He introduced some innovative ways of doing ministry. But very few bought into his vision. Some of the charter members met in homes, plotting how to get rid of Walt. In those early years, Walt was extremely discouraged. In fact, one night he received a call that the church kitchen was on fire. *Let it burn,* he thought to himself."

As I listened to Paul, I was intrigued. The church had clearly overcome some major obstacles in its early years.

Paul continued with a slight grin. "In Walt's first year as CCOJ's senior pastor, the church 'grew' from two hundred members to one hundred. He felt like a failure. He was ready to throw in the towel. But God touched his heart with the confidence that this wasn't Walt's mission but God's mission. Walt hung in there through the rough times. Then things started to change."

I noticed a couple of other people trickle into the room. Undeterred, I asked Paul to go on.

"This passion to reach the lost and take risks for God was seared deeply into the soul of the leaders, including me. Over the years, thousands have experienced Jesus for the first time ever. Very few traditional, mainline churches ever have as many adult baptisms as we have."

Paul shared his excitement over the spirit of joy he felt when he first arrived, and how the church lived up to its name. He talked about his shock in realizing a traditional church could reach so many broken people, with support groups in every classroom and a constant stream of counseling.

As he talked, I noticed that the other people in the room were sitting at the table, doodling on notepads. Not everyone appeared to share Paul's enthusiasm. Nobody spoke to me. Sensing Paul had more to say, I interrupted him.

"Why am I here?" I asked.

Paul shifted uncomfortably. "We used to laugh together—"

Before he could finish his thought, his cell phone rang.

After excusing himself, Paul walked to a corner to take the call. I was anxious to get started, as I had a plane to catch. Despite numerous empty chairs, I suggested we begin the meeting. As people responded to my introductory questions, I kept hearing about "Walt's dreams" of reaching the unchurched. How CCOJ was seeker driven with cutting-edge media, music, drama, and relevant messages. How the 170-acre campus was designed to resemble an upscale mall because unchurched people could relate to that. How Walt had this vision of outreach where he could provide services and products from "cradle to grave."

I couldn't help but notice that only a few people spoke and that their answers seemed rote, almost memorized. Knowing my scheduled departure time and growing apprehensive, I decided on the direct approach again: "Why am I here?"

When no one volunteered a response, I plodded ahead. "Judging by my drive onto your campus, it seems you have been incredibly successful at accomplishing these goals."

From the outside, it looked like CCOJ was thriving. But clearly something was wrong.

The Successful Church

Like CCOJ, the contemporary church in America could be judged a success in terms of growth and power. Consider the following statistics:

- Between 1970 and 2006, the number of churches with an average weekly attendance of more than 2,000 jumped from 10 to 835.
- According to a recent Gallup Poll, 43 percent of Americans said they had attended church in the past week (up from previous decades of stagnation).
- Church construction in the United States is now a $6-billion-a-year business.
- Despite rising secularism, there are now more churches in the United States than there were 20, 50, or 100 years ago.

In many ways, the church is stronger and more influential than it has been in a long time. The buildings and programs and designs and numbers speak for themselves. At the same time, as I consult with church after church, I am forced to ask two deeper and more unsettling questions:

- Can we always equate success with health?
- Is relevance synonymous with transformation?

Community Church of Joy: "We Used to Laugh Together"

No one in the conference room had answered my question, so I was forced to ask it once again: "Why am I here?" Still no response.

I tried a different approach. "How many members do you have?" I asked. "Four or five thousand?"

"Thirteen thousand," one of the pastors corrected me perfunctorily. The room fell silent again. More doodles. Bored looks out the window. Fingers tapping on tables.

Left with no real alternative, I decided to wait them out. I fought hard to keep from checking my watch and calculating the minutes before my departure time. I listened to the air conditioner hum. I waited.

Finally, someone spoke up. "We have a huge amount of debt—almost seventeen million dollars."

After a few more seconds, another voice: "It feels like a corporation around here." Finally, the feedback started to flow.

"We have an incredible amount of respect for Walt's vision, and he's really a great leader, but we're not sure we can pull it off."

"It feels like each one of us is an island, doing our own thing."

"We are growing too fast and don't have the necessary resources."

"We used to all laugh together—"

Then Walt Kallestad walked into the room. As the leaders had been talking about their senior pastor's dreams and vision, I pictured him in my mind's eye: a man about six foot four, with a chiseled body and jaw, a commanding voice and presence.

The real Walt was quite different. Lanky. Average looking. Humble. He stumbled over himself apologizing for his tardiness. He told me how much he appreciated my being there, and spoke of how my uncle Billy Graham had impacted the direction of his ministry in 1974. He was thoughtful and kind, speaking with genuine appreciation about a book I had written.

I shifted gears. As we began to discuss some basic concepts of organizational health—good communication, general leadership principles, the difference between vision and focus, understanding identity, and establishing healthy boundaries—Walt listened intently. I found him a man of great evangelistic passion, highly relational, and incredibly curious.

But spirits in the room were low.

There was one complaint that stood out: "We can't even talk about the issues."

So I started and ended there. I asked the group if they would commit, over the next few months, to explore why they couldn't talk about the issues. Walt said that was an excellent idea. The others agreed, but with no great enthusiasm.

We would communicate over the phone and e-mails and set a time for another meeting. I walked outside into the dry desert heat, climbed into my rental car, heaved a few sighs, waved at a lot of smiling pedestrians, and drove to Phoenix Sky Harbor International Airport.

The Transforming Church

Most contemporary church strategy is focused on achieving success. There is nothing inherently wrong with that. But the goal is to be a transforming church—to aid in transforming people to the image of Christ—and this requires congregational health. The longer I serve as a church consultant, the more I wonder if success is the same thing as health.

In my early years at TAG Consulting, I scrambled for ways to measure congregational health. Specifically, I wanted to know what metrics would indicate how well a church was doing. I assumed that statistics about worship attendance, giving per member, and the size and quality of the church's facilities would be indicators of health. Gradually, it dawned on me that the very way I was framing the questions was part of the problem.

In our search to quantify church health, we have a tendency to measure the wrong things—church attendance, political muscle, buildings, and budgets. Again, these things are not bad in and of themselves, but the fact is churches can be large, influential, financially secure, and have a beautiful facility yet still be desperately unhealthy. Outward success does not guarantee inner health.

As TAG Consulting began to frame questions around the issue of church health instead of "success," the Transforming Church Index became a useful gauge for us. Primarily, the TCIndex attempts to define a church's ability to thrive in change—with the focus of *well-being* instead of *doing well*. It is a fundamental premise that if a church *is* well (healthy) it will also *do* well (be successful in its mission). The five key indicators I introduced in the previous chapter tell us how well a church is.

Along the journey of transformation, each indicator marks a "fork in the road" where a church can choose a healthy path or be detoured by cultural dysfunction. You will remember the five key indicators and their continuums:

- Consumerism ↔ Community
- Incongruence ↔ Code

- Autocracy ↔ Shared Leadership
- Cloister ↔ Missional
- Inertia ↔ Reinvention

There is a reason why we list *consumerism ↔ community* first. The way that people relate to one another largely defines the rest of the list of indicators. Whether a church is defined by consumerism or community tells us whether the relational system of the church is toxic or life-giving.

The Church Down the Road

Several years ago, I consulted with a church in California. By all outward appearances, this church was successful. More than two thousand people gathered weekly for worship, the music was cutting-edge, the landscape was perfectly maintained, everyone loved the pastor's sermons, and the children's programs were creative and engaging.

But the pastor suspected something was fundamentally wrong. After visiting with the staff, I met with some focus groups composed of people who attended the church. I asked the participants to give me their general perceptions of the church.

"I love it here." "Things are great." "It's the best church I have attended."

What specifically made the church so appealing?

"The music rocks!" "The dramas make me laugh and cry." "The pastor's sermons are so relevant to my needs." "My teenager plays the bass in the youth band." "My children meet in rooms with jungle creatures painted on the walls." "Everything here is always high quality."

I wondered aloud what would happen if the pastor left or the worship leader resigned or the children's ministry declined in quality.

Not one of them batted an eye. Without hesitation, one after the other, the responses flowed: "I would leave." "I saw this really cool Web site for Hope Community." "I'll take my kids wherever I can find the best program."

I was headed toward an "aha" moment, one of those flashes of intuition consultants pray for. But I wasn't there yet.

I asked each group: "Has your participation in this church changed your life?"

Without exception the members of the focus groups talked about the programs of the church and how much they and their families enjoyed attending.

Not one person mentioned personal transformation, or anything akin to being "sent" into their home, work, or neighborhood as a representative of Christ. Sure, some of them had "grown" at a personal level. But that usually meant they had learned more about the Bible or theology.

My "aha" moment turned into a crystal-clear conviction: The members of this church—and many others like it—were part of a dysfunctional human system. On the outside, the church looked vibrant and healthy. But a look inside revealed a group of people who were "consuming" the church's products without connecting to one another in meaningful relationships or engaging in the local community with the transforming power of the gospel.

A "successful" church can offer outstanding programs and ministries, but if its members are not being transformed, it is not a healthy church.

The church in California scored well on several parts of the Transforming Church Index. But their lowest scores, compared to national norms, were all related to how people perceived their level of connection to the church. Some of those statements included:

- I am regularly involved in a smaller group within the church.
- I have a clear understanding of my role in fulfilling the church's mission.
- I am valued around here.
- I have a clearly defined role in the church.
- My actions influence this church.
- Our church enjoys a healthy sense of fellowship and community.

The quality of the community is the quintessential test of the health of a church. But few church leaders are skilled at developing an environment where meaningful and transforming relationships will occur. They desire community but often don't know how to build it, and they fail to recognize the impact the American consumer culture has on the church.

The journey from consumerism to community is not a quick one, because the problem of consumerism has deep roots.

The Pursuit of Happiness

Consumerism has its roots in the dawning of the era of Enlightenment and the beginning of the modern world, with its attendant philosophy— modernism. During the modern era, God was often viewed as stripped of His relevance because He was invisible to the empiricist—and irrelevant to the five senses. Reason replaced faith as the arbiter of truth. And in a world without God, the autonomous individual replaced community as the center of reality.

The philosophy of individualism was foundational to the forming of our nation. Following the Jeffersonian belief that every person is entitled to "life, liberty, and the pursuit of happiness," our Constitution began a grand experiment with individualism.

Before World War II, American individualism was tempered by a society dominated by sacrifice and an emphasis on the "greater good."

Consider, for example, the advent of the concept of the "teenager." Prior to the end of World War II, teens typically went to school, helped the family with chores, and worked in the family business or farm. Every hour of their time was needed for the family to survive. But the convergence of new technologies, dual-income families, and increased mobility created a teenage phenomenon: free time. Teens turned to television, hanging out with other teens, and playing games. The constructive use of time was replaced by a consumer use of time.

Along with the emergence of leisure time, technological advances began to create a new set of needs and wants in American culture. Businesses became virtual, no longer requiring proximity. Boomers moved farther out from the cities, and even commuted between cities. Both parents started working to keep up with mortgage payments on new homes in the suburbs.

This began creating divisions between work, home, and social life. Meals began shifting from relationship-building events to efficient means of consumption where convenience was king. Fast-food restaurants boomed as busy parents waited in line at the drive-through. As the consumer moved more into the center of our culture in the 1970s, the philosophy of consumerism took root. Simply put, consumerism is the idea that personal happiness is equated with acquiring and consuming products—usually alone. We choose our "community" based on our "consumption." When our individual tastes or desires change, so do our friends.

Disturbing Trends

Over time, the rise of consumerism has created at least two dangerous trends.

From Creativity to Passivity

The phrase *killing time* is a recent entry into our culture's shared vocabulary. And the phrase is misleading because it implies an active engagement. Look at the ways Americans typically kill time, and you'll see it is a much more passive endeavor that is no longer a teenage phenomenon— watching television, playing video games, surfing the Internet, or listening to iPods. We seek to fill time more than kill it. In fact, the ideology— and economic machinery—of consumerism is geared toward passive consumption. The individual, at the center, is to be served. The consumer, not the broader community, is the reference point.

From Real to Imitation

In his revolutionary work *Habits of the Heart,* Robert Bellah describes how consumerism often creates false community. It works like this. The premise is that acquiring and consuming leads to the good life—for the individual. But a life of consumption leads to boredom. As a result, we seek out others who share common interests—from Trekkies to chocolate aficionados to wine tasters to Harley riders to Porsche owners to urban gangs. You name it, and there's a "lifestyle enclave" formed around it.

At its heart, each enclave is formed around pursuit of the product, not on significant relationships. Among the members loyalty varies, and nothing stands in the way of moving from group to group or interest to interest. As a result, lifestyle interests become a substitute for genuine community. This is all the more dangerous because it can fool us into thinking we are experiencing the real thing.

The late Neil Postman suggested that Las Vegas is the metaphor of the American psyche. He writes, "Las Vegas is a city entirely dedicated to the idea of entertainment, and as such proclaims the spirit of a culture in which all public discourse increasingly takes the form of entertainment.... The result is that we are a people on the verge of amusing ourselves to death."[10]

Consumerism is individualism on steroids. It is the logical end product of living for self. Consumerism paves the way for the worship of self, and self-worship leaves us alone with the object of our devotion.

Together Alone

The other day I was at the Fair Oaks Mall, which is not too far from my home in Virginia, doing some last-minute Christmas shopping. Stopping for a few minutes to "people watch," I saw three teenage girls walking, each listening to music on her own iPod. I saw several children playing in the "Kid's Zone" but not interacting with one another, while their parents, sitting by themselves, watched. I also saw dozens of individuals bounding from shop to shop, avoiding eye contact with clerks and other shoppers. And I saw all of this in just five minutes.

Hundreds of people in the same mall … and each one an island. As I reflected on the paradox, it occurred to me: I was people watching by myself.

While foundational to the development of a powerful democracy, our cultural focus on self-interest has also contributed to a society filled with individuals who are alienated, lonely, disconnected, and rootless. Americans tend to live in one place, work in another, and socialize in yet another. We have constructed a society that encourages retreat. Front porches are a thing of the past. In the suburbs, garage doors open and close, shutting us off from our neighbors. In cities with congested traffic, highways often have designated lanes as a reward for the few who actually carpool.

From the 1950s through the 1990s, we became increasingly disconnected from others. The best-selling book *Bowling Alone* describes this shift.[11] Bowling leagues and teams had all but died out in the 1990s. Bowling alleys, a metaphor for American life, were populated by individuals bowling alone.

The Ultimate Consumer

C. S. Lewis once wrote that the greatest evil was a good thing slightly twisted. An emphasis on the individual can be good. Without a proper understanding of the value of each individual life, history teaches us that human abuse is likely. Organizations like World Vision, the Salvation Army, and the International Justice Mission continually fight to raise awareness of individual rights in impoverished places. An emphasis on the importance of the individual was partially responsible for the abolition of slavery, women's suffrage, and the civil-rights movement.

The problem is not recognizing the *importance* of the individual. The problem is the *glorification* of the individual. When the individual self is glorified over the greater good of the community, rights begin to take precedence over responsibility, isolated pursuits replace the struggle for the common good, desires are twisted to resemble needs, and the imitation is presented as the real thing.

In the transformation of the hobbit Sméagol into Gollum, J. R. R. Tolkien painted the ultimate picture of self run amok: the consumer. Gollum, the ultimate consumer who initially killed to obtain the magic

Ring and owned it for centuries, was eventually consumed by its power. Disconnected from community, self, and soul, Gollum existed only for the empty and circular pursuit of personal appetite. Granted long life, invisibility, and greater power to satiate those desires by the coercive force of the Ring, his extended number of days were a mockery of disappointment, suffering, and deep emptiness. In *The Fellowship of the Ring,* Tolkien writes of the character of Gollum under control of the Ring. He could just as well have been writing about many of the souls who populate our contemporary consumer culture. In fact, his words might serve as a clinical description for one under the power of addiction.

> All the great secrets under the mountains had turned out to be just empty night; there was nothing more to find out, nothing worth doing, only nasty furtive eating and resentful remembering. He was altogether wretched. He hated the dark, and he hated the light more; he hated everything, and the Ring most of all…. He hated it and loved it, as he hated and loved himself.[12]

We can see Gollum in ourselves. We long for something deeper than the enslavement of addiction or the ongoing satiation of personal appetite. As many sociologists point toward a cultural shift back toward the importance of being connected with others, the American church has an opportunity to lead the way. Sadly, most churches struggle to live in community.

Community Church of Joy: Fundamentally Flawed

In the months following my initial meeting with the leaders of the Community Church of Joy, people began to open up. Over the phone, through e-mails, from information collected from two hundred staff surveys, and during a series of follow-up meetings, the adaptive issues began to emerge.

Although CCOJ scored high on the TCIndex in areas of program excellence, innovation, and missional focus, we identified significant dysfunctions requiring leadership attention.

In particular, the church scored well below the national average in developing community. Although hundreds of people were flocking through the many front doors of CCOJ, almost as many were leaving through a large back door. Although some leaders were tempted to explain this away by pointing to the transient nature of the Glendale community—more than one-third of the population moved every year—Walt Kallestad was increasingly disheartened by the fact that seekers were not being transformed into disciples. Although Walt confessed an inability to pinpoint the underlying and foundational problems, he intuitively understood that something was fundamentally flawed. Something was lurking deep down—at the level of core values and identity.

As staff and leaders began to open up, healthy conflict emerged. Since one of the critical problems at CCOJ had been conflict avoidance, we took great care to keep people's anxiety at a tolerable level.

Along with one of my partners, Joe Jurkowski, I asked CCOJ's senior leadership team to gather for a weekend retreat. From the start Joe and I emphasized the goal: to raise the tough issues in a safe context. Our aim was to move the ministry of CCOJ forward and not to cast blame or unleash personal, built-up grudges.

With characteristic humility, Walt urged the team to speak their minds freely.

"We have a complicated set of problems here," he said, "and we don't even know where to start." Over the next couple of days we set out to identify the problems. The list quickly grew into a long one.

Low staff morale. Conflict avoidance. Meetings ending in tears or anger. Lack of organization. Lack of staff productivity. Staff not showing up for worship services. A decline in worship attendance. Accusations of nepotism. Employees not tithing. No more laughter. Lack of accountability. Not knowing what anyone else was doing or how the parts formed a whole. Trying to grow too fast. Lack of volunteers committing to ministry. Lack of giving by the members. A huge debt. Not being able to do what they had signed up to do.

As we began to talk through the issues, looking for common threads, many of the leaders pointed to the more external issues, the symptoms rather than the causes. *If* was always the telltale word. If the members would just give more or the volunteers commit more ... If less qualified family members were not hired and shown favor ... If the vision were communicated better ... If Susie weren't so quick to cry or take offense ... If we didn't have so many crises ...

As Joe and I processed the information, we began to weave together the themes into threads. Two critical—and interconnected—issues became clear. The church was plagued by

- a lack of community among the senior leadership team; and
- an absence of shared values.

"What happens at the leadership level," Joe told them, "is reflected symptomatically in the rest of the church. If the leadership team does not model community, that plays itself out among the staff and then throughout the congregation."

Values That Endure

We spent the remainder of the retreat discovering, or rediscovering, CCOJ's core values—the values that drew them together in the first place. Even if the values weren't on paper, they were alive and shared:

- Healthy relationships
- Innovative excellence
- A Lutheran understanding of the gospel
- A focus on mission
- Integrity

As the leaders reflected on their shared values, they began to define "healthy relationships." They began to explore how they could make decisions in a healthy and collaborative way, as partners in the ministry of the gospel. And they established commitments to figure out how they would work together in healthy relationships. They redefined decision-making parameters. They reorganized the staff.

Walt Kallestad, naturally a relational man, began to understand how he had drifted into the role of a corporate chieftain and the impact this had had on the rest of the team.

"The drift from the centrality of loving relationships was very slow, and I wasn't really consciously aware of it," Walt says. "Over time, and without really noticing it, the business of church took precedence to developing real community and relationship. The larger and quicker you grow, the more pressure there is to produce.

"I lost sight of people," Walt continues. "I took on more of the CEO role and became focused simply on oiling the machinery and creating the necessary structures to keep up with our growth and the spiritual needs we were trying to meet. I became more concerned about feeding the animal instead of living out the gospel through loving relationships."

Joe and I understood that our process was only the first step in their journey. Core values had been discovered. The adaptive issues were identified. But reorganizations and a handful of commitments written on a flip chart never really bring about transformation.

A Problem of the Heart

On January 7, 2002, Walt Kallestad suffered a nearly catastrophic heart attack. His treatment set a record at a Phoenix hospital: the first six-bypass surgery. His doctors were stunned he survived. As Walt came back to consciousness from a morphine dream, he understood what was to become a defining metaphor of his new journey: His heart needed to be miraculously healed.

3

CONSUMERISM/COMMUNITY, PART 2

Creating Community

*They devoted themselves to the apostles' teaching and to
the fellowship, to the breaking of bread and to prayer....
Every day they continued to meet together in the
temple courts. They broke bread in their homes and ate
together with glad and sincere hearts, praising God and
enjoying the favor of all the people. And the Lord added
to their number daily those who were being saved.*
—Acts 2:42, 46–47

Consumerism is so deeply rooted in our culture that it has become part of
the air we breathe. It's one of the unchallenged assumptions that shape our
way of believing, living, and relating. The journey from consumerism to
community is not easy or obvious, but it is vitally important. Fortunately, the
roots of community grow far more deeply than the roots of consumerism.

Twin Purposes: In His Image

The place to start to understand community is found in the opening
pages of the Bible. In Genesis, the first pairing of subject and verb is "God
created." The crown of God's creation was mankind: "'Let Us make man in
Our image, according to Our likeness....' So God created man in His own
image, in the image of God He created him; male and female He created
them" (Gen. 1:26–27 NKJV).

To be made in God's image means that we are like God in significant
ways. And the most important thing that the early pages of the Bible tell us

about God is that He exists in community: Let *Us* make man in *Our* image. He is Father, Son, and Spirit, the Three in One.

Community is God's essence. He not only created community, but He Himself also experiences it as part of His very nature. To say that God exists in community means that He is not isolated but is in reciprocal relationship. He knows others and is known. He gives and receives. For humans, being part of a community means that we are bound together in love and that we are aware of others' needs and put them ahead of our own (Phil. 2:3–4). Not only do we develop meaningful relationships, but also we are united by a common mission. This is a great mystery. But it is not mysterious at all to say that if we exist in God's image, and if God exists in community, then we are created for community as well.

Another aspect of God's image is that He is incessantly creative. From a biblical perspective, the verb *create* is not limited to artistic expression but refers more broadly to our purpose: to participate with God in His redemptive work. In the Genesis narrative that is so central to God's initial design for community, God sets up His inextricably connected mandates for humanity: creation and redemption. In Genesis 1 and 2, the creation story unfolds with a call for humanity to participate with God in creation (Gen. 1:26–28). After the fall, in Genesis 3, we learn that God's plan is to include us in the redemption of the world (Gen. 3:15).

We were made to be creative within the context of life in community. Relationships inspire us to create, and creativity happens best in the context of relationships.

Several years ago, I led a business seminar on innovation and creativity. I was teaching some basic principles about the creative process. I pulled in the best business thinking from ad agencies, toy manufacturers, software companies, songwriters, and film producers. I thought I had covered the creative process pretty well.

But when I placed the participants in breakout groups for input, another common theme emerged, one that I had not even thought about in my presentation. For the members of the seminar, every single act of creativity they experienced came through a process of collaboration. Even those who had written songs or created paintings saw their individual creativity as an expression of community. One person spoke of a play he had written—and how it didn't take life until the production crew got involved and began collaborating. A songwriter spoke of the "middle of the night" solitude of writing and how that emerged from a troubled relationship with one person and comfort from another. A painter described how she saw every painting as a reflection of her total environment—the moods of her children, the crispness of the air, and even the frustrating conversations she was having with a domineering mother-in-law!

Creativity and community cannot be separated. They are central to God's design for all of humanity. God has called the church to a dual purpose: community and creativity. Community defines the nature of relationships with God, each other, and the world around us. Creativity defines the kind of redemptive and purposeful activity taking place in our relationships with God, each other, and the world around us. God simultaneously demonstrates these two characteristics in the creation story.

We cannot be genuinely creative outside of community—and we cannot be a true community without creativity. God calls us to "creating community." The transforming church is a community of people participating with God and one another in the creative process.

To explain the functioning of the church, Paul chose the body as his primary metaphor (1 Cor. 12). A body is a set of mysterious, interconnected, and dynamic relationships that create and sustain life. Although God has designed local churches to differ from one another in many ways, one thing is not optional: unified community. A healthy body, by design and definition, is never a collection of disconnected individual parts.

I love the scene in the movie *The Fellowship of the Ring* when Frodo tries to separate himself from the rest of the company. To save them suffering, he determines to attempt the trek to Mount Doom by himself. Following the chaos of battle, Frodo finds a boat, pushes it into the river, jumps in, and sets off. Sam, emerging from the woods, sees his master paddling away and instinctively runs into the water after him.

"Frodo, no! Frodo! Mr. Frodo!" he screams.

"No, Sam," Frodo says, continuing to paddle farther away. "Go back, Sam! I'm going to Mordor alone."

"Of course you are," Sam replies, splashing water frenetically, "and I'm coming with you!"

"You can't swim! Sam!" Frodo shouts as Sam begins to get in over his head. In slow motion, you see Sam sinking slowly farther and farther into the water—the sun shimmering on the surface, his arms floating limply as he descends. Suddenly Frodo's hand reaches down and grabs Sam's wrist. Sam tightens his hand around Frodo's. Frodo pulls him out of the water and up into the boat, and Sam tumbles in.

Recovering his breath, Sam explains that he had given his word to the wizard Gandalf that he would take care of Frodo all through the journey to Mordor: "I made a promise, Mr. Frodo. A promise! 'Don't you leave him, Samwise Gamgee.' And I don't mean to! I don't mean to." Together, floating on a river to almost certain destruction, far away from home in a strange world filled with terror, the two hobbits embrace each other.

The scene paints a beautiful picture of what creative community was designed to be.

Recovering the Heart of Community

As he began the long recovery from six-bypass surgery, Walt Kallestad came to understand his heart was broken in more than a physical sense. On a three-month sabbatical from his duties as senior pastor of the Community Church of Joy, Kallestad did some deep soul-searching. After starting so well, how had CCOJ lost its way? Why were people not connecting in significant relationships? What would it take to get back on the right road?

All was not bleak at CCOJ. It had been nearly four years since I had first met with the leadership team, and they had been making progress. Staff members were meeting more regularly in team settings. There was general consensus on the core values. Some who didn't buy into the mission and values had moved on. But community was still noticeably absent. Despite his best efforts—and maybe because of them—Walt had himself become more unhealthy. As he says, "[I was] burned out, overworked, overwhelmed, and near to death, but I didn't know it."

The difficulty was that consumerism was rooted in parts of the church's strategy and structure. Designing the campus around the model of a mall, for example, was a bad idea. "What we became," Walt says, "was a dispenser of religious goods and services where people came to get instead of a missions station where people are launched to give.

"By creating excellent spiritual products, we believed we could eventually change the consumer mind-set and transition people into ministry," Walt continues. "But what we found is that the transition rarely occurred because we were forced to neglect the very process along which the transformation takes place—loving and healthy relationships in the community of God. As I began to realize how far we were missing the mark in terms of community, I began to die inside."

The Antithesis of Community

In his quest to rediscover the healthy heart of community, Walt came to understand that meeting individual needs solely by creating excellent programs and products was doomed to fail. He came to believe that consumerism is the antithesis of creative community. "To consume" is the opposite of "to create." Central to community is "we"; consumerism is "me."

- Community requires being missional; consumerism demands internal satiation.
- Community shares responsibilities greater than self; consumerism demands entitlements.
- Community expresses itself in service; consumerism feeds an endless hunger.

- Community leads to a shared freedom; consumerism leads to singular addiction.
- Community actively creates; consumerism passively devours.

It is a mistake to think that the church can adopt a consumer-oriented strategy, reach people, and then convert them into lovers of creative community. Too many churches succumb to this "bait and switch" type of strategy. In my work as a consultant, I have seen this strategy fail again and again.

There are two fatal flaws inherent in this failed strategy. First, consumers resist change. You can lure them in, but a consumer-oriented strategy will fail to transform them. Second, the consumer is never satisfied. Rather than being transformed into a life of sacrifice and service, the consumer will demand more and more of others.

In an article in *USA Today*, Philip Kenneson is quoted as saying, "Part of becoming a Christian is coming to see that what you thought you wanted deeply is not what you most wanted. It's having your wants retrained. So it's pretty hard to appeal to this old set of desires to get people in the door and then all of a sudden say, 'You know, we didn't quite tell you the whole thing.' Then people feel betrayed."[13]

In fact, the strategy of consumerism rises and falls with the truth that people "can't get enough of what they don't really need," which is a great description of the inherent nature and power of addiction. Why should it be any different with the creation of excellent "spiritual" products? By placing the insatiable desires of the individual at the center of a church's efforts, the individual is reduced to a state of isolated passivity—a shopper.

We think we need "spiritual products" and keep reaching for them, but in the process we often miss the thing that should be driving us: an intimate relationship with God and a life based on following Him that includes commitment to loving and serving others.

Remember the question I posed to the focus group at the church in California? "What would happen if the pastor left, the level of excellence in children's programming dropped, or the worship leader resigned?" Without hesitation, each person gave me the same kind of response: "I would leave." "I saw this really cool Web site for a new church, Hope Community. I hear the music is really good there." "I have a friend who goes there, and she says her kids love it."

In a consumer-oriented society, consumer-oriented churches will lose their "market share" as soon as another church with flashier offerings hits town. It is simply the nature of the beast.

Like CCOJ, a church can become wildly successful in attracting and serving consumers. With about thirteen thousand members and a campus of services for people "from cradle to grave," the Community Church of Joy had earned a reputation for success. It was nicknamed "the Willow Creek of mainline denominations." Pastors and church leaders from across the nation and world flocked to the suburb of Phoenix to learn from its model of ministry.

But following his heart attack, Walt wasn't buying it anymore. To his great credit, Walt chose to care more for his church's health than its success. He realized that, in a transforming church, health defines success.

Fries with That?

Franchising is a great business model, if you can capitalize on a strong brand of burgers or basketball shoes or home electronics or lattes. But franchising church is less effective. There is no "McDonald's of churches" offering a standardized package of ministry that can be imported anywhere (at least not yet). But a preoccupation with emulating successful ministry models betrays much of the thinking behind franchising.

By emphasizing models of ministry, the church risks sacrificing critical concepts at the very heart of creative community. Instead of reaching out in a creative way with a unique identity and purpose to a specific local culture and context, the consumer church settles for cloning, imitation, or franchising. The desire is to reproduce success. The franchise operates on the central concept that a Quarter Pounder tastes the same in Austin as it does in Kenosha. Or that a Nike shoe can be mass-produced in China as well as in Oregon. Likewise, a consumer church believes similar "spiritual" products can be manufactured regardless of the community and culture it inhabits.

Why do some people prefer Burger King to Wendy's (and vice versa)? Certainly, it's not the quality of the food so much as it is the brand—the images of identification. In the consumer church, often on a subconscious level, the brand is more important than community. In fact, the brand itself often becomes a substitute for community. In more contemporary churches, the brand may include a dynamic preacher, powerful performance art, and slick Web sites. For more traditional churches, consumers are looking for a brand they are familiar with—liturgies, responsive readings, the old hymns.

Don't get me wrong. The problem is not whether or not a church has a dynamic preacher, a worship band, or liturgy. The problem is that too many churches, consciously or not, have emphasized production of spiritual goods to satisfy individual appetites. As people who attend church, we may not have been asked yet if we would like to add fries to the order of faith, but we have learned how to look for what we like. And if we don't find it or it mysteriously disappears, then, like the members of the focus groups, the next step is obvious: Head down the road a mile or two to the next McChurch.

Broken beyond Belief

In addition to the difficulty he faced in building community, Walt also was troubled by the church's inability to attract the next generation of believers. He sensed "the seeker style of ministry was becoming a tradition unto itself." As he began to plead with God for the future of CCOJ, he studied, prayed, and reflected on the church in the postmodern or emerging culture.

Walt's near-death experience also caused him to consider a successor. At a conference of pastors in Washington DC, Walt shared the idea of looking for a successor in a casual conversation with another pastor. The man's response was stunning. "Why would anyone want your church?" he asked. "Anyone who is serious about ministry today does not want to be stuck raising money for maintaining buildings and mortgages. They want to be on the cutting edge of making a difference."

The comment cut to Walt's core. He knew change was necessary, but he had no idea how to reverse the momentum of consumerism in his church and was on the brink of despair. In a moment of deep agony, Walt can remember falling to his knees in prayer, sobbing uncontrollably. "God, I'm broken. I don't know what to do," he cried.

He remembers his body going ice cold and his heart pounding hard and fast. Then he heard a soft and gentle voice: "I have healed you."

But what did that mean?

The Endless Production Cycle

I recently worked with a church in Woodbury, Minnesota—a fast-growing suburb of the Twin Cities. The church was growing by leaps and bounds (234 percent over seven years). Members sincerely loved the church. There was unanimous praise for the church's excellent programs and services. At the same time, members also expressed concerns: "I'm worried about the quality of sermons. They're just not fresh anymore." "The music isn't consistently excellent anymore." "My kid doesn't drive, and the youth group is becoming terribly inconvenient for me."

I met with the senior pastor and the staff. Despite their successes, I found troubling symptoms of consumerism. The senior pastor, working seventy- to eighty-hour weeks, required a sabbatical. The staff members were weary and struggling to find enough volunteers while remaining focused on providing top-notch services and special events. The demand of consumerism was snowballing out of control.

Like so many churches I have consulted with, their church was about to "implode from success."

There is a subtle and destructive process at work in a consumer-oriented church. Without knowing it, the church that operates as a provider of spiritual products sets in motion an endless cycle of production that, in the end, cannot be sustained. Eventually, the church ends up asking some troubling questions. If everyone consumes, who produces? If the ever-increasing appetite of the consumer is not met with a corresponding rise in both the quality and quantity of products, what will happen?

Although a consumer-oriented church may intend to foster community, transform lives, and impact culture, the focus on production will never produce the intended results. To continue to produce the right—and better—products, staff burns out, the focus remains inward, and creating community becomes something "we will get to." The fundamental relationships of those attending the church become twisted by the consumer church's emphasis on production. Even the vocabulary changes meaning. Think of the words *volunteer* and *member*.

In a consumer-oriented church, a volunteer is a person needed to perform tasks in the production of a church's programs and operations. Little attention or honor is given to those who are focused on loving a neighbor, forgiving an unforgiving boss, developing a relationship with the boy next door who has no father, or any of the other countless ways the gospel can be exhibited in loving relationships. Every week, the church bulletin publishes the church's internal needs, and over time, the message is unintended but clear: Only "official" ministry really counts. Those who are involved in the "production" are valued, while those who are on the front line are not.

Often, such volunteer efforts are simply connected to getting tasks done, with little or no focus on building community. Instead of feeling connected to a life and mission larger than self, the volunteer often feels reduced. Over time, such a person, valued simply because of his or her "willingness to show up and do the task," will often end up feeling used and will disconnect from the church.

In much the same way, the concept of "member" has also been twisted by consumerism. In the New Testament, Paul used it to convey the reality of being a living part of an interconnected and dynamic body. But in a consumer culture, the meaning shifts from a shared responsibility to an individual entitlement. I pay dues for privileges. As a member of a country club, I get to play golf and dine in private facilities. In one major denomination, a member is someone who communes and gives once a year. That is all that is required. Once met, these requirements entitle the member to baptisms, confirmations, weddings, and funerals. In some cases, the church will even throw in scholarship assistance to a private school.

In most consumer-oriented churches, what is defined as "community" is often little more than enlistment into a lifestyle enclave. Church leaders assume that their people are experiencing biblical community when in fact they may simply be sharing in an interest or hobby—essentially a club or support group focused on mountain biking, piecing quilts, or rearing toddlers.

Let me be clear—casual relationships are a building block in creating community. I don't believe that groups organized around shared interests are inherently bad things. But I am simply posing the question: Once the interest is no longer shared, does the community sustain itself?

A substantial difference between real community and a shared lifestyle interest is that community is focused outward—on making a difference in the lives of others who are outside the community. Because a true community is called to participate in God's creative activities and redemptive work, shared interests cannot solely define it. A lifestyle enclave, founded on sharing individual pursuits, often amounts to little more than a collection of individuals who help each other avoid reality. The seduction is that it often looks and feels like something deeper, but in fact it prevents us from going deeper.

Walt Can No Longer Manage

As God began to reveal to Walt Kallestad the danger of building a consumer-oriented church, he realized that building a transforming church would start with the hard work of creating biblical community. And for Walt this meant learning a whole new way to lead.

"I used to feel that a management-driven church was the best leadership style to adopt," Walt says. "I hired staff to oversee various ministries and groups in the church, and I managed the staff. Management is an easier road to follow, because management does not pursue change; it seeks to maintain the status quo. The environment around our church did not stand still, but we continued to maintain what we had already achieved."

In a postmodern, technological world, Walt realized that culture changes rapidly. "The more I managed," he admits, "the further removed I became from the community of our church. I realized that I needed to return to leading rather than managing."

He also believed he could not lead alone. The leaders of transforming churches are passionate collaborators, knowing that they need the insights, gifts, and abilities of a diverse team.

Rooting out the cultural dysfunction of consumerism is a never-ending, collaborative, and adaptive work. As we will see in upcoming chapters, it is beyond what one person can do—no matter how gifted, charismatic, brilliant, or heroic the leader. Instead of coming up with the right answers, the leader is the one who begins to frame the right questions and invites others to join the process.

Once the issue has been reframed and people are working on the right problems, practical steps can be taken to build community.

Based on our research and experience, five essential building blocks are needed to create community:

1. Mentor mission partners
2. Invite input
3. Create a structure for assimilation
4. Develop small groups
5. Build a third place

Mentor Mission Partners

In the business world, the rank of partner is one of the most prestigious and powerful titles one can earn. Many lawyers, for example, work their entire lives to have their names listed on firms' stationery: White & Dalton & Fosmire & Shelton. The church offers a better deal. Every follower of Christ is, by definition, a full partner in the kingdom.

As we have already noted, the vocabulary of *member* and *volunteer* has been deeply corrupted by consumerism. I often suggest that churches refer to their members as partners.

My own company, TAG Consulting, has partners. We don't have employees. What this means is that every partner at TAG Consulting is responsible for the overall effectiveness of the organization. We all share responsibility for living our values and fulfilling our mission. Each partner is responsible for developing business, serving clients, and helping lead the company. Our consulting work is often rewarding. But there are no entitlements at TAG Consulting. A partner—or whatever more suitable name a church can come up with—is someone who is engaged with its organization's mission.

In contrast to a focus on internal "volunteers," ministry outside of the operations of the church matters. While the church needs Sunday-school teachers, it is equally important to value parents who are trying to raise their kids to follow Jesus. Every church needs people to help manage finances. But if the accountants in our congregation understand that conducting their workday jobs with integrity brings glory to God, they will begin to connect their everyday lives to the church's mission. Many churches commission their missionaries to short-term or long-term Christian work. But what if our churches started commissioning our truck drivers, doctors, businesspeople, and parents? This message would become clear: "Your everyday life is an extension of our church's mission!" Partners are those who engage in creating community both inside and outside the walls of the church.

Invite Input

To feel as if they are part of the community, partners often need to be connected to the church's internal processes and decisions. Whenever I conduct a strategic planning session with a church, I require that we have a process that gathers as much input as possible from as many people as possible. We start with the Transforming Church Index—an opportunity for every person in the congregation to give his or her feedback about the church. I then follow up with a series of focus groups, hoping to have representation from every major constituency or demographic segment within the church. Next, I take the leadership through a process of reviewing the input, clarifying key issues, and developing a strategic plan. Finally, the leaders take the plan back to the people as a work emerging largely from the fruit of their input.

I'm not suggesting that a strategic plan is built on consensus. Leaders may make decisions that run counter to the input that was gathered. But when people are included in the process, they feel more connected to community.

Create a Structure for Assimilation

I've consulted with hundreds of churches. It constantly amazes me how many leaders assume people will find a way to connect. One pastor recently expressed his frustration to me. "People just don't get involved. Our giving is down this year. We are really hurting for Sunday-school teachers."

When I asked the pastor what his church's strengths were, he was able to name several—worship services, student ministries, and missions. When I followed up by asking who the leaders of those ministries were, he was able to quickly give me a string of names. Then I asked, "Who is leading your assimilation team?" With a deer-in-the-headlights look, he responded, "We don't have an assimilation team."

The clearest sign of what a church values is where it puts its resources. I've observed an emerging trend, even among smaller churches, to hire an assimilation director, whose responsibilities include developing effective communications tools and teams of people who follow up with newcomers and longtimers alike, as well as creating processes to make it easy for people to use their gifts and talents both inside and outside the church.

Assimilation, though, must move beyond the work of one person; it is a shared responsibility. In a transforming church, pastors communicate the personal fulfillment of being involved in ministry, testimonies of ministry involvement are published in newsletters, and the teaching of new members goes beyond one class on Sunday morning. Often a church fails to assimilate new people because it relies on impersonal communication channels—assuming people will learn about the church through welcome brochures, bulletins, the church newsletter, or its Web site. Assimilation is a highly relational process. The ultimate goal is to connect each person to others as well as discover and utilize his or her gifts both inside and outside the church. You cannot assume this will just happen on its own.

Transforming churches build an intentional process of assimilation into everything they do.

Develop Small Groups

When newcomers connect with a group of seven to fifteen people within their first three months at a church, they are much more likely to stay involved over the long haul. Our own data shows churches that intentionally emphasize small groups are much healthier than those that don't. But it doesn't have to be one particular model of small groups. Such groups can take any number of shapes and forms—Bible studies, mountain-biking clubs, breakfast meetings—as long as they are missional and foster genuine relationships and a common mission rather than mere hobby sharing.

When I conduct focus groups at a church, I often ask people whom they would call if they had a crisis at 3:00 a.m. If they identify someone from a small group within the church, then I know the church is pretty healthy. At the same time, we have found that the level of participation in small groups is not extremely high, even in healthy churches. Some people just don't like small groups. Different people have different ways of connecting. Some will connect through small groups, some won't. Everyone needs intimate relationships, but they don't have to occur in small groups. If people have one or two close friends at church, then the "intimacy factor" is secure.

Build a Third Place

Many churches have a tendency to overemphasize intimacy. Not every relationship in a church must involve a deep connection with another person. The development of casual relationships is every bit as important. While casual relationships can develop anywhere, our research indicates there is a correspondence between a church's buildings and its effectiveness.

In his book *Celebrating the Third Place,* sociologist Ray Oldenburg suggests that the lack of casual relationships puts too much strain on family and work relationships. First place is home. Second place is the workplace. A third place is where casual relationships occur. Sometimes it's a coffee shop. Sometimes it's a football field or a recreation center. Sometimes it's just an open and inviting lobby.

A basic principle of organizational dynamics is that structure creates behavior. If a church is meeting in an elementary school, it must find a place where people naturally gather apart from Sunday morning. If the church's narthex or fellowship space isn't conducive to interaction, it must find an alternative.

But too often, the physical space itself becomes a roadblock to community, and the alternatives are insufficient. And when churches start to grow, the tendency is to add multiple services, which further cripples casual relationships.

The concept of a third place is one where people have a place to hang out, meet new friends, and talk with old friends. The Latin word *trivium* means the intersection of three roads—a place where people on a journey would stop to socialize and talk about everyday things. It's where we get the words *trivia* and *trivial.* Small talk. But small talk is not unimportant talk—it is an essential part of community.

We live in the most suburban nation in the world. We work in one place, live in another, and worship in yet another. What's missing in American culture, according to Oldenburg, is a place to hang out. In Munich, they hang out in the biergartens. In Tokyo, it's the teahouses. In London, it's the pubs. We long for a third place, but rarely find it. That's why so much of what's on TV is popular—it helps us meet a need vicariously. *Cheers* is a place where everybody knows your name. In *Friends,* Chandler, Phoebe, and the gang hang out at Central Perk. In *Seinfeld,* they gather at the diner. Companies like Starbucks and Panera Bread Company have developed profitable businesses catering not just to people's desire for a good cup of coffee or a slice of fresh bread, but for the even deeper hunger to find a place to connect with others. And many churches throughout the United States are starting to build third places.

As you begin to connect people to the church's mission and help them develop intimate relationships, you can't ignore the importance of casual relationships. Look around on Sunday morning. Are people hanging out before and after services? Do people gather informally on Tuesday afternoons or Friday mornings? The concept of a third place doesn't have to be limited to your church's facilities. You can find a third place anywhere. It just has to be easily accessible, help strangers make new friends, and provide a place where old friends can catch up.

Partnering to Lead Change

As Walt Kallestad began to search for ways to move his church from consumerism to community, he called a former professor and asked him if he knew of a church that was successfully reaching the next generation, building authentic community, and transforming the culture. The answer: St. Thomas' Church in Sheffield, England.

When Walt arrived unannounced at "St. Tom's," what he saw, in many ways, was the opposite of what he had built in Phoenix. While CCOJ was invested in campus development and programs, the two thousand members of St. Tom's met mostly in homes. Where CCOJ was focused on large events and entertaining corporate worship, St. Tom's emphasized small groups and met only once a month collectively. Where CCOJ was heavily burdened with mortgage, debt, and organizational demands, St. Tom's was relatively free to invest into the hearts and lives of its people, especially the small-group leaders. Where CCOJ relied almost exclusively on ordained pastors and paid staff for leadership, St. Tom's ministry was almost completely empowered by lay leadership.

Within two days of his visit, Walt believed he had found the kind of dynamic church and principles he had been looking for. He believed CCOJ needed to move from "more and bigger and better" to "smaller and deeper and authentic."

When Walt met Mike Breen, the rector and team leader of St. Thomas' Church, he felt an instant connection: Both men were straightforward, unassuming, and passionate about church. As it turned out, Breen was going through a personal transition; he believed he had taken St. Tom's as far as he could and was listening for the still, small voice of God's new direction for his ministry. On the day after Breen announced his resignation, Walt's voice may have sounded mysteriously divine. He met with Mike and said, "I think God is calling you to America to work with us."

In the summer of 2004, Mike moved to Glendale to join the staff of Community Church of Joy. Walt Kallestad, Mike Breen, Paul Sorensen, and the other leaders at CCOJ partnered together in the first steps of transformation. During the first two years, the results were mixed, depending on your perspective. Membership declined, but giving per member increased. Attendance dropped, but participation in small groups grew. Many members and employees left, and some were even angry. Others engaged in more significant levels of ministry both inside and outside the church. Change is never easy. And the effectiveness of the change process is never in the hands of the consultant—whether an outsider like me or an insider like Mike Breen. The transformation process is always in the hands of the community.

Paul Sorensen, the first person I met at CCOJ, has become a good friend and partner in ministry over the years. I recently asked him about how he personally was experiencing the transitions at CCOJ. Early in the journey, he says he is seeing real signs of transformation.

"It all started with our leaders. More specifically, I realized change had to start with me. It has been painful. I had to let go of my tendency to control others. I have had to learn how to build leaders rather than maintain a program. I'm still in process, for sure, but now other leaders are learning how to equip people as well. We've moved away from a program focus and toward a discipleship emphasis. The seeker model was the right model at one time. We had great people serving here. But that model was no longer effective in fulfilling our mission. We had to change. We had to sacrifice a model of ministry in order to gain a way of life. Some of our numbers may be down. But our most important numbers are up.

"More laypeople than ever are stepping up to serve. For example, a lay couple has stepped into a previously staffed role with our missions team. They have multiplied our impact locally and globally. Worship has become a rich and engaging experience of God's presence. In recent weeks, literally hundreds of previously passive spectators are praying for each other and coming to the altar area to respond to the message and receive personal prayer. Instead of a staff-driven program of small groups, leaders are being mentored and are launching other groups everywhere. Sunday sermons have become focused upon Scripture. Leaders are drawn just to hang out with each other. Community has become more than a stated value but is becoming the fabric of our lives."

We can never predict the future. But we can prepare for it by building a strong community. Despite good intentions and well-laid plans, the quest is often filled with sharp turns in the road. It is, after all, a journey of change, much of it unexpected.

CONSUMERISM/COMMUNITY SPEED BUMP

Transforming Church Checkup

1. Do you have a large number of members who are not on board with the church's stated direction?

2. Does your church have difficulty filling volunteer positions?

3. Are your staff and lay leaders discouraged or on the verge of burnout?

4. Is your church's worship attendance significantly higher than the number of people involved in ministry?

Travel Tips

Consumers resist change. People must feel connected to the community before they will embrace change. To build a creative community:

1. Help people see how their Monday-through-Friday lives connect to your church's mission. *Communion people fa their daily lives*

2. Connect individuals to the bigger picture by including a wide range of people in major decisions.

3. Don't expect congregational meetings and "town hall" events to foster community. Rather, intentionally and personally invite people to participate in focus groups or individual discussions about the church.

4. Design a process that makes it easy for newcomers to connect with a smaller group within the church.

5. Make sure you take advantage of ways your buildings can facilitate community.

Reflections

1. When you consider the statement "A 'successful' church can offer outstanding programs and ministries, but if its members are not being transformed, it is not a healthy church," what do you think about the health of your own church?

2. Which is a better description of your church: "A dispenser of religious goods and services where people come to receive" or "A missions station where people are launched to give"? Why do you feel that way? What changes would you like to see?

4

INCONGRUENCE/CODE, PART 1

Out of Sync

There are different kinds of gifts, but the same Spirit. There are different kinds of service, but the same Lord. There are different kinds of working, but the same God works all of them in all men. Now to each one the manifestation of the Spirit is given for the common good.
—1 Corinthians 12:4–7

Anabel and Leighton, my two daughters, have very different personalities.

Anabel is loud, full of energy, and loves to be the life of the party. Although Leighton is younger, we began noticing her uniqueness only a month or two after she was born. She is quieter than Anabel. She loves the feeling of being cuddled; Anabel has always been our explorer and won't sit still for long. Leighton doesn't cry much. Even when her eardrum nearly burst from an ear infection, she hardly made a sound. Anabel lets us know immediately if she's upset.

Some of these characteristics are genetic. Others have been shaped by our daughters' experiences. If you are a parent, you understand. At times, you see yourself in each child. At other times, you wonder if you might have picked up the wrong child in the hospital nursery.

In the same way that the forces of nature and nurture shape our children into different people, the men and women who make up the body of Christ—the church—are vastly different as well. Paul employed the metaphor of the human body with all its diverse parts and varied functions to illustrate the fact that the church is a teeming mass of very different people. And this is part of its glory.

Such diversity within unity was modeled from a time before time—in the unique and shared existence of each of the Three Persons in One. By design, each person within the body of each church—and each church within the larger body of the global church—is designed to reflect God's image in unique and varied ways (Eph. 4:11–13).

Obviously Incongruent?

Pastor Rich pointed out his car window. "See this neighborhood?" he asked me. "Could it be more obvious that our church needs to change?"

I saw a run-down neighborhood populated mostly by older Hispanics, with very few hints of a former prosperity.

"When First Baptist was first started sixty years ago," Pastor Rich continued, "this was a predominately white community with lots of prosperous young families. We averaged about fifteen hundred in worship. But for the last ten to twenty years, economic decline has drastically altered the makeup of the neighborhood, and we're down to about a hundred fifty in worship.

"Ninety-seven percent of our church is white," the pastor told me. "Do you see anything incongruent about that?"

The church's founding pastor had served nine years. In the most recent ten years, nine pastors had served. Rich was the tenth. If things did not change soon, he believed there would soon be an eleventh.

He turned to me. "How many white families do you see in this neighborhood?" I looked around and could see none. "Every time I suggest reaching out to the diversity in our community—maybe a simple suggestion like teaching English as a second language—I am always greeted by resistance. The remaining members usually counter by telling me that I should focus on reviving our ailing children's and youth ministries. So tell me, how many kids do you see in the neighborhood?"

I looked around and had to say, "None."

"If it's so obvious to you and me," he said, turning down the road leading to his church, "then why doesn't anyone else get it?"

Code: Collective Personality

Transforming churches are congruent—they have a relationship to a fixed point, which serves as a true north. Our consulting firm, TAG Consulting, calls this fixed point the church's *code*. Every church has its own unique code that defines its identity and clarifies its focus.

Code can be tricky to define. We can talk about code as the essence or soul of a church. We can talk about what code does, which is to shape the face of how the church displays itself to the world. Code shapes tradition, values, and mission. Code is not usually rational. Most often, it reveals itself indirectly and symbolically, through the myths, heroes, and stories that give a church its texture and flavor.

Code, in fact, is most easily understood when things are out of alignment, when something isn't right. When code functions, it is almost invisible, like the air we breathe. A church incongruent with its code is the single greatest cause of conflict we see at TAG Consulting, and it creates far more damage than clashes over personal differences, worship styles, or even theology. Churches fail to change because they don't know who they are. Or they deny who they are and try to live in a way that is inconsistent with their code.

In much the same way a person falters in life without a sense of identity, a church that does not know itself is fated to struggle. When people don't know who they are, a gap appears between what they claim to be and who they really have come to be. We hardly blink a collective eye anymore when the president of the United States looks squarely into the camera and says with deep conviction, "I did not have sex with that woman," or, "No new taxes." We barely crack a smile when a professional baseball player, closing in on a remarkable career of five hundred home runs and three thousand hits, tests positive for steroids and then denies the charge with this defense: "Why would I do that? That would be really stupid of me."

The cultural dysfunction of being disconnected from one's true identity has infected the church. Sadly, most Americans see the results of this infection.

On *Seinfeld*, Elaine assumes her boyfriend is an uptight dork because his car radio is preset to Christian stations. On *King of the Hill*, the pastor of the Lutheran church is a nerdy woman who is obsessed with stinky fish. Homer Simpson's neighbor is a stick-in-the-mud Holy Roller. A vast majority of the mainstream press lumps all Christians in with right-wing political movements and tends to ignore every other expression of Christian faith. Many Americans use the word *hypocritical* as their adjective of choice for Christians, especially Christian leaders.

Obviously the stereotypes are an exaggeration. But I wonder: How are we really doing? Churches go to great pains to define their stands on controversial issues and to distinguish themselves from theological rivals. But do we understand who we really are, deep down underneath the ideological and political labels?

Incongruence is not limited to the church world.

Sears failed miserably when they launched the "softer side of Sears" campaign. Why? Because when people think of Sears, they visualize power tools and appliances. By focusing on the softer side to attract a neglected market segment, Sears shocked their loyal customers. Who wants to buy lingerie in the same checkout line as a chain saw?

When 7-Eleven sent their cashiers through customer-service training, they focused on a model similar to the Ritz-Carlton hotel's training programs. Cashiers were trained to look people in the eye, engage them in conversation, and ask, "How may I be of service to you?" and a litany of similar questions. Sales plummeted. Why? People visit 7-Eleven because it's quick and convenient. They want 7-Eleven, not the Ritz-Carlton.

In 1996, McDonald's lost millions on a line of sandwiches targeting adults—the Arch Deluxe. The executives learned the hard way that Ronald McDonald just doesn't appeal to many adults. Since then, they've learned to focus on Happy Meals and playgrounds. They've learned that their ancillary adult products (salads and healthier sandwiches) will only succeed if they are true to their code.

When Carly Fiorina became the CEO of Hewlett-Packard, many of her initial moves—including her first major proposal, to merge with Compaq—violated the company code known as the HP Way. When founders David Packard and Bill Hewlett cooked hot dogs at the company picnics and refused many of the accoutrements of success, they helped form a deep code about respect for employees—including empowerment and shifting decision making to the least expensive part of the organization. But the merger with Compaq resulted in fifteen thousand HP layoffs and was a direct frontal attack on the HP Way.

People will resist change when decisions don't align with the code.

As a consultant, I help many of the churches I serve discover their unique code. Every church has one. But very few have taken the time to discover what it is. In part, this is because, to do so, a church must fight three cultural obstacles to the creative, intuitive understanding of code:

- Reason
- Manipulation
- The Next Big Thing

The Nameless Age of Reason

As I was working on this chapter, I was speaking at a conference. An assistant to the bishop came up to me at a break and said, "I just don't get this whole code thing."

She explained that she consults with churches in her Lutheran synod on conflict, strategy, and change. I asked her to explain her methods and approaches. She told me she reviews financials and attendance trends, and conducts a demographic assessment. She also has a questionnaire for members, measuring the effectiveness of church programs. She then uses the well-known Natural Church Development tool to assess vitality.

Curious, I asked if she ever asks members about their memories of the church. No, she said. Did she ask people what the architecture communicates? Again, no. I asked if she looks for the metaphors that people use to describe the church. I got a blank stare. Her assessment was all left-brained. She was missing the intuitive, and most powerful, parts of the church's identity. I then asked if there were times she knew something was amiss, even if she couldn't find it on paper. At that, she perked up. Yes! She often consulted with churches where something was out of sync, but she found herself unable to put her finger on just what that was.

Our culture places a high premium on defining reality through logic. But at its essence, identity is right-brained. Code is deeply embedded in the symbols that draw people together in community. It cannot be flushed to the surface by reason alone; intuition must play a part.

The forensic scientists on *CSI* discover the truth through a ruthless examination of the "facts"—bloodstains, fingerprints, cigarette ashes, fragments of carpet on the soles of shoes. If I tried to reach the inner life of a church using similar scientific methods, I would be helpless as a consultant.

Understanding the code of your church requires the soul of an artist more than the tools of a scientist. It requires skillful listening to intuition more than the ability to read charts, graphs, and financial statements. Sound too mystical? For now, just consider that reason alone does not reveal everything that is true about a person—or a church. People can know my age, my college GPA, my job performance, and facts about my family, but they can't *really* know me unless they talk to me and walk with me to experience my passions.

Manipulation: Vision instead of Insight

Our culture also places a premium on control. In our mechanistic society, we have come to believe we can manipulate destiny through the correct techniques. In other words, we no longer discover reality so much as we create it. In the late 1980s, I recorded a CD of mostly original music. I wrote the lyrics, music, and chord charts. I did the vocals and some of the guitar work. It was not very good. But it was a process of self-discovery. Today, by contrast, I can produce an entire CD of "original" songs by manipulating software programs on a computer—without ever writing my own melodies, lyrics, or chord charts. By simply weaving together bits and pieces of computer-generated sounds and chord progressions, I can "create" original music. I'm sure the quality of my new production would be much higher than my feeble "rock star" attempts of the eighties. But the manipulated version certainly wouldn't capture the essence of my heart and soul.

In a similar fashion, when seeking to determine what their code is, many churches get it wrong. They try to define a code rather than discover the one that's already there. They start predetermined ministries and ask people to serve. They carve out a set of core values or craft a mission statement on flip charts using a left-brained voting process. No one ever stops to consider that the process itself may be flawed.

Instead of starting ministry with a program, it is much more effective to begin with a person (or better yet, a group of people) with specific gifts and passions and form a ministry around him or her (or them). Not only does this process give the ministry a better chance of success, it enables leaders to more clearly identify the genetic makeup of the church's code.

The Next Big Thing: Copying the Church down the Street

Americans love to pursue the next big thing. Whether it is a hot stock tip, a "can't miss" business proposition, this year's "in" fashions, or the cool car my neighbor just bought, we want the newest, the biggest, and the most promising.

Churches are not so different. It is tempting to identify "models" of ministry from churches that have experienced rapid growth and import their practices without paying any attention to a unique identity within the context of a unique community. This process of adopting the next big thing has a number of negative unintended consequences:

- A tendency toward mimicry, which inhibits true creativity
- A lack of a unique code to bond people together in shared ministry
- A lack of attention to the critical role of local context in the formation of a church's focus
- A depersonalization of ministry as leaders find themselves spending all their time keeping the machine running smoothly

Perhaps the most damaging consequence is that relationships—the very lifeblood of ministry in the transforming church—are sacrificed on the altar of success.

Megachurch Wannabe

At one point, River Oaks Community Church was a rising star in the megachurch-wannabe world. The church's gifted founders experienced personal transformation and inspiration when they encountered the Willow Creek model, and so they set up shop in Carmel, Indiana, with a mind to import the strategies, principles, and tactics of one of the nation's largest churches. And it worked.

Within the first few years, River Oaks—the nineteenth church to join the Willow Creek Association—had grown significantly. And then, unexpectedly, with little warning, trouble hit. The pastor left. Conflicts set in among leadership, membership declined, and eventually the church divided.

A new pastor, Marcus Warner, was called. When I first consulted with Marcus several years later, he wore the look of despair I have come to expect from frustrated pastors. He knew his church lacked direction, but he was beginning to doubt if he had what it took to lead the necessary change. In talking to the current staff, leaders, and members—as well as some who had left—I asked a few questions focused on the question of identity:

- What are your defining values?
- Does the church have clearly defined groups of people it is trying to reach?
- Why do people choose your church?
- In what ways is your community unique?
- What are your best memories of this church?

Most of the people were able to answer the questions succinctly. But they would do so by prefacing their responses with "It's the same as Willow Creek" or "They wanted to be the Willow Creek of Indianapolis" or "The seeker model didn't work for the founders."

When responding to questions about code, rarely did people use a possessive personal pronoun—*our* or *ours*. While they may have believed in the strategy and vision, few ever owned it. By simply borrowing the Willow Creek model and hoping to clone it, the leaders of River Oaks never localized the distinctive context, mission, and culture of the church. They never asked the most important question: Given the uniqueness of each person and the context of Carmel, who are we?

Earl Thornton was excited about a new men's ministry for the church he pastors near Chicago—First Assembly of God, Joliet. The same ministry had taken off at a church in Arkansas, and Earl had a member of his congregation who was willing to champion it. First Assembly, a large and growing church, routinely launched new ministries with great enthusiasm. He anticipated nothing short of success with the new men's ministry.

Much to Earl's surprise, the men's ministry flopped. Looking back, he notes several reasons why. The leader was new to the congregation and had not built connections to other people. Several of the church's small groups were lukewarm in their support because their members already felt overcommitted. But most significantly, the new ministry focused on large events rather than small, relational settings, which symbolized the code of First Assembly.

Good ministry. Great success in Arkansas. A flop in Joliet for two main reasons: The ministry was incongruous with the church's code, and mimicry is rarely an effective strategy.

The Model of Relationship: The Beginnings of Code

In our postmodern world, the primacy of autonomy and reason as the twin arbiters of reality continues to fade, while the primacy of relationship continues to rise. Code emerges from those relationships. We can think of code as the collective identity of a given culture and as the shared norms adopted by groups within that culture. In other words, code exists at both macro and micro levels.

For example, Americans share elements of a common code. Freedom, pioneering, exploration, and discovery help to form what it means to be an American. But unique codes exist at smaller levels within the broader context of the American code. The code of Texans is quite different from the code of New Yorkers or Californians. And the cultural personality of folks who live in Corpus Christi differs from those in Dallas.

In much the same way, every church is connected to a macrocode within the larger context of the biblical narrative and church history. I look at the Bible as a series of short stories, each providing context and meaning within the scope of a larger narrative; in other words, the *metanarrative*—the one Story that explains and encompasses all others.

The Bible forms the metanarrative of the church. For example, within the context of the sixty-six books of the Bible is the story of God's relationship with His people—first Israel and then the church. Very early in the Bible, we can see the main themes emerge. At the end of Exodus 5, Moses complains to God that the fate of the Israelites has steadily deteriorated since God directed Moses to approach Pharaoh and request the Israelites' freedom. "You have not rescued your people at all," Moses accuses (v. 23). God's response, recorded in 6:1–8, is to show who He is. He is a God of redemption; He is a God of covenant relationship; He is a God of revelation; and He is a God of promise.

And He is our Father. In these critical ways, we should be and look like Him. That is our DNA. As we read the Old and New Testaments, we find the same themes of *redemption, covenant, revelation*, and *promise.* When any church lives outside of these four elements, it becomes incongruous with its genetic and experiential relationship with its Father. Every church must participate in God's work of redemption: sharing the gospel and making the world a better place. Every church must function as a covenant community, loving and caring for one another in self-sacrifice. Every church must seek to understand how God has revealed Himself—in general revelation through the laws of nature and in specific revelation through the Bible, the Son, and the Spirit. And every church must have an eschatological hope that drives it toward God's future promise. When any local church misses these basics, it falls out of alignment with God's plan for the church.

At the same time, each individual church has a different role to play within the greater metanarrative. That role is formed around a church's code. The collective personality of a local body of believers is formed in much the same way as the personality of an individual. Like people, churches are shaped in part by their unique histories, experiences, and contexts. Two Baptist churches may share the same theological perspectives but have very different codes. Each church has a unique story, or defining code, within the larger story of its denomination. And within the code of a specific local church, each person, connecting with others in creative community, has a particular role to play expressed through a personal code. Through a complex and interconnected series of relationships, we experience unity within diversity, unique roles toward a shared end, and the body functioning over time and space as something much more than just a collection of parts.

A body implies the dynamic and interconnected nature of life-giving and life-forming relationships—unique and living parts, connected together mysteriously and symbiotically, each performing a specific role for the greater good. In a sense, the local church is not simply a collection of individual personalities. The necessary and critical reality of being in relationships with one another helps define a collective personality—the church's code.

Emotional Imprints

Anthropologists suggest that human beings are the most susceptible to learning during highly emotional periods. As a result, early childhood and adolescence tend to be the most formative times in the development of human personality. Because a church is a collection of human personalities, it makes good sense that a church's personality, its code, would be developed along the same lines.

In his thought-provoking book *7 Secrets of Marketing in a Multi-Cultural World*, G. Clotaire Rapaille argues that every person has strong emotional "imprints" early in life that help form lifelong perceptions. These experiential imprints combine with our genetic makeup to form a personal code. While psychologists often point to shattering moments of abuse or positive experiences of love, Rapaille suggests that imprints are not confined to the dramatic. Early imprints form our lifelong reactions to things both great and small. They may involve things as mundane (and glorious) as coffee.

A large coffee company was losing market share. They hired a market research firm to figure out what consumers were looking for—taste, price, quantity, and so forth. The research firm quantified the results and helped launch an ad campaign. The campaign failed miserably. So the company hired Rapaille, a cultural anthropologist, who took a different approach. He looked for early imprints related to coffee. He asked people about their recollections of coffee during early childhood and adolescence—and discovered these focused mainly on its aroma.

People described to him how they would lie in bed as a child and wake up and smell coffee brewing. During his research, he learned most Americans didn't actually taste coffee until adolescence—and they didn't like it, so they added cream and lots of sugar. His conclusion? Americans don't really like coffee. We like the aroma, because it symbolizes home, family, and safety.[14]

The early imprints discovered by Rapaille revolutionized the coffee industry. Think of Starbucks or Caribou Coffee. Walk in the front door and notice the aroma and all the people having coffee with friends. And then look at all the different options—from caffe mocha to vanilla syrup—that mask the taste of the coffee itself!

Emotional imprints define all areas of our lives, including our understanding of church. Adults tend to gravitate toward (or away from) churches based on early memories of church. One young lady in Chicago recently told me that her most prominent childhood memory of church was sitting in her mom's lap while Mom stroked her hair. Is it any wonder that she was drawn to a church with a code of nurturing? An older man from the same church told me about his sense of pleasure as a five-year-old at church with an extended family—mom, dad, grandpa, and grandma. A young business executive in Toledo recalled his most striking memory: sitting bored on a hard pew, receiving stern looks from his priest. In fact, he remembers the same priest spanking him with a wooden spoon for failing to memorize his catechism. The negative imprint caused him to seek out a church where worship is energetic and theology nonjudgmental. We often gravitate toward church because of strong emotional imprints, which affect—even drive—us on mostly subconscious levels.

When the strong imprints occurred is just as important as *what* they were. Consider the postconfirmation exodus that happens in many mainline churches. Many of these churches emphasize getting children to church, which is a great thing. But it doesn't take long for these children subconsciously to notice that their parents are attending primarily for the sake of the children. The imprint is formed. They leave church during their teenage or early adult years and then return when they have children of their own. They gravitate toward churches that have the same message: Church is something you do as a family for the sake of your children. Likewise, people whose experiences with church were strongest during adolescence—possibly a summer camp or youth group—tend to link up with churches that have a more individual or experiential emphasis. And those whose experiences were largely negative, at either development stage, are those who are most likely to look for something totally different, if they even look for a church at all.

Shared Intuitions

A person's decision to attend your church is usually made in a moment. If someone is looking for a church, she will drive by the facility and decide within three seconds if it might be a fit. If she actually shows up, she determines in another three seconds whether to return—even before meeting another person, singing a song, or hearing a sermon. The rest of her experience will merely confirm or challenge the initial impression. This "three second response" is rooted in the brain's limbic system—which determines instantly what sensory inputs will be accepted or rejected. The limbic system is the center of emotion. While the right brain and left brain represent our conscious thought processes, the limbic system determines which messages will go to the neocortex at a subconscious level. It alerts us to danger or safety; to stress or comfort; to fit or no fit.

People often make decisions about which church to attend based on those early imprints. We take in the visual clues and instantly determine the fit between our code and the church's code. Biologists and psychologists have long understood the power of intuition to mine subconscious experiences empowered by emotion. Even before we can "think" about what church to attend, that decision has often been made.

Porsche drivers, at least those who are honest, are not concerned about a car's fuel efficiency or cost. Mac users are drawn to the visual elegance and simplicity of their computers. Most of us didn't choose a spouse for logical reasons. All of us make significant life decisions based on intuition, not reason. We can't always explain why—but we recognize when something deep inside of our personalities resonates with a particular code. I believe most of the people who attend a particular church do so less for reasons of denomination, values, ministries, services, or even theology than for the subconscious pull of a church's code. For the most part, people attend a particular church because they intuitively sense that their personal code is similar to the church's code. The archetype is the bond.

And it is the code of a church that binds us together.

Unless we violate it.

Do Not Violate Your Code

Aurora Advent Christian Church, located just outside of Chicago, was stuck. The church was dynamic in a lot of ways but really struggled on the leadership level. The leaders were highly motivated, talented, and committed. But as a unit, something was wrong.

The first things I noticed were the signs—in the office, in the gymnasium, on the doors to the bathroom. The place was plastered with "do nots." Do not bounce balls on the wall. Do not wear black-soled shoes. Do not leave the lights on. Do not remove the books. Do not take the stapler. Do not sit in these seats. Each notice was signed "The Trustees." I attended a few meetings, which were formal, focused on procedure and rules.

Yet everyone seemed so friendly, warm, and passionate about ministry. When I took a direct, left-brained approach and told leaders they were overly focused on the business of the church, it did not go well. I was challenging their way of operating, and they weren't about to budge. Nothing changed. Aurora remained stuck.

On a return visit, I focused on trying to better understand the church's code. I took a more intuitive, right-brained approach. In focus groups, I asked people to go back as far as they could in memory and recall first or powerful experiences with church. I expected to hear lots of legalism and rules—since that seemed to be what the church was all about. I was amazed to hear their stories. "It was the one place each week where Mom and Dad were with me." "I remember holding Mom's hand, and it was the only place where I held her hand each week." "I remember going to Grandma's house after church." Nearly all of the people I talked to told me of deep experiences relating to family. It didn't take a genius to figure it out: The church's code was all about family—warmth, caring, and connection. In leading the church like a business, Aurora Advent Christian had become a stranger to its own code.

In meeting with the leaders, I made an appeal for change based on their own code. I posed this question: "In your board meetings, do you function more like a government agency or a family?"

There was a long silence. The question stunned them. One by one, they had to admit: government agency. They vowed to be more like a family. By appealing to their code, I gave them "permission" to change how they were operating.

Six months later, Pastor Kenny sent me an e-mail saying the board meetings were the best they had been in his twelve years at the church. They took a few minutes for business and spent the rest of the time interacting like a healthy family—sharing with one another, praying for one another, reading together.

The only way for a church to move forward is to look back. Paradoxically, change can come only when the good past is guarded with passion.

Code shapes church culture, values, focus, and mission. It creates the core ideology. It creates a context for vision and strategy to emerge. It shapes the stories we tell, the rituals we observe, and the unspoken rules we follow. It is crucial that all the people in the church be committed to a healthy code, since the code sets the direction for all the members of the church.

I recently went white-water rafting. Before we began, our guide told us that when we were in rough water, it was imperative that we stay in sync, listening for his commands. If we did not work together, we would quickly be over our heads in trouble. The first time we hit Class 4 rapids, we nearly capsized. We had heard the leader's voice and reacted frantically. The next time, though, we managed the rapids a little more smoothly together. By the time the trip ended, something interesting happened: None of us were really listening to the guide's specific words; instead, we fell into the rhythm of his voice. That's what it's like when a church clearly defines and protects its code over a long period of time. With just a little guidance, people instinctively know what to do. Code is the rhythm they fall into.

The Power of a Discovered Code

Pastor Rich nearly became the tenth pastor in eleven years to leave First Baptist. Blame was circulating as fast as a fan on a summer day. Rich wanted to blame the lay leadership for not understanding how drastically the neighborhood had changed—from a prosperous white community of young families to an aging Hispanic community fighting against crime, drugs, and prostitution. Other leaders blamed Rich for failing to jump-start the failing youth ministry and for pursuing his own agenda. The blaming missed the point. Pastor Rich was failing for one central reason: First Baptist's code was ignored.

On a return visit to Rich's church, I began to seek to understand the code, which was submerged. When I asked members what they thought it was, most of them suggested "family." The founding pastor, who had served for nine years, loved and served the people. He visited them on a regular basis and made everyone feel safe and secure.

I was perplexed, because that didn't explain why the church had so much trouble with change. A church's code never prevents a church from adapting. Rather, it acts as a launching pad for change. I began to question if "family" was the real code. As I probed deeper, I began to understand that "family" was simply a metaphoric expression of the church's real code: safety.

The members wanted a place to feel safe, and the changing community posed threats. Pastor Rich's vision didn't seem to protect the church's code, the need for safety. But once we understood the church's code, we were able to move forward in the planning process. The leaders developed a new church slogan: A Safe Place. They created core values that were congruent with the code: a safe community, unconditional acceptance, focus on people, loving our neighborhood.

Once the lay leaders began to feel safe, they were able to move into a strategic plan—one that protected the code. Interestingly, the code became the launching pad for a new direction. The lay leaders began to realize their current ministries were not "safe" for the Hispanic and elderly populations. The church wasn't a safe place for the poor in their community or the young Latino gang members. As a result, existing programs for the nonexistent young families were closed down. New ministries geared toward the area's demographics were created. The church bought an old grocery store and turned it into a community outreach center, with a food pantry, a teen room, and a senior citizens' ministry. They offered ESL classes and started a career development center. Although the church lost a few members in the process, nearly everyone was excited about the new direction.

First Baptist was beginning to discover its code. Just as important, it was beginning to live in a way that was congruent with that code.

5

INCONGRUENCE/CODE, PART 2

Cracking the Code

*For we are God's workmanship, created in Christ Jesus to do
good works, which God prepared in advance for us to do.*
—Ephesians 2:10

There is no easy way to get to Moultrie, Georgia, without making a good long
drive. It's not a big place; I had to find my reading (magnifying) glasses when
I consulted my atlas. I booked a flight into Jacksonville, Florida, the nearest
direct flight from Washington Dulles. On the three-hour drive to Moultrie, I
crossed vast unpopulated spaces, checked my gas gauge a lot, and wondered
what I was getting myself into. When I finally arrived in the town of fewer
than twenty thousand, I discovered pretty much what I had expected: Other
than a Wal-Mart and three used-car dealerships, there's really not much
there—unless you like barbecue places that close around seven at night.

On my drive to Heritage Church, which even MapQuest couldn't
find, I took special notice of the other churches in town. They were mostly
Baptist or Methodist with colonnades, high white spires, and the easy
charm that marks so much of the South. My suspicion (later confirmed)
was that Moultrie was a sleepy, conservative town whose central rule was
"Don't break the rules." Especially when it comes to church.

Pastors do the pastoring, members show up in their Sunday best, and
visitors are greeted with smiles. Churches look like churches. Church music
shouldn't have a beat. Church is the place where you see your friends and
raise your kids (not your hands)—and don't try to make it more than that.
Play it safe; play by the rules. That's the way it has always been.

But when I finally pulled into the parking lot, Heritage blew all my preconceived notions away.

Code as Essence

Code is the defining essence of a church. Healthy growth is the result of a church's congruence with its code; poor health is caused by incongruence. It is important to understand that there is no such thing as a "bad" code. Code is value neutral. It is neither good nor bad. It just is. The culture that emerges from a church's code, however, can be positive or negative, a conduit for both good and evil. I once consulted with a church in South Carolina whose code was built around technological innovations. The church was an early innovator in multisite worship experiences, featuring live feeds of the pastor's sermons and reaching people they could never have reached otherwise. The same innovations, however, provided a means for the pastor to view and send pornographic material over the Internet.

Code is like a magnet in that it attracts people who resonate with it and are eager to be part of a similarly committed community.

Code is like a picture frame. It provides boundaries, color, and shape, but it is rarely the thing that we pay attention to.

My favorite metaphor for code, though, is a big, ugly machine.

A few months after Hurricane Ivan destroyed much of the panhandle of Florida in 2004, I was driving on a recently reopened road on Pensacola Beach. Despite nearly round-the-clock work to restore the beach community, it still looked like a war zone. Once-luxurious homes were littered like giant toothpicks, and the beaches themselves were rearranged and nearly destroyed. As I drove along, I noticed the center of activity for the restoration work: a series of giant machines, each at least the length of a freight car. Sand was being pumped and filtered continually into each of these machines. The debris—every imaginable form of glass, wood, steel, and plastic—was emptied into giant piles as the filtered sand was returned to the beach. For months, the machines worked round the clock to filter miles and miles of beach. Years after the hurricane, the work of filtering and refining continues.

That is how code works: It acts as a filter for what the church is and what it becomes. A code screens and sifts, keeping out programs that do not fit the code while empowering new ones that do.

Several years ago, I facilitated a strategic planning session with First United Methodist in Fort Dodge, Iowa. The church was struggling to clarify new strategies and was failing to attract children and youth. The long-term members routinely shot down each new idea from the pastor, Gordon Watson. When I interviewed the members, I asked them to talk about the church's history. Each one of them told me of the glory days when the church had a bus ministry. Every Sunday, the church's bus meandered through the town, picking up children and then dropping them home again after the church service and Sunday school. When I asked them what the church should do in the future, I was not surprised when they suggested bringing back the bus ministry.

While I was tempted to dismiss the old guard's suggestion for lack of present-day relevance, I was more interested in discovering what the bus ministry represented. It was symbolic of the church's code: ministry outside the walls of the church. More specifically, "ministry on wheels" was a significant element of the church's code. The specific expression of the church's code in an earlier era had been the bus ministry. Over the years the bus ministry gradually faded, and there was little chance of resurrecting that particular ministry again due to a variety of factors— changing demographics in Fort Dodge, regulatory and liability issues, and the general lack of interest from the community. But a church's code never dies, and this church needed a new outlet.

As Gordon and I discussed the church's code, I asked about his passion and experiences, trying to discover his personal code. I was shocked to learn that Gordon was a former truck driver who saw driving a truck as a way to share the gospel with people. Ministry on wheels! The church's code and Gordon's code were in sync. It was now simply a matter of leveraging the code in new ways.

As we discussed the church's code during the planning session, one long-term member said, "Hey, I've got an idea. Gordon still has an eighteen-wheeler in his backyard, and I'm sure his neighbors are thrilled about that. Why don't we use the truck to take the ministry to the people?" With that, a new ministry was launched. About once a month, First United Methodist Church takes a truck throughout Fort Dodge. A short worship service—complete with a band, puppets, dramas, and a short message—attracts kids and families from all over town. The local newspaper recently featured the ministry, which is now called "Taking It to the People." First United Methodist had cracked their code and is now leveraging "ministry on wheels" for a new generation.

Once your church has cracked its code, you will want to filter everything through it. Your stated values will help protect the code. Your mission statement will reinforce your code. Your code should determine everything your church does—from ministries and programs to decisions about who leads. Your members will resist any change that is in conflict with the church's code. But they will also resist change if they don't perceive that leaders are intentionally preserving the church's code. By discovering and preserving your church's code, you will give your members a sense of safety so that they will be more open to change. In other words, they resonate with the church's code at a subconscious level. People will be more open to change if they know that you understand and value who they are—even if they are not conscious of their own connection to the code.

In my business consulting, I can tell a lot about a company's code, culture, and values simply by walking through the front door and looking around. I may see a dingy, depressing sweatshop that values money more than people. Or I may see a place of light and color where creativity and inspiration take precedence over efficiency. Whatever I see when I look at the building that houses an organization, I can be sure of one thing: I have seen the *soul* of that organization. The same can be said of a church.

Unless, of course, the church is incongruent with its own code.

Imagine, if you will, a series of expanding concentric circles. The innermost circle is the code, and the outermost circle is the face of the church—how it presents itself in stories, symbols, architecture, and style. The degree of congruence between the outward expression of a church and its code is critical in determining the health of a church. In fact, in a real way, it *is* the health of a church. A church can present itself in a manner incongruent with its essential code—its collective personality, shared intuition, and cultural archetypes. When this happens, disease feeds off the incongruence and grows to become a consuming cancer.

On the Face of It: Heritage Church

Heritage Church was nothing like I expected. Instead of an ornately designed building with elegant lines and warm tones reflective of Southern charm, I found a warehouse with bare concrete floors and heating ducts snaking along the ceiling. Instead of driving along the carefully manicured lawns and precisely landscaped acres of the town's "real" churches, my car kicked up a plume of dust as I navigated a rutty dirt road leading to an unpaved parking lot. Instead of the polite, genteel worship experienced in most Southern churches, the service was enthusiastic, almost fervent, and roiling with raw energy. Clearly, this church presented itself differently than the other churches in Moultrie, Georgia.

But that was about to change. The church, which had been started six years earlier by a group of lay leaders, had outgrown its warehouse. With a seating capacity of 550, their facility, which previously housed a recreation business and was rented out for dances and parties, was bursting at its corrugated seams. Worship attendance—driven by highly participatory music, solid biblical preaching, and strong lay leadership—was increasing exponentially. Heritage was out of space and wasn't exactly sure what to do. They owned a lot of land and knew they could build something much better without relocating.

"We just thought we'd build a nice building," said Pastor David Oaks during my first visit. Initial conversations with a local architect presumed

Heritage Church would construct a somewhat traditional sanctuary. When they brought in TAG Consulting for strategic planning, they assumed we would help them develop a series of action steps, charts, and budgets for a five-year period. They also thought we'd help them select a design-build firm, a fund-raising consultant, and so forth. The new building was going to cost about four million dollars, they reasoned, so why not spend a few thousand dollars to develop a good plan?

Something Doesn't Feel Right

At a critical point in the church's history—the construction of a new facility—leaders sensed uneasiness, but they couldn't identify the source of the disquiet.

On many different levels, Heritage's story is instructive. In most cases when I am called in to consult with a church, the initial issue presented is not the "real" one. The problems reside much deeper, even in a very healthy church such as Heritage. Although Heritage invited me in on the premise that I would facilitate a strategic plan, I didn't have to probe very deep to find a different, more important question: Was this direction really congruent with what the church was?

Incongruence almost always initially presents itself as "something I can't quite put my finger on." Something just doesn't feel right. It wakes you up at night. You can't quite explain it, but you feel restless. You sense something lurking in the shadows just outside of consciousness. In your head, the pieces aren't quite fitting. As a leader, you need to pay attention to those unsettling feelings, even when they are coming from other people. Sometimes the uneasiness will go away as the church adapts to a new set of realities. Sometimes these feelings represent a valuable piece of information attempting to leap from the subconscious to the conscious. Other times they are a leading from the Holy Spirit. Or they may come from a combination of factors.

Time after time, I have heard leaders bemoan a critical decision gone awry by saying, "I knew in my gut this might not be right." When you experience a similar intuition, make sure you take time to explore the matter with other leaders and members: "Is it just me, or does someone else feel this way?" The more the congregation shares a similar feeling, the greater the need to probe deeper.

Cracking the Code

A good leader is a good detective. A church discovers its code in much the same fashion as a team of crime-scene investigators breaks a case. Start with the obvious clues, and often through intuitive leaps, you can work yourself into deeper levels of defining motive. To understand how to crack a church's code, leaders must understand the process of how a church expresses its personality. I have found it helpful to imagine a series of expanding concentric circles. The process of identifying your church's code is not purely linear. Each concentric circle interacts with all of the rest, and different aspects of your code may reveal themselves at different times. But we can note some core principles and tendencies

Break the Code

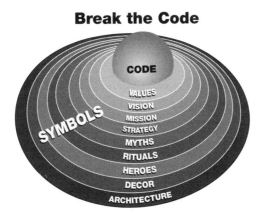

- The code is the core of identity, containing the blueprints of genetic makeup and shared experiences.
- The next four inner levels—values, vision, mission, and strategy—represent conscious intentions to define and unleash code through action.

- The outermost levels—myths, rituals, heroes, decor, and architecture—are *symbolic* expressions of code residing and expressed mostly beyond conscious awareness.

At any level the possibility exists for corruption of the code. These are the places where dysfunctions will take up residence.

"They Care More about People Than Programs"

We met in rooms with no carpet to begin to crack the code of Heritage Church. I began my consulting work as I usually do, by inviting the participation of people who are representative of the church at various levels of involvement—newcomers, longer-term members, staff, sporadic attendees, and leaders. In focus groups and one-on-one interviews, I began to ask a series of questions designed to answer this central question: Who are you as a church? Because Heritage had completed the Transforming Church Index, I already had answers to some of the more straightforward questions related to code:

- Do you feel the church has a clear statement of faith?
- Does the church have a clearly defined vision of the future?
- Has the church clearly differentiated itself from other churches?
- Are you excited about where your church is headed in the next few years?
- Do you love telling your friends about your church?
- Do you have a personal commitment to the church's future?
- Does your church have a clearly defined group(s) of people you are trying to reach and serve?
- Are the church's goals and direction clear to you?
- Do visitors quickly experience what your church is about?
- Do the church's ministries reflect its values?

These questions are geared more at the left brain—the conscious perceptions of church members. They are helpful in identifying symptoms of disease or signs of health; varying responses to these questions often point to deeper issues. The TCIndex will never tell us what the church's code is. It will only tell us whether the code is clear and congruent.

At Heritage, member responses to these questions were generally positive, compared to national norms. But a couple of the questions scored low. On paper, I couldn't figure out what the discrepancies were all about, so I knew I had to tap in to the right brain to understand the church's code. I designed a set of questions to explore the code's expression in the most outward—and largely symbolic—manifestations.

The best way to crack the code of a church is to get people to tell stories. So that's what I did. I asked questions such as, What is your most meaningful memory of this church? What first attracted you to Heritage? Can you describe your earliest experience of church? How is this church different from or the same as the one you remember going to as a child? What is most noticeably different about your life since coming to this church? As I listened, I began to see consistent messages expressed in slightly different ways.

- "This church doesn't waste money on buildings."
- "This is the first place where I felt like I could really be myself."
- "I feel loved here."
- "They care more about people than programs."
- "The leaders don't ask us to do anything they aren't doing themselves."
- "No one cares about who gets the credit here; we are all in this together."
- "Everyone is treated equally here, whether you are a bank president or a janitor."
- "It's the first time I really believed I could make a difference in the lives of others."

- "Status and position don't matter much here, compared to the church we came from."
- "This church believes I can and should be involved in a ministry. It's not the pastor's job to do the ministry; it's a job that we all share."
- "Most churches in the area focus on following rules and looking good, putting on a smile. This church lets me be real."

For Heritage, the church was clearly about the people, not the building. Across the divide of how much money each made or what he or she did for a living, they were connected to one another in the purpose of ministry. By intuitively understanding their code, a people of great diversity lived, worked, and worshipped together.

Detective Work

If congruence with code is so critical to a church's health and future, why do so many continue to fail at this level? My first answer is that incongruence is easy to detect but difficult to pinpoint. We know that something is wrong, but we don't always know what. My second answer is that most people seek to apply the wrong solutions to the wrong problems. Imagine the distress that First United Methodist would have experienced if they had failed after investing thousands of dollars to revive a defunct bus ministry.

Identifying and leveraging code requires a subtle, complex, and intuitive approach. Most of the critical information must be coaxed from areas beyond conscious awareness. That's why symbols are so important.

The dictionary defines *symbol* as "something that represents something else by association, resemblance, or convention." It works by imparting meaning, evoking emotion, and creating an "aha" understanding. We can learn much about its meaning by considering its antonym: *diabol*, the root of *diabolic*. The Devil's work is to divide, create confusion, and make reality disconnected.

G. Clotaire Rapaille writes, "A symbol is the unconscious expression of a cultural archetype. Members of a culture all relate to the same symbols without knowing why. If a symbol is wrong, it just doesn't ring a bell. If it is right, it taps into their emotions."[15]

The most difficult—and revealing—work of cracking a church's code is through symbolic understanding. Symbols take many forms. Some are intangible and almost unconsciously adopted and used, such as a particular style of body language, gestures, vocabulary, phrases, and jargon employed within the culture of a church. Other symbols are solid, tangible, and prominent, like the buildings that house the church's services and programs. Some have meaning only for the members of the church, while others are used to represent the church in the wider community and the marketplace. As a church evolves over time, some symbols remain timeless and unchanged, some disappear, and others arise to take their place.

You can begin to crack your church's code by looking at the symbols. Symbols are discovered in four primary forms:

- Myths
- Rituals
- Heroes
- Visuals

Myths

Myths symbolize the story line and historic meaning of a church. They explain, in story form, what the church is all about.

In our culture, the idea of myth has generally been denigrated to mean untrue and, therefore, untrustworthy. That is because we default to understanding reality in purely rational terms. What I mean by *myth* is a story that has taken on larger-than-life meaning. Although there are usually varying levels of factual veracity at the core of myth, its power is not dependent on the facts but on its ability to provide symbolic and meaningful communication.

Several years ago, I consulted with a church outside of Chicago. They told me about the Sunday when the church was out of money. The pastor put the unpaid bills in the narthex and challenged the members to "take a bill home and pay it." At the end of the day, all the bills were paid. That story was well over twenty years old, but it was told over and over again. The details of the story—if the church was completely out of money or if every bill was paid—don't really matter. What does matter is that the myth communicated part of the church's code: When faced with a struggle, we will overcome all odds against us.

Typically, a myth tells the story of the founding of the church or key passages in a church's growth and development. As a myth unfolds and is embellished, it sets the tone of the church's story. Sometimes the myth is related as a tragedy and other times as a comedy or even a romance. Though myths may play fast and loose with the facts, they always point to deeper truths.

Rituals

Rituals symbolize the beliefs, archetypes, behavior patterns, and ideals of a church. Rituals are collective activities that do not serve a pragmatic purpose but that the church considers socially and even spiritually essential. Rituals are carried out for their own sake. Examples of rituals in a church include traditional events, ceremonies, and gatherings; ceremonial ways of recognizing individual achievements and milestones; and traditional ways of greeting and paying respect to one another. Some rituals are formalized and intentional. Others are practiced in a subconscious way. What are the rituals at your church? A Sunday potluck? A particular manner for conducting baptisms? A time of open prayer in worship? An expected worship-service format? A certain style and curriculum for Sunday school or confirmation classes? A holiday feast or party? These may be expressions of your code. So be very cautious when making changes.

Heroes

Heroes come to symbolize the code of an organization. The hero of Microsoft is Bill Gates, whose intensely driven personality has left an indelible mark on the company he founded. The hero of Wal-Mart is Sam Walton; the hero of IBM is Thomas J. Watson Sr.; the hero of Willow Creek is Bill Hybels; and the hero of Disney is, well, Walt Disney. Heroes can be living legends or departed saints. They can even be imaginary creations, such as Mickey Mouse. A hero is any personality who possesses highly prized characteristics that symbolize the church. A church in Omaha valued "unassuming service" above all. Their hero was a soft-spoken elderly woman who cooked meals for the homeless every week, even after she could no longer drive a car. The entire church came together to assist her in delivering her home-cooked meals. Heroes populate the church's myths and give meaning and emotional power to the unfolding story of a community of people.

Visual Style

Visual style is the symbolic face a church shows to the world. A church's visual style is reflected in its logos, bulletins, Web sites, choice of paint colors, architecture, design, and the way the parking lot flows. The way a church looks often reveals how well it is connected to its code. For example, I once consulted with Orchard Hill Reformed Church in Grand Rapids, a church that took great care to host beautiful art galleries in its narthex. They employed a full-time art director who changed the art seasonally and promoted aesthetics in every aspect of the church's ministry. However, the church's exterior facade was plain and utilitarian. The incongruence was apparent to me, but not to them. What I discovered, however, made the incongruence understandable. The church was the product of a merger fourteen years prior to my consultation, and the two codes never quite became one.

Visual style extends from the exterior to the interior, from the artwork hanging on the walls to the dress code of the members. All aspects of the visual style of a transforming church are coordinated and mutually complementary, signaling that the members are in sync with, and immersed in, the church's code.

The Heritage of Heritage

Through the symbolic expressions of the people at Heritage—the stories, heroes, and rituals that were told, honored, and repeated—it was a rather simple task to decide that the church's new building plans were wrong. The proposed architecture and cost would be incongruent with the code of the church. Most of the other churches in town were focused on budgets and buildings. They were run like businesses at best and country clubs at worst. But Heritage was designed to be different. It was genuinely focused on ministry. The building was incidental. In fact, meeting in a warehouse communicated something very important to the members and visitors about the church's priorities.

At the core of the Heritage code was a simple value statement: People are more important than programs, and so ministry takes precedence over buildings.

"We bought the original building on the second Sunday we met as a church," explains Randy Benner, one of the founding elders. "When we bought it, we understood it was not attractive. But we believed people who would come to Heritage would do so for different reasons than how it looked."

The building was the ultimate illustration of the church's code. "We wanted to use our money for people and not for property, programs, and buildings." Before the church was even able to articulate its core values, the founders shaped what it was to become. Three of the founding laypeople had met for Bible study every Tuesday for fourteen years prior to starting a church. They shared a history of honest and life-transforming community. When the church started with a handful of laypeople, they had no pastor, but they shared a vision of empowered relationships and ministry by the people. "We had the mentality that whatever we did, we would do it together. We only made decisions if they were unanimous. We knew, loved, and trusted each other and wanted to mutually submit to each other and to our mission. We had many years together of mutual accountability around our sense of mission and purpose."

In our strategic planning meeting, the building decision was perhaps the quickest I've ever witnessed. Leadership discovered the incongruence of building a new facility similar to other churches in Moultrie. Instead, they were able to redefine a new building plan—a bigger warehouse costing less than half of the original estimate.

The money saved could be redirected toward ministry consistent with their code—building authentic and meaningful relationships, working in teams, and involving every member in ministry. But that was not the greatest payoff of cracking the Heritage code. As they plan for the future, understanding their code has helped them to identify and articulate core values, develop a vision, and create ministries that flow consistently out of their code.

"We realized that our church loved the warehouse," David Oaks told me recently. "It communicates who we are—a functional facility that allows us to do ministry. Our vision is to be a passionate community of disciples who significantly impact their world for Jesus. That vision was developed in our first strategy session with TAG Consulting after we identified and preserved our code. And we live it and breathe it every single day. Every member knows what we're about. But if we had just built a nice building and developed a series of steps to get there, we would have killed our church—and wasted millions of dollars in the process!"

The Lasting Value of Code

Unlike many churches, Heritage Church never experienced an initial decline in attendance after announcing the building plan. In fact, their growth skyrocketed. Shortly before moving to the new facility, they were cramming 600 people into their warehouse, 350 people in small groups, and nearly every member in some form of ministry. What most members understood intuitively, they now understood with the other lobe of their brains. Because they knew who they were, they better understood what they were to do.

I consulted with Heritage again about four years after our first meeting.

The new warehouse was in its final stages of development. I was amazed when I met with the newcomer focus group, people who had been at the church for six months or less. When I asked them what it meant to be a part of Heritage, every single person told me about the ministry he or she was involved in—working with homeless people, helping another service agency in town, leading a small group for teenagers. They all talked about the importance of getting involved in ministry and how the leaders were on the front line. The code of "ministry over buildings" and "every member in ministry" was clear, even to the people who had not been aware of the building question four years earlier.

Once your church has cracked its code, you can begin to put your "core ideology" in writing. If the core values and mission, however, are incongruent with the code, they are meaningless words that gather dust on a shelf or take up valuable space in your church's bulletin. Sometimes they just don't ring true—and so they lead to no real action. In the worst-case scenario, they create a high level of cynicism when the stated values and purpose don't match reality.

The Outflow from Code

A church's core values and mission flow from its code. If your church is in sync with its code, the flow is natural and free. But if your church's life is incongruent, the flow is interrupted or polluted.

Core Values

These are our deep-seated understandings about who we are. It is not enough for a business to say, "Our core values are honesty, integrity, quality, and service." Every organization says that. Likewise, it is not enough for a church to proclaim, "Our core values are fellowship, discipleship, and evangelism." Your church must define its values in ways more related to personality, experience, genetics, and style.

I've consulted with some churches that have descriptive core values, like "meeting God in unexpected ways," "innovative excellence," "chasing truth together," and "serving on the edge." Those core values give their people a greater sense of the personality and style of the church.

Core values are not the same things as aspired values. Aspired values are what we want. Core values are what we have. An aspired value might be "shared ministry between clergy and laity" when the current reality doesn't match. It's okay for a church to move toward an aspired value, but we shouldn't call it a core value. Core values are also not the same as operating values. Operating values are the negative values preventing a church from moving forward. They are the unspoken norms that have developed and need to be changed. The operating values often become clues to our code. "Take care of the wealthy members or they might leave" might be an unhealthy expression of one positive element of a church's code: leaving a legacy for the next generation. "Don't rock the boat" might be an unhealthy expression of a genuine and healthy desire for a loving community. The practice rather than the code is what becomes problematic.

Core values are not the same as core beliefs. Core beliefs govern our theology. Core beliefs may include things like the death and resurrection of Jesus, the virgin birth, the inspiration of the Bible. Core beliefs may be specific to a particular theological perspective such as Calvinism, Lutheranism, or dispensationalism. They can reflect certain practices such as infant baptism or believer's baptism. But two churches may have identical core beliefs and very different core values.

Core values are positive and present within the current environment. They are also enduring. A church should have no more than four or five core values. Any more than five, and you start to dilute the ones that are really important. I once worked with a church that had twenty-nine stated core values. The leadership began to ignore the stated values because there was zero sense of priority.

To discover your church's core values, you will want to ask some right-brained questions of your members: Tell me about your most meaningful experience at this church. What is the best decision that this church has ever made? Then begin to look at the themes that emerge from the stories that people tell. Do you see any themes generally expressed across a majority of members? If so, you've got your core values.

Mission

The mission (purpose) of a church flows directly from its values. It is the church's collective reason for existing within a specific context. A mission serves as a set of guardrails to keep the church focused and on course. It is like the bank that defines the course of a river. But mission is not quite as enduring as core values.

Mission is defined, to some extent, by context. Over time, the river may begin to move the walls of the bank and change direction. Like code, a mission is part of the larger narrative of God's work through the church. Every church is part of the Great Commandment (love God and neighbor) and the Great Commission (go into the world and make disciples). But an effective mission statement takes context into account. Why does your church exist at this time in history and at this location?

An effective mission statement should be congruent with the church's code and values. But it is an expression of the church's identity in action. A good mission statement tells a church what it does and what it doesn't do. Normally, a mission statement should be short and concise, capturing the church's reason for existence, an intended outcome, and a primary beneficiary.

For example, the mission of Southwest Church in Springboro, Ohio, is "sharing Jesus with unchurched people in southwest Ohio and leading them to become wholehearted, devoted followers of Christ." Their purpose is clear: to reach out. Their intended outcome is clear: so the unchurched become passionate followers of Christ. And their primary beneficiary is clear: unchurched people in southwest Ohio. A clear mission does not mean your church won't love and serve people who are outside the scope of your mission statement. Rather, it gives your leadership team a way to make tough decisions about priorities.

When ministry flows from a transforming church's code, the church is a healthy one. It experiences both growth and deepening. Myths, rituals, heroes, architecture, and decor point to a deeper identity. The leaders identify core values, which protect and preserve that identity in the face of changing circumstances. And mission expands the reach of the church's code and influence.

Warehouse Style

Heritage Church opened the doors to its new facility in December 2005. For eighty-five hours prior to the first service, the people of the church shared in around-the-clock prayer and Scripture reading—speaking into a sound system that echoed throughout the building. After the last verse was read by one of the children from the youth ministry, a kid with Down syndrome, the leaders openly wept. And then nearly 1,100 people flowed in—more than twice the capacity of the previous facility.

When Pastor David Oaks looked around, he didn't notice so much the enhanced warehouse style—the larger heating ducts, the greater spread of concrete, and the dust kicked up from the parking lot. His focus was elsewhere—on the impassioned faces of those waiting to be launched into and even greater ministry.

INCONGRUENCE/CODE SPEED BUMP

Transforming Church Checkup

1. Do members of your church overreact to decisions?

2. Have you tried new things that should have been successful but ended up failing?

3. Has the leadership of your church made decisions they later came to regret?

4. Is your church out of sync with its neighborhood or community?

5. Do people give lip service to certain values, without any real commitment?

Travel Tips

1. You must know your church's code before you can introduce change successfully.

2. Your church's code will probably never change. Paradoxically, that fact is what enables your church to change its practices, norms, and strategies.

3. Your church's code is neither good nor bad. It just is.

4. If you challenge your church's code, you will lose.

5. The best way to discover your church's code is through your church's symbols; stories that take on larger-than-life meaning; activities, rituals, and programs that generate an enthusiastic response; and facilities and decor that seem to attract people.

6. Just as you might help children discover and leverage their unique talents and passions, your church's code becomes a launching pad for transformation.

Reflections

1. Why do people choose your church?

2. Does your church have a clearly defined group(s) of people you are trying to reach and serve? What are those group(s)?

3. How has your church differentiated itself from other churches?

6

AUTOCRACY/SHARED LEADERSHIP, PART 1

Leadership (the Noun)

Also, if two lie down together, they will keep warm.
But how can one keep warm alone? Though one
may be overpowered, two can defend themselves.
A cord of three strands is not quickly broken.
—Ecclesiastes 4:11–12

For Ken Shigematsu, the call to pastor the Tenth Avenue Church in the heart of Vancouver, British Columbia, was more like a whimper at first.

"I went to visit the church and sensed immediately that this would *not* be the place for me," he says. As a twenty-nine-year-old Japanese Canadian, Ken considered himself too young, too ethnic, and generally too unfit to lead Tenth Avenue.

Besides, at the time, the church already had a senior pastor.

But then things got weird. Ken, who had sensed God leading him from California back to Canada, was now living in the town of White Rock, British Columbia, located near the U.S. border. On the third day of a fast asking God for direction, he distinctly heard the words, "Tenth Avenue Church." And on the fifth day: "Senior pastor."

Within the next few months, the senior pastor of Tenth Avenue resigned and Ken was asked to candidate. But the more he learned about the church, the less he liked the idea.

Tenth Avenue Church was in rapid decline. "In its heyday," Ken says, "the church had over a thousand people attending and a vibrant Sunday-school ministry. Canadian churches aren't large like many American churches, so this was really huge for Canada. It was innovative in both its outreaches and in raising money for overseas missions. In the 1950s and 1960s, Tenth Avenue was considered the flagship church for the Christian and Missionary Alliance denomination in western Canada. But over the next three decades, the church went through a period of significant decline—from over one thousand to below two hundred at its lowest point. It also cycled through twenty pastors and associate pastors in twenty years."

The statistics were bad enough. But the real deal killer appeared to be the basic incompatibility between Ken and the church.

Tenth Avenue was composed mostly of Caucasians who had never lived outside of North America; Ken was a Japanese Canadian who had lived all over the world.

Tenth Avenue catered mostly to the middle and upper-middle classes; Ken desired to lead a church engaged in social justice.

Tenth Avenue was stuck in a passion to get back to its glory days; Ken liked to live with at least one foot in the future.

Tenth Avenue, at various points during the decline, had toyed with the idea of selling the inner-city church facility and moving into the suburbs; Ken was passionate about ministry in an urban context.

Tenth Avenue was inwardly focused; Ken's eyes were always toward the next horizon.

Leadership as a Noun

Recently I was in a meeting of pastors to discuss a research grant. A Christian-oriented Fortune 500 company was interested in funding a think tank to study various models of church transformation. The pastors in the meeting were mostly unknown outside of their own congregations. But one attendee, running late, was an internationally known pastor and author.

The group began to discuss the nature of leadership while we waited for his arrival. We talked about how to engage people in the tough issues and deal with conflict, the value and place of vision, and how to handle disappointment. In the middle of this lively conversation, the famous pastor walked into the room. More accurately, he strutted in like a rock star. Even though he had heard only the last ten seconds or so of our conversation, he proceeded to launch into a twenty-minute monologue.

"You know the problem with you guys?" he asked with a winning smile. He paused a moment for effect. "The problem is that you are all talking about the *questions*." Another perfectly timed delay. "When you should be talking about the answers." He had our attention. "The problem is that Christian leaders aren't very good at coming up with solutions. A leader is someone who has the answers for the people!"

For the next twenty minutes he proceeded to do just that—give us all the answers. "People need certainty in their lives. They need someone they can follow. They want someone with answers and not more questions." As he pounded the table and walked about the room, his audience had grown mesmerized. He was charming. Charismatic. Captivating. I looked around the room. Everyone was nodding enthusiastically. Without waiting for feedback, comments, or questions, he got up to leave. His performance was over. But just as he reached for the doorknob, I couldn't resist asking a question. "Was Hitler a good leader?"

Immediately an awkward silence filled the room. The world-famous pastor stopped in his tracks.

"I mean, for a nation in despair, didn't Hitler have all the answers?"

Another stunned pause.

"By your definition, then, was he an effective leader?"

Having recovered, the pastor motioned to his watch, made his apologies, and fled the room.

I'll have to confess to feeling disappointed—I was looking forward to his answer.

This rock-star pastor represents the defining perspective of much of contemporary strategy—*leadership as a noun*.

In this perspective, the focus is on the person of the leader. Unwittingly, we have equated leadership with power. The function of a leader is to acquire and exercise power by any means necessary—leveraging position, using coercion, playing political hardball, or outworking everyone else. When exercising power is the central value of leadership, the questions revolve around who is in charge and who makes the decisions. People defer responsibility to the leader, who then becomes in charge of everything. When leadership is defined by power, the people are not mobilized for action. More often, they are listless, fearful, or simply uninvolved.

In our consumer-oriented culture, we the people are expected to buy what leaders are selling and then complain about the leaders when our needs are not met. The all-powerful and all-knowing leader is expected to produce the answers. During former president Bill Clinton's run for reelection, a participant in a town-hall meeting rose to his feet, leaned into the microphone, and asked, "Mr. President, we are your children. What will you do to take care of and provide for us?" President Clinton appeared momentarily taken aback. But he quickly recovered his composure and did what leaders are expected to do when leadership is a noun—he set out to name all the things *he* would attempt to do to improve life for the American people.

When leadership is identified with the leader, we judge success by statistics. We keep score by counting the number of followers or the size of budgets or growth percentage. If you have ever been to a pastors' conference, you know what I mean. ("So how many is *your* church running?" asks the insecure and overcaffeinated pastor during the coffee break.)

But the true test of leadership is in the legacy, or the positive impact the leader leaves behind. In fact, the very act of defining *leadership* as a noun—a leader with a certain number of followers—runs counter to true leadership, which is all about mobilizing others to take initiative, to fulfill their calling, and to make a difference for the sake of the kingdom.

Leadership, Power, and Authority

When leadership is defined as a noun, two choices are available to a leader:

- Exercise power to coerce
- Seek authority to please

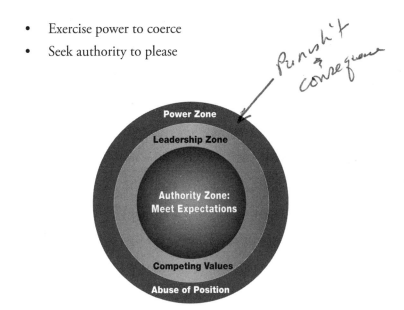

Punish't → consequence

After listening to Harvard professor Marty Linsky at a TAG Consulting roundtable, I developed a graph to illustrate what he was teaching. I was surprised to find that he was verbalizing so much of what we had learned through our research. As the graph indicates, power, authority, and leadership are not the same things. Power is taken. Authority is granted. Leadership is exercised.

A leader operating in the *power zone* relies on punishment and consequence. The way that I'm defining it, power is abusive by definition. It's an appeal to position our self-interest at the expense of the greater good. Even when used with the best of intentions, power immobilizes people in the long run. It may produce a short-term result but fails to create ownership or true adaptation. Power is a destructive force. It is something that is taken, not given. A dictator is not elected. He uses force to take over a country. A corporate raider capitalizes on the power of money to take over a company. In the power zone, a leader enforces his will upon the people by demanding that they "buy into" his vision.

In *The Lord of the Rings*, the Gondor steward Denethor leads by coercion. Even worse, he appeals to the good—loyalty and courage—as leverage for others to follow his demands. As he orders his own son into a battle that cannot be won and very likely will end in death, Denethor asks, "Is there a captain here who still has the courage to do his lord's will?" In a perhaps less dramatic—but still damaging—fashion, how many of us have heard church leaders use a similar technique, appealing through guilt to the cause of the gospel?

A leader operating in the *authority zone* delivers what people want and desire. People *authorize* leaders to do the things they want the leader to do. Authority is all about understanding and meeting people's expectations. When a leader does so, he is often granted more authority—and the circle expands. Pastors are expected to *do* certain things—teaching, preaching, ministering to the sick, administering the sacraments, and fulfilling other essential pastoral tasks. As a pastor does these things and does them well, his congregants cede greater and greater authority to him. Within limits.

The use of authority is essentially about maintenance—protecting people, keeping order, and establishing parameters. Meeting expectations, though, is more about management than leadership. People never authorize a leader to do things that cause pain or discomfort. As a leader, you must also be aware that what you are authorized to do is rarely communicated outright. A job description or bylaw may give you the right to do certain things, but exercising those rights may very well put you into the power zone. Authority is based on discovering what people really expect, regardless of what they say.

As we will discuss in the next chapter, a person operating in the *leadership zone* raises conflicted but important issues, even if they cause distress among the people. A leader must meet basic expectations. But if a person only meets expectations, then he is not exercising leadership.

A leader who leverages power is illegitimate. A leader who relies only on authority will never lead change; at the best, he will be a competent manager proficient in technical strategies. But technically proficient managers do not lead transforming churches. Transforming leadership goes far deeper and requires much more of both leaders and followers. They must be willing to engage the real problems, and they must be willing to grapple with competing values, which always emerge when you face the real problems.

Engaging Problems

Fountain Hills Presbyterian Church is located in the desert hills just east of Scottsdale, Arizona. When the leaders called me to work with them, they described Fountain Hills as a retirement community. The demographics of the church certainly validated this presupposition—more than 70 percent of the members were over sixty years of age. When I showed up, no one could put a finger on precisely what was wrong in the church. But everyone agreed that the church was stuck. Something was awry in the system.

Senior pastor Ewen Holmes had been at the church for five years. When he was considering the position, he let the search leaders know that he saw himself as a pastor, not a CEO. That came as good news to the leaders of the church. The previous pastor operated as a CEO, and their desire was to hire a leader with a pastor's heart. In addition, they wanted Ewen to help the church become more intergenerational—a tough sell in a retirement community. Ewen had three young kids of his own and so was personally motivated to see the church reach out to young families. It seemed to be a match made in heaven.

Five years later, it was clear that something had gone wrong. Ewen had to resist an unrelenting pull to function as a CEO. And the church had made no progress in becoming intergenerational. To help reveal the issues, I formed some focus groups and listened. "We would love to involve young families in the church," I heard. "But this is a retirement community. There simply aren't that many young families living here!" Because this concern surfaced over and over, I decided to do some research. What I discovered shocked me. The median age in Fountain Hills was only forty-six! And only 25 percent of the city's population was over the age of sixty. While forty-six is substantially older than the national median, the church was actually much older than the town. The age issue was simply a convenient excuse to avoid facing the real issues.

Upon closer examination, I began to get to the heart of the matter. It soon became clear that the church lacked a sense of its identity. No one knew the code. They possessed no sense of focus or priorities, and they lacked true community. They had relied for years on a talented pastor to provide all of the leadership. And all they asked was that he meet their expectations and fix the basic problems. Any efforts to create focus, to reach out, or to become genuinely intergenerational were shot down. For example, the church initiated an alternative worship service with paid musicians and a café-style atmosphere, with the notion that this would attract younger families. In reality, the alternative service, averaging twenty-five people per week, primarily served the Sunday-school teachers who missed the first service—and there was no child care provided, even though young families were the intended audience. But as long as the alternative service didn't interfere with other things, everything was fine. However, the alternative service was meeting in the fellowship hall, and an issue of space began to surface. Older members began to criticize the service, especially because it was costing a lot of money and using valuable fellowship space.

The bottom line was that many people expected the pastor to solve the significant problems. When he couldn't, he became a convenient scapegoat, distracting the church from dealing with deeper unresolved issues around identity and purpose. I have seen this pattern repeated more times than I can count. Fortunately, Fountain Hills Presbyterian is beginning its journey of change.

Pay Me Now, Pay Me Later

Like many churches I have consulted with, Fountain Hills chose to attempt technical fixes for adaptive, or deeper, issues.

Underlying the concept of leadership as a noun are powerful cultural dysfunctions, such as the passive entitlement of consumerism, the arrogance and self-preoccupation of a leader with the answers, and the misdirected idea that a journey of significance can be achieved without loss and sacrifice. By endlessly focusing on the technical fix—solutions within the scope of a leader's skill—the most subtle and powerful illusion of change is created: the win-win scenario. Many of our churches have bought into the lie that change can occur without conflict. And, given the right leader, a technical fix or series of fixes can solve the problems without too much pain or too much change.

Technical fixes can be Band-Aid solutions that don't address the core issues. I know of one church that attempts to deal with its ongoing problem of a lack of volunteers by continuing to increase the font size in its bulletin announcements. Another church, which lacked any real impact on the local community, placed great emphasis on being first on a list of donors to the American Red Cross's blood drive. I have seen countless churches use suggestion boxes as a substitute for real input. I visited an aging church that rented out space to a preschool in hopes of attracting young families.

Some churches continue to exercise technical fixes long after they show any sign of providing effective solutions and, in fact, actually exacerbate the problems. Why? Primarily for three reasons: *ignorance, camouflage,* and *distraction.*

First, many churches simply don't know other options exist. Deeply mired in dysfunction, so far down a dead-end street, the churches can't imagine any other road out. When I see churches engaged in the endless process of trying to fix adaptive problems by using technical fixes, I am reminded of the catchphrase from the old television commercial for a car-repair chain: "You can pay me now, or you can pay me later." Undiagnosed and untreated problems always get worse. The key is to have the courage to acknowledge when change is imperative. Technical fixes can also camouflage the real issue. By refusing to deal with attitudes, values, or behaviors, a church can focus on the right issue but continually apply the wrong solution.

I once worked with a bank that struggled to implement its strategic plan. The bank added more and more "training programs" but failed to make progress. They knew what the problem was: failure to implement the strategic plan. But if a little training didn't work, they figured a lot of training would. They wasted a great deal of time and money on more and more training without ever looking for a different kind of solution.

A technical fix can also distract leaders from facing the adaptive issue. I recently worked with a church where the leaders had argued for three years about whether or not to purchase a projection system for the sanctuary. But in reality, the projection system was only a distraction from dealing with the deeper issues of how decisions are actually made.

In general, there are three types of situations requiring change:

Type I: The problem can be fixed by someone with the authority and technical knowledge. I break my leg; the doctor sets it. The doctor, as leader, has the authority and expertise to provide a technical fix for the problem.

Type II: The authority has a technical solution in mind, but he or she cannot implement it because the other person has to do the hard work. My doctor tells me that my cholesterol is too high. He can recommend diet, exercise, and lifestyle changes, but the work is in my hands, not his.

Type III: The problem is not clear-cut, and there are no available technical fixes. My community is suffering from an outbreak of a new viral disease. The doctor can't even diagnose the problem.

I have gone to great lengths to argue that technical fixes born out of the use of authority are not sufficient for the kind of adaptive problems standing in the way of building a transforming church. So given that, what is needed? The process begins with the heart of leadership. And at the heart is the challenging task of raising competing values.[16]

Raising Competing Values

I recently worked with a church that was growing rapidly. They had a long history of deep community, which was attractive to newcomers. For years, the church held an hour-long coffee break between two services—the primary place where informal fellowship occurred. But as the church outgrew its space, they added a third service and canned the coffee hour. After a couple of years, the church was experiencing all kinds of conflict. Nobody could figure out what went wrong. But as I listened to the members and leaders, it became apparent that two values were competing with each other: the value of room to grow versus the value of fellowship. As the church grew, it became harder to emphasize the foundational value of community. Unfortunately, the leaders had focused on various minor conflicts for two years through technical fixes without ever addressing the competing values. They kept trying to meet expectations, as they always had, but they were now failing for the first time.

If you are a note taker, write this down: *Changing circumstances lead to competing values.* How a church deals with competing values largely determines its health. The primary reason leadership as a noun fails is that no one leader can solve the problems raised by a clash of competing values. Remember, leadership as a noun relies on either authority (the meeting of expectations) or power (the exercise of will to coerce change). The pendulum swings back and forth from authority to power to authority to power. Often, this sets up a recursive pattern. Pleasing people gives way to coercing people, which gives way to pleasing people. In fact, genuine leadership is defined neither by authority nor power.

Leaders of transforming churches become skilled at raising competing values—in other words, acknowledging them and bringing them to the congregation's attention. The clash over values creates acute discomfort, but transforming leaders navigate this, knowing that it leads to change. Hear me well: Having competing values is a good, even a necessary thing. When adaptive issues are on the table, no one ever wins by trying to create a win-win situation. Win-win, in the end, always ends up lose-lose. A solution that doesn't step on anyone's toes or reveal the primary issue may be easy, but in the long run it is useless. Adaptive work is difficult on a number of levels for one primary reason: It involves closing the gap between circumstances and competing values. Ron Heifetz nails it:

"Leadership will consist not of answers or assured visions but of taking action to clarify values."[17]

This is the prevailing cultural notion of leadership turned upside down. Transforming leadership is not the exercise of either authority or power. Rather, it is raising the right questions and making sure that competing values come to the surface and are dealt with.

Heifetz says, "[In] the old definition of leadership the leader has the answers—the vision—and everything else is a sales job to persuade people to sign up for it. Leaders certainly provide direction but that often means posing well-structured questions rather than offering definitive answers. Imagine the differences in behavior between leaders who operate with the idea that 'leadership means influencing the organization to follow the leader's vision' and those who operate with the idea that 'leadership means influencing the organization to face its problems and to live into its opportunities.' That second idea—mobilizing people to tackle tough challenges—is what defines the new job of the leader."[18]

While authority relies on meeting expectations, leadership challenges them. True leadership means releasing power for the sake of empowering others. Leadership is an art, and it's more like a walk on a high wire than a march down a well-ordered path. A leader must always balance authority (meeting people's unspoken expectations), conflict (challenging those unspoken expectations), and change (helping people deal with loss). Change always involves loss. I recently helped a church in Corpus Christi develop its strategic plan. Toward the end of our last session, an elderly woman tentatively raised her hand and said, "Kevin, I think we're missing the boat. We're talking about strategies and plans. But this is a good church. We really don't need to change much."

I sat back and observed as the group responded to her: "Mary, we have to change if we're going to be relevant to our community!" one person pronounced. Another jumped in. "These strategies will help us become more focused so that we aren't as scattered and frazzled." One by one they tried to sell her on the vision and why the strategies were so important. But the more they tried, the more visibly resistant she became.

After twenty minutes of listening to the dialogue, I interrupted. "Mary, I think you represent a lot of people in this church who aren't at this meeting today. And I think they may have some of the same concerns that you have. Your thoughts are very important to this process. Can you tell me what you think they will be afraid of?" All of a sudden, her demeanor changed. I wasn't trying to sell her. I was trying to understand and value her. Rather than focusing on the vision, I tried to understand what she perceived might be a loss to herself and others. She responded by talking about the 8:00 a.m. worship service and how important that was to her. I then said, "Mary, do you think people would be willing to make only minor changes to that service if we don't change anything else? Do you think they would support the rest of the strategic plan if they knew that their service wasn't going to change too drastically?" She smiled and gave an enthusiastic thumbs-up.

The group had missed the boat by trying to sell her on the vision. As the leader in that moment, I focused on helping her deal with the sense of personal loss that the strategic plan represented to her. There are times when a leader must slow down the change process to regain authority. And there are times when a leader must orchestrate conflict to begin challenging expectations. In this case with Mary, I was able to do both.

None of this is easy, and all of it will involve a necessary measure of pain and risk.

Desperation or Sanity?

When the Tenth Avenue Church board hired Ken Shigematsu as their senior pastor, following a string of twenty pastors in as many years, they finally understood that the status quo had failed. They could not retreat to move forward. More technical fixes would destroy them. Because the church had little left to lose, they were finally open to facing loss. Hiring a thirty-year-old Japanese Canadian constituted an act of both desperation and sanity.

During one of his first days as senior pastor, Ken was contemplating the road ahead. Intuitively, he understood the church had drifted far from a sustaining mission and had lost touch—both with its changing community and with its original code. He also had a gut-level sense that his work as a leader required complex, painful, collaborative, and multidimensional change.

Suddenly, he was interrupted from his thinking. The church secretary walked into his office and said, "I just wanted you to know that if the church sinks now, everyone will blame you, since you were the last person holding the baton."

She pivoted on her heel and walked out.

7

AUTOCRACY/SHARED LEADERSHIP, PART 2

Leadership (the Verb)

If you have any encouragement from being united with Christ, if any comfort from his love, if any fellowship with the Spirit, if any tenderness and compassion, then make my joy complete by being like-minded, having the same love, being one in spirit and purpose.
—Philippians 2:1–2

We've seen that leadership is not a noun. Furthermore, it is not a pronoun, as in *I*. What is it, then? My high school English teacher might not agree, but I argue that leadership is in fact a verb.

I choose to call leadership a verb for several reasons. First, a verb defines action, and action, more than anything else, defines leadership. A verb also connects a subject with its object, and leadership involves engaging people in the critical issues requiring adaptive change. Leadership as a verb connects people and problems in the active context of stepping out in faith and up to the plate. Unlike a noun, a verb is rarely static. Its work never ends. In the same way, leading adaptive change is an ongoing quest with no guarantee of ever getting to the finish line.

Leadership as a verb is not about who makes the decisions. In transforming churches, leadership is about the leader mobilizing others for ministry. Finally and perhaps most important, a verb demands energy, and adaptive leadership requires endless energy. The work of rooting out deep cultural dysfunctions is ongoing and painful. Stress, pain, and loss are inevitable. Without the source of ongoing energy, seeded in the

Holy Spirit's work and springing through creative community, the job is impossible.

It takes energy and courage to lead well. According to Ron Heifetz, "Many people have a 'smiley face' view of what it means to lead. They get a rude awakening when they find themselves with a leadership opportunity. Exercising leadership generates resistance—and pain. People are afraid that they will lose something that's worthwhile. They're afraid that they're going to have to give up something that they're comfortable with."[19]

The coronation of Aragorn in *The Return of the King* is a majestic and moving ceremony. Aragorn is a great ruler because he understands that leadership is a shared responsibility. After being crowned king of Gondor by the wizard Gandalf, Aragorn stands before the cheering masses. He immediately recognizes the shared reality of the day.

"This day does not belong to one man but to all," he says. "Let us together rebuild this world that we may share in the days of peace." In addition to calling people into shared leadership, he also honors those who have played critical roles in securing victory. As he approaches the four small hobbits who were part of the Fellowship, they begin to bow to the new king. However, Aragorn refuses the gesture. "My friends, you bow to no one," he says to them. And then the king bows to them.

Leadership shares power. It invites rather than coerces. It recognizes rather than manipulates. It engages rather than separates. It serves rather than rules.

Leadership is active. The verbs that most define the activities of a leader in a transforming church are:

- *Build* rapport
- *Distinguish* between technical and adaptive change
- *Engage* the issues
- *Manage* your red zone
- *Mobilize* others for ministry
- *Orchestrate* the speed and stress of conflict[20]

Build Rapport

When Ken Shigematsu arrived at Tenth Avenue Church, he wanted to hit the ground running. Immediately he developed a list of hundred-day goals: create a vision statement, define core values, and craft a new logo, to name just a few. At the same time, Ken intuited a need to move beyond tasks to develop relationships. Along with some core members of the church, he gradually turned the church's prayer committee (which, at the time of his arrival, spent more time planning prayer than praying) into a group of people who prayed together over critical personal and corporate matters.

"From the start I came to an understanding that Tenth would change not because we implemented a new program or because of some fancy new methodology," says Ken. "I believed change would only emerge as the hearts of the leaders connected organically in a deep dependence upon God and the Spirit to renew us. As I look back, that was critical to the adaptive change the church has experienced."

Ken, consistent with his type-A personality, met all of his hundred-day goals. As it turned out, however, he would end up scrapping most of his initial thoughts. "We started with a vision statement, and we cranked out an elegant one that was written in parallelism," he remembers. "It really read well, but at the same time, it seemed kind of wooden. It was more from the head than the heart." It would have looked great on a polished annual report or a professionally crafted capital campaign brochure. But like so many "vision" statements, it didn't actually bring about change. The real sense of mission developed naturally in an atmosphere of trust—out of heart-to-heart conversations, over time, emerging from the church's code. It was born out of the creative community.

Trust is the starting point for shared ministry. In church after church, I have seen leaders fail because their passion for change far exceeded the trust they had earned. Building trust requires time. Churches often hire pastors to lead change and then resist every step of the way. But when things get to crisis mode, people will typically trust more quickly. In many ways, Ken was lucky. He was hired to be a catalyst for change—and the board was actually ready for change, having burned through twenty pastors in as many years. However, they had no clue what sort of change was needed.

For Ken to be effective, he had to understand the real expectations of the congregation—and generally meet them. By doing so, he began to fulfill the contract of authority, which earned trust from the people he was leading. In time, Ken slowly began to introduce change. He understood that timing is critical. Some leaders introduce change too quickly and sacrifice trust. Others, waiting for some magical point of no resistance, move far too slowly. If there's no resistance, there's no leadership. At the same time, overwhelming resistance fails to produce transformation. Good leaders understand the balance: Trust must be earned, but resistance will never be completely overcome. Trust is the bridge that will allow you to deal with the inevitable resistance. Real change will create both trust and resistance, often at the same time.

Ken's first major change—introducing a more contemporary music style—gained widespread support. But it also generated significant resistance among some members. One man, after sitting through the first service with drums, commented, "If Jesus saw those drums on the platform, He would roll over in His grave." Instead of correcting the man in his theology or arguing the point, Ken gracefully listened. He demonstrated care for the man and honestly valued his opinion. At the same time, Ken spoke of the need to connect in a more dynamic fashion to a dying world (a reality that actually did cause Jesus to roll over in the grave).

Distinguish between Technical and Adaptive Change

Ken arrived at Tenth Avenue with a passion for social justice and a consuming desire to see the church reach out to the economically disadvantaged in Vancouver. While many members of the church paid lip service to this idea, the change necessary to make such outreach part of the church's focus was of a higher order than Ken had anticipated.

For example, a Filipino church was renting Tenth Avenue's facility for church services. Although Ken was delighted to see the church open up the space, he challenged a policy that stated the Filipinos could not use the church's parking facility. As a person of racial minority himself, he helped his congregation see the issue from a slightly different perspective. Although the policy was implemented for good reasons—to allow more parking for guests and new people attending Tenth Avenue—a minority group would experience this as a kind of racial oppression, though they would likely never verbally express that. With the issue reframed, the church lifted the policy in favor of a first-come, first-served basis.

As relations deepened between Tenth Avenue and the Filipino church, the group often used Tenth Avenue's facility for other events, including meals. The smell of Filipino food can be pungent and offensive to Westerners, and Tenth Avenue would often have to open the windows the next day to clear out the smell. Some of the Tenth Avenue members wanted to prevent the Filipino meals. Once again, Ken reframed the issue as one of outreach to the community. After all, the original founders of Tenth Avenue, while still meeting in a saloon, often had to clear the air of the smells of smoke and beer before a Sunday service.

Although the initial issues Ken chose to focus on may seem minor—a dispute over parking and some cooking smells—the first steps of adaptive work were critical to a new direction. The full transformation would require a change in the members' values and beliefs. More critically, these first steps also moved the leadership focus from simply meeting expectations to challenging them.

Ken began to learn how differently authority is used when making technical change as opposed to adaptive change, as the following chart indicates:[21]

Leadership Function	Technical Fix: Meeting Expectations	Adaptive Change: Raising Competing Values
Direction	Person in authority provides problem definition and solution.	Leader identifies the adaptive challenge, provides diagnosis of condition, and produces questions about problem definitions and solutions.
Protection	Person in authority protects people from external threat.	Leader discloses external threat.
Role clarification	Person in authority helps people understand typical roles and positions.	Leader disorients current roles or resists pressure to orient people in new roles too quickly.
Controlling conflict	Person in authority restores order.	Leader exposes conflict or lets it emerge.
Norm maintenance	Person in authority maintains norms and customs.	Leader challenges norms or allows them to be challenged.

Leadership is more art than science. A person in a position of authority has to fulfill expectations (middle column) at a basic level in order to have enough credibility to challenge the more significant expectations (right column). Think of it this way: You generally want to meet expectations about 80 to 90 percent of the time, while challenging expectations about 10 to 20 percent of the time. Ken did just that. He fell in line with enough of the church's norms that he had adequate credibility to raise the adaptive issues.

Engage the Issues

The central task of adaptive change is to raise competing values. This is not because leaders enjoy the tensions and conflicts that inevitably come when values are shown to be in conflict. Rather, it is because the values that are part of a church's code can only be defined with clarity when they are forced into the open.

Part of Tenth Avenue's code was creating a safe place for spiritual exploration, where people with a diversity of beliefs and backgrounds could investigate important issues together. The church, started in a saloon, had been deeply concerned about reaching their local community. Diversity and relevance to the local community had long been part of their code. But one of the operating values of the church had become protecting the church's homogeneity, because this created comfort and perceived safety. The homogeneity included social class, economic status, and theological perspectives. Ken chose to expose the conflict between diversity and homogeneity. He decided to challenge the operating value rather than accept the status quo. He appealed to the church's code.

As the church began to grow, the board hoped to hire a pastor of discipleship and small groups. The most qualified person in Ken's mind, however, turned out to be a person who did not line up completely with Alliance doctrine—specifically in his view of eschatology, or end times. As a result, a faction of the search committee opposed the candidate adamantly. Ken took the matter to the board with a suggestion of compromise: If the candidate was accredited by the denomination, he would be hired. If not, the search would continue for another person. When the man was formally accredited, a powerful member of the search committee formed a small posse of influential members who threatened not only to end their tithing (which was significant) but also to leave the church altogether. This raised yet another values conflict: playing it safe to retain people of means versus taking a risk for the sake of the church's mission. Although Ken attempted to reframe the issue to focus on greater impact rather than minor theological differences, the posse refused to listen. If the man was hired, they would leave. Graciously, Ken informed them, "It will be a board matter. I hope you choose to stay, but if you feel you would like to move on then that's up to you."

The man was hired, and the posse members left.

Although Ken was sorry to see longtime members leave, the issue resulted in adaptive change. "The issue generated a great deal of passionate and heated discussion among the board of elders about the ethos of our church. Should we follow a doctrinal statement or the Bible? One of our most highly respected and influential board members insisted that the doctrinal statement—and not Scripture—should be the guide. I remember him saying, 'If we study the Bible too much, we might end up getting funny ideas.'" Ken, as well as many others, recognized the absurdity of that statement. For Tenth Avenue, the decision to be biblically driven marked a critical transition—another line crossed, another circle of impact expanded outward.

Each time competing values surfaced at Tenth Avenue, Ken framed the issues through the church's code—a place where everyone, regardless of race, class, belief system, or lifestyle, could feel safe and at home and engage in a spiritual quest. The code became the filter.

Manage Your Red Zone

Competing values also occur within individuals. A good leader, therefore, must be able to face unresolved personal issues arising from competing values. In their book *Thriving through Ministry Conflict*, my colleagues at TAG Consulting, Jim Osterhaus, Joe Jurkowski, and Todd Hahn, engage this paradox of leadership. They believe unresolved personal issues (what they call the "red zone") lead to unhealthy behavior patterns and conflict in ministry. In contrast, healthy conflict (the "blue zone") is centered around values, mission, and strategy. My colleagues identify four basic red-zone tendencies that best describe a leader's engagement with others: *survival, acceptance, control,* and *competence.* Each has a positive and negative sides (see following chart).

When we have unresolved issues, they tend to mask themselves in positive ways. For example, I have a pastor friend, Greg, who never felt accepted as a child. He has spent most of his life dealing with unresolved issues surrounding acceptance. He comes across as very "others-centered"— caring and compassionate. But the caring disposition crosses over lines of

Red-Zone Issue	Self-Description	Positive Side	Negative Side
Survival	"I must take care of myself. The world is full of peril, so I must enjoy the moment."	People who deal with this issue are competent, self-reliant, and responsible.	These people are unable to trust others and tend to be wary and troubled in relationships. They have little interest in anything but what is of practical benefit. They become angry and panicky (red zone) whenever they feel their emotional or psychological "survival" has been threatened.
Acceptance	"I will do anything to be loved and accepted by others. I am a people pleaser."	These people have a heart for serving others and are very attentive to others' needs and feelings.	People with acceptance issues are overly compliant and self-effacing. They tend to be rescuers. They become angry and carry personal grudges (red zone) whenever they feel they have been rejected.
Control	"The world is a threatening place, and the only way I can feel safe is if I can control every situation and the people around me."	People with control issues tend to have strong leadership qualities. They are vigilant, highly organized, and have high expectations of themselves.	These people often wall themselves off emotionally. They do not let others get too close to them. They can be overly controlling toward others—bossy, directive, demanding, rigid, and nit-picky. They impose perfectionistic demands on others. They become anxious and angry (red zone) whenever anyone or anything threatens their control.
Competence	"I am loved only on the basis of my performance. My performance is never good enough, so I never feel worthy of being loved."	These people tend to be high achievers. If you are a leader, you want these people on your team, because they will work hard to achieve a great performance.	People who struggle with competence are never satisfied with their achievements. They have a hard time receiving from other people. They impose perfectionistic demands on themselves. They are defensive and easily angered (red zone) whenever they perceive that their competence has been questioned.

health as he is overly tolerant of unhealthy behaviors from his church members, even to the point of allowing verbal abuse. Over time, his tolerance of such behaviors has come back to haunt him. His lack of backbone has caused him to fail repeatedly in ministry. He now feels completely unacceptable.

The need to feel accepted is common. I have another friend who is a former pastor. He has major acceptance issues, which makes him very effective relationally. At the same time, his unresolved issues have led to unhealthy relationships—crossing emotional and even sexual boundaries. His moral failure eventually caused him to lose his job. He felt devastated by his sin but also by the sense of rejection that he experienced in the process. This rejection simply exacerbated his need for acceptance, leading to a cycle of more and more destructive behavior. Every time his red-zone issue of acceptance took over, he invariably experienced more and more rejection.

Like these two men, Ken Shigematsu also struggled with acceptance issues. He never felt at home as a Japanese Canadian. In Japan, he was too Canadian. In Canada, he was too Japanese. He never felt at home in London, Boston, or Los Angeles. A significant part of Ken's personal code was wrapped around "a longing for home." In many ways, Ken's personal code served him well. His passion to serve the homeless (physically, spiritually, and emotionally) helped to attract others of like mind and bent. It helped reconnect Tenth Avenue with its original code.

In his wanderings, his desire to find and create a place to call home, Ken rarely felt accepted for who he was. The unresolved need drove him in good ways and bad. "Envisioning the future, framing the broad issues, and releasing people to solve problems comes fairly naturally to me, but I am not as strong at guiding people through the hands-on, nitty-gritty process of actually implementing the change," Ken says. "The desire to be accepted and liked at times causes me to hold back from intervening in healthy conflict until it was absolutely necessary." At one point, Ken's vulnerability to his need for acceptance became so serious it nearly cost him his ministry.

Red-zone problems—an individual's unresolved issues—become self-fulfilling prophecies. Red-zone issues distract leaders from the more important blue-zone stresses of leadership—conflicts around mission, values, and strategic focus. For a leader to be effective as a leader, he must (a) become aware of his own red zone and (b) monitor his reaction in situations where his need for acceptance (or survival, control, or competence) distracts him from being an effective leader. This is one of the most important parts of a leader's personal, spiritual, and emotional development. To fail at either (a) or (b) can bring disaster, as unresolved personal issues tend to unravel in destructive fashion.

Mobilize Others for Ministry

Good leaders mobilize others for ministry, using authority appropriately. In more than one case, people other than Ken produced the greatest steps forward in Tenth Avenue's ministry. There is no better example than the work of Don Cowie, who was an associate pastor at Tenth when Ken arrived as senior pastor.

Says Ken, "Don preceded me by three to four years. As I began to dialogue with Don, I realized he had a real heart and passion for social justice. But his role at Tenth Avenue had always been to work with youth, young adults, and family to get more people to come. I began to look for opportunities to align his work more with his passion."

Ken and Don's dialogue was accelerated by a tragedy. A homeless person, who was mentally ill, died on the church's property. It attracted media coverage in Vancouver and shook a lot of the members of Tenth Avenue. "I made a personal vow that nothing like this would ever happen here again," Ken says. "From that moment forward, we began to look for a way to develop a ministry to the homeless."

A church on the east side of Vancouver had a ministry, which some of the members of Tenth Avenue participated in. At about the same time,

Don was granted a study sabbatical by the board, and he immersed himself in the book of Isaiah and issues of social justice. When Don returned, Ken shifted his job responsibilities from "pastor to youth and young families" to "minister of social justice and outreach." Through Don's leadership, Tenth Avenue launched "Out of the Cold," a ministry to the homeless of Vancouver, which currently feeds up to 175 people every Monday night and houses up to 25 people overnight. At first, there was some resistance to the ministry—an indicator that leadership was being exercised. "As we started having homeless and marginal people show up to Tenth Avenue," Ken says, "some eyebrows were raised and some lips grumbled." However, gradual exposure—from the terrible reality of a homeless man dying on their property to connecting people with the faces of real need—began to shift the focus of the church outward. A case in point: An elderly and longtime member, whom Ken describes as "fairly well-to-do," volunteered one day to help for a lunch program and was moved by the desperate need of the people. As a result of that one encounter, she shows up every Tuesday to make lunch for several hundred homeless people.

Once the adaptive change was in full swing, things began to speed up. The church added other ministries focused on social justice—a halfway recovery house for people struggling with drug addiction, a refugee sponsorship ministry, a center for the underemployed and mentally ill. Eventually, Don planted a daughter church called Mosaic, which ministers in innovative ways to the underprivileged and is supported by Tenth Avenue.

Ken recalls, "We were able to create a structure where people could dream and grow. Although these hopes had been in my heart, Don was a better leader for these ministries because he embodied that vision to a greater degree than I did." Over the years, the desire to connect with the community across cultural and economic lines has worked itself out in ever-expanding circles of impact. Recently, a missions pastor was hired and a new dream was born. "Our dream," says Ken, "is to mobilize as much of the congregation as possible. We're adopting a place in Mexico for the next five years to do humanitarian work. When you expose people to need, the Spirit will work in people's hearts."

Orchestrate the Speed and Stress of Conflict

Two things about adaptive change are key: It often needs to be slow, and it will always generate resistance. Because adaptive change essentially means dealing with competing values, which creates tension and conflict, it is important to carefully monitor and regulate the level of anxiety in the congregation. Too much anxiety immobilizes people. Conversely, people become complacent when there is too little anxiety.

For Ken, such pacing was a critical factor in moving his church to reconnect with its code. He often quoted one of his former seminary professors, Haddon Robinson, who used to say, "When you change the music on a particular Sunday, don't have the ushers come in through the window at the same time."

Marty Linsky, a Harvard University professor and author, identifies three critical verbs in facilitating change: *observe, interpret,* and *intervene.* At a TAG Consulting roundtable, Linsky defined each of those tasks. Observation, he said, is about taking a step back to look at patterns, competing values, and stakeholder viewpoints. Interpretation is about trying to make sense of why people do what they do, which provides the perspective to reframe issues. Intervention is the process of helping people deal with an adaptive change.

A leader must understand when it is necessary to challenge a prevailing view of a problem. And the leader must be willing to intervene—not with a definitive answer, but with the suggestion that another possibility exists. If the stated problem has not been solved despite numerous attempts, the people are probably trying to solve the wrong problem. An effective leader never presumes the stated problem is the correct problem.

Adaptive change is never easy. Fortunately, difficult things can sometimes be made more manageable by using a well-defined process. In facing adaptive change, an effective leader will:

- Create a safe place in which problems can be faced
- Keep people focused on the competing values
- Investigate problems at a collective, rather than individual, level
- Reframe unsolvable problems into solvable ones
- Create conflict around competing values when conflict isn't present
- Allow overheated conflict to cool off
- Care for people as they deal with the inevitable loss that comes with change

The 3-D Method

Effective leaders know that too much change too fast creates anxiety, uncertainty, and unnecessary opposition. As a result, they introduce change incrementally—one step at a time. At TAG Consulting, we encourage leaders to use a simple but profound tool to introduce change while regulating stress. We call it the 3-D Method.

The 3-D Method allows for change to be introduced in three phases: dialogue, discussion, and decision. Each phase has different ground rules, and each may require a different amount of time to complete. I'll illustrate the process with a consultation.

Recently I was hired to help Immanuel Lutheran Church in Puyallup, Washington, develop a strategic plan. They were struggling to clarify what they were about, what their mission was, and where they should focus their resources. ILC scored well in some areas of the Transforming Church Index, but they scored lower on responses to the following statements:

- Our pastors and leaders do an excellent job of communicating expectations to members.
- When concerns are voiced to leadership, those concerns are taken seriously.
- When big decisions are made, many people are included in the decision-making process.

- Our leaders accept constructive feedback.

- Our leaders effectively mentor other people into leadership roles.

- When unpopular changes occur, people who disagree are still cared for in this church.

- Our church keeps up with the changing needs of our community.

- Changes at our church rarely catch me by surprise.

- Great efforts are made to understand various points of view.

- Conflicts are handled well by leadership.

After developing a strategic plan, there was a sense we had not quite finished. On paper, the plan was fine. But nobody thought they would be able to execute it. They told me that the church couldn't deal with conflict and, as a result, would not be able to focus on some things to the exclusion of others. I asked the staff and council to identify all of the issues causing conflict. Using a flip chart, I wrote down the emerging issues. We decided to work through one issue—Should the church continue to offer scholarships to Concordia Lutheran School?—using the 3-D Method.

Dialogue Phase

In the dialogue phase, people simply state personal opinions without feedback or interruption from others. Each person in the meeting has to share an opinion. The goal is to gather as much information as possible. Look to outside resources. Listen to each person. In a group setting, this usually happens when people go around the circle and state their opinion about what the key issues are and what they think should be done. The purpose is to capture the data. The leader's task here is to use positional authority to enforce the ground rules: no interruptions, no feedback, no reaction. Then stop.

As we began dialoguing, some people were surprised. For some, this "issue" had been a problem for well over ten years. For others, this was the first time they had heard about it. Staff and council members believed that the only issue on the table was whether the scholarships to the school should be continued or discontinued. But as each person spoke, it became clear that assumption was false.

One person said, "I think the issue is more related to our mission as a church. Providing scholarship assistance to families who simply sign up for membership doesn't seem to fit with our mission. But getting rid of scholarship assistance altogether doesn't make sense either." A long-term member recalled, "A lot of us were invested in starting that school. It's an important part of our legacy. To get rid of the scholarships would be a slap in the face to many older members." Another person spoke up: "The people who are receiving scholarships may never have contact with any church. They join our church to get the scholarship, but would they have any connection to a church otherwise? We can't think of them as inactive members who are looking for a free ride. We have to view them as our mission field!"

One by one the group shared different perspectives and experiences. Ten years' worth of either-or polarity was replaced by a spectrum of views. After forty-five minutes, we concluded the dialogue phase. People sat in amazement.

"I've learned more about this issue in forty-five minutes than I have in ten years," was the comment from many people. Mission accomplished: Dialogue led to deeper understanding. More important, the church discovered they could actually talk about a very intense issue in a healthy way.

Discussion Phase

The discussion phase occurs in a separate meeting, sometimes days or months after the dialogue phase, depending on how hot the topic is. No decisions are made in this phase, but unlike the dialogue phase, participants are free to agree or disagree with each other. The goal is to identify the competing values, clarify the issues, and provide scenarios or options. Healthy competing values, such as community versus outreach, need to be kept in some sort of balance at a macrolevel. In other words, while leaders need to choose one of the competing values in each unique situation, the two values should remain in dynamic tension in the life of the church.

Other competing values may be "self-interest" versus "common good," and in these situations, the task of leadership is to frame the discussion toward the church's mission. Some people will experience this as a personal loss, so they need to understand their voices have been heard. Remember, the goal of this process is not consensus. The goal is to raise the competing values so that leaders fully consider them when a decision is made. Consensus is rarely achieved up front. Rather, consensus is the by-product of a series of good decisions. It occurs after the fact.

When the staff and council members at Immanuel Lutheran reconvened, there was a different spirit in the room. In the absence of a dividing polarity, people were eager to go deeper. Based on the dialogue phase, we began to tease out the competing values: maintaining loyalty to denominational traditions; reaching out to unchurched people; affirming Christian education; raising the bar for church "membership"; focusing on our mission; valuing the people who helped found the school; and supporting other organizations beyond the local church.

After about two hours, the group was exhausted. The competing values were clear. But here was the really fascinating result: Those same competing values were identified as the source of conflict for all of the other unresolved issues within the church. "If we can solve this issue, which is relatively minor," said Pastor John Biermann, "we can make progress on the other issues that are keeping us back." No decision was allowed. But people left the room that day with a deeper understanding of the church's competing values—and even more hope in dealing with other unresolved issues.

Decision Phase

The decision phase occurs after the discussion phase. At the decision point, conflict will emerge, but it will be much less significant because the group has already processed the issue through dialogue and discussion. If this phase becomes too personal, each participant shares the responsibility of helping to make the conversation more objective. At some point, the authorized leaders make a decision, based on what they perceive is the right direction for the church. The leader earns his pay.

Although dialogue and discussion are inherently democratic in nature, the final decision belongs to the leader (or leaders). As I mentioned earlier, consensus decision making is usually a bad idea because it plays to the lowest common denominator. At a November 2002 TAG Consulting roundtable discussion, Jim Collins, author of *Good to Great*, stated his belief that "consensus decision making was the biggest mistake of twenty-first-century management." Leaders, he said, are responsible for making the right decisions.

It's important to note that we're not talking about decision-making structures here. This gets back to the notion of reliance upon a "position" to be able to make decisions. Sometimes a leader (regardless of position) has to make decisions even if it violates polity. Of course the most effective leaders will find that their decisions are usually supported by the polity if they have listened to and valued the people involved. The "congregational vote" often becomes the reason leaders fail to exercise leadership. They think of leadership in terms of structure/position/polity (the power zone) rather than working a process that mobilizes people to face the adaptive issues.

The leaders at Immanuel still have some work to do before they make a decision about offering school scholarships. The dialogue and discussion phases should include as many stakeholders as possible before decisions are made. Immanuel's leaders need to talk with the parents, students, teachers, the principal, and school board members. I am confident, however, that their decision will be the right one. But beyond the final decision on one relatively minor issue, the process we walked through was helpful because it opened a new way of handling competing values. After having worked through the conflict on one particular issue, the church is able to move more quickly on the other conflicted issues.

This does not mean stress and conflict have been eliminated. They have simply been regulated and monitored, creating a healthy level of anxiety so the church can continuously move forward. Instead of the leader "fixing" the problem, the people were called to engage in the adaptive process and ultimately created a situation where many more people were connected to the church's mission.

Two Snapshots of a Dynamic Process

In his mind, Ken Shigematsu has two snapshots of the transformation of Tenth Avenue Church. The first is from an actual photo he found while rummaging through some old boxes—a black-and-white picture of the congregation, which was probably taken during the late 1950s or early 1960s. Everyone in the photo is white. Most of the men are wearing suits, the women dresses. They appear to be prosperous, content, proper. The second snapshot has been engraved in Ken's mind as a kind of defining metaphor of what he desires the church to be. It is based on a true story. In the picture, a desperate woman in dirty clothes pours out a series of woes to one of the few people she knows, who happens to be her pimp. She tells him she is near the end of her rope and doesn't know whom to turn to. Standing in a drizzly gray afternoon in Stanley Park, the prostitute is weeping hysterically. Partly out of a motivation to help and partly to get rid of her, the pimp makes a suggestion. "I don't know how to help you, but maybe you should try going to the Tenth Avenue Church."

For Ken, the distance between these two snapshots cannot simply be measured by passing years. "By God's grace and through a community of people who have been willing to embrace change, we have emerged as a community where people of all different backgrounds—racial, ethnic, socioeconomic, generational, or spiritual—can come and in their time experience a relationship with God through Christ.

"Tenth Avenue Church has the privilege of serving people who are professionals—doctors, university professors, CEOs of high-tech companies—as well as artists, students, homemakers, the homeless, and the sexually and emotionally broken."

In nearly every way, Tenth Avenue reflects the city of Vancouver. It is in the process of becoming a transforming church, unleashing the power of the gospel in its community.

AUTOCRACY/SHARED LEADERSHIP SPEED BUMP

Transforming Church Checkup

1. Are people in your church overly concerned with how decisions are made?

2. Are your leadership meetings focused on trivial issues?

3. Do people tend to question every decision?

4. Does the vocal minority have too much influence in your church?

5. Is there a tendency for people in the church to make power plays?

6. Does leadership tend to make decisions too quickly? Or not quickly enough?

7. Would your church view leadership as a noun or a verb?

Travel Tips

1. Don't equate leadership with authority or power.

2. Be careful not to appeal to your position as a leader, as this will only diminish your effectiveness over time.

3. Resist the temptation to fix adaptive issues with technical solutions.

4. Determine when to meet people's expectations and when to challenge those expectations.

5. Change cannot occur without healthy conflict.

6. When people are complacent, your task is to raise conflict.

7. When people are anxious, your job is to slow things down.

8. Use the 3-D Method to engage people in problems, rather than suggest solutions too quickly.

Reflections

1. What are some adaptive problems that your church has tried to solve with technical fixes? How effective have the fixes been to solving the problem?

2. Which red-zone issue do you personally struggle with the most? How has that issue negatively impacted your ability to lead? When has that issue had a positive effect in a leadership situation?

3. As a leader, how do you handle change and conflict?

4. What is the process by which decisions are made?

8

CLOISTER/MISSIONAL, PART 1

The Cloister

When Jesus had called the Twelve together, he gave
them power and authority to drive out all demons and
to cure diseases, and he sent them out to preach the
kingdom of God and to heal the sick.
—Luke 9:1–2

We all believe life should lead somewhere. The idea of life as a journey is deeply embedded in our hearts and in our cultural memories. Many of the great stories and myths tell of heroic, harrowing journeys. Modern literature tells stories of inward journeys across the psychological landscape.

These are journeys with a purpose—with a destination in mind. Traveling in circles frustrates us, whether on a trip to the beach or on our inner journeys. A sure sign of this is the title of the biggest publishing phenomenon of recent years: Rick Warren's *The Purpose-Driven Life*. Millions of people seem to be thirsting for direction in their lives.

The best journeys are usually those taken with others, "road trips" with good friends. This is a reflection of the very nature of God, who exists in a dynamic, living community of love. The church takes its cue from God Himself. Our mission is to participate in the outworking of God's transforming love as it reshapes the whole created order. Two biblical mandates for the church, the Great Commission and the Great Commandment, both emphasize love and service to those outside the boundaries of our own group. This kind of missional focus is central to the biblical purpose of the church, and it can only be done effectively and biblically as a community.

We all desire creative community. We long to be part of something bigger than self, to be connected with others. We want to be involved in a journey focused on the creative and redemptive restoration of people made in the image of God. So why is it that we rarely live that experience? If, by definition, the mission of the church is outward, why do relatively few churches have an impact beyond their own walls?

How many of us have been involved in a church that started out with great intention and enthusiasm to "make a difference" but came to feel sidelined or disappointed or burned out somewhere along the way? And how many pastors, having set out to lead their churches to transform their communities, now feel like they are presiding over a country club or a voluntary association filled with demanding members? Why is it so few churches seem to make an ongoing impact?

The Quest

Two months after the birth of our first daughter, Anabel, we were ready for an escape. Sleepless nights and nearly endless spells of crying had taken their toll on my wife, Caroline, and me. Sensing our need to get away, my parents had arranged for all of us to stay free at a house on the beach. It was a rare opportunity for the extended Ford family to spend a few days together in seclusion, beauty, and privacy.

It was a wonderful time. Caroline and I spent countless hours in the hot tub talking with Mom, Dad, my sister Debbie, and my brother-in-law Craig. Anabel was in heaven with all the attention. If all that wasn't enough, our free house on Sea Island was part of one of the most expensive and exclusive country clubs in the United States—The Cloister.

Private dining facilities, private tennis courts, private pools, and private golf courses. Who could ask for anything more? Complete seclusion. No goals. No deadlines. No demands. Just sitting by the pool, dining when we wanted to, and strolling along the beach. It was a wonderful vacation and a reenergizing retreat. But that's all it was. After five luxurious days, we crossed the bridge from the island and headed back to the real world.

Many churches are on a permanent retreat from the world. One dictionary defines *cloister* as a verb: "to shut away from the world."[22] Of course, there are many reasons for this retreat. Fundamentally, though, I have come to believe that most churches cloister because they misunderstand what it means to move outward.

The church is often eager to point out the need to be missional. I don't know of a single church whose mission statement comes out against the Great Commission. The church understands the *necessity* of a journey focused on sharing the gospel and seeing lives changed. What it often doesn't fully understand is that true transformation of people and communities depends on the *kind* of journey.

I believe most churches fail in the journey of change because they start off offering people an adventure rather than a quest. As I state in chapter 1, Tolkien writes that an adventurer seeks treasure without the necessity of transformation, while someone on a quest is forever changed, often in the very process of losing a treasure. Church leaders often promise that being a Christian will yield great treasure, but they fail to understand Christ's central paradox concerning purpose: "If you give up your life for me, you will find it" (Matt. 10:39 NLT). Reaching out involves loss—a loss of comfort, a loss of self-focus, and perhaps a loss of some personal enjoyment.

The transforming journey outward involves a loss as much as it does a gain.

Advancing across a Great Divide

Craig Lotz started out with a strong missional focus. As arts director for Grace Community Church near Asheville, North Carolina, he understood the church's potential to heal the wounds of a region pummeled by "culture wars." Nestled in the mountains of western North Carolina, Grace literally stands in a great cultural divide—between Asheville (a liberal community composed mostly of artists and New Agers) and Hendersonville (a conservative town firmly in the buckle of the Bible Belt). On his drive to work, on any given day and on any given car bumper, Craig might see the divide spelled out:

Don't put a question mark where God put a period.

Hate is not a family value.

I still pray.

So Many Right-Wing Christians. So Few Lions.

An integral part of the code and theology of Grace is to build bridges to the community. Instead of pointing out what divides us, the church's focus has been on what we all share: the image of God and a continuing need for grace. Art, Craig believes, is uniquely capable of creating connections between the church and community. Operating on Francis Schaeffer's principle that all truth and beauty belong to God, Craig worked to discard labels of *believer* and *nonbeliever* and *us* and *them*.

As his philosophy of art has evolved (he once used to burn secular albums), he discarded the notion of the "Christian artist." Good art, he believes, points to transcendent realities and, therefore, to God. Because all artists share the image of God and the common grace of creation, such truth and beauty is as likely to surface in bars as in church sanctuaries.

Craig's method of being missional was to produce events designed to build bridges between the church and the community. He wanted artists to grasp glimpses of deeper realities on shared ground. Instead of limiting his bookings to Christians, Craig opened the doors to those who did not label themselves as such. Singer-songwriter David Wilcox, for example, has performed numerous concerts throughout the country and has achieved celebrity status in the Asheville region. A local director, not connected with the church and professing no particular belief, directed the play *Shadowlands,* which portrays C. S. Lewis's marriage to Joy Davidman, at Grace. Juried art shows displaying the works of artists from western North Carolina are on display annually in Grace's foyer.

Intuitively, Craig understood the need for community to empower and sustain such creativity. He knew being missional springs from relational connections. But his plan bypassed the building of community. Instead, he reduced his strategy to: Build it and they will come. Craig says, "We believed if we could give a place for artists to create out of the gospel, they would flock to come, be involved, and build this great community. So the focus became the event." Craig excelled. The events were highly successful on many levels. Most plays and concerts sold out, people who would never consider stepping inside the walls of a church did so, and dialogues were started in a region where shouting matches were the norm.

But as time passed, the pressure of producing high-caliber events took its toll. The creative community Craig longed for—and desperately needed—never materialized. "I realized our focus was always on the next event—that this was going to be the thing that finally put us over the top." In an effort to create even more innovative events, he was forced to focus resources on the production instead of developing relationships. "Community was always something that we would finally be able to get to after the next event. Artists were participating in the events, and many people had heard of the church, but no one was being transformed."

During the production of *Shadowlands,* Craig was putting in eighty-hour weeks. On the edge of exhaustion, he decided to take a break—hitting golf balls with his then four-year-old son, Bryce. That's when a couple of realizations were driven home:

- There was no other place on the planet he wanted to be more than with his son.
- His mission of making a lasting impact on the Asheville community would never be realized without some kind of deeper change.

Selling an Adventure

What Craig offered—both to the people who came and to those few who helped produce—was an event. It promised personal satisfaction, whether spectacle and entertainment for those who watched or a self-fulfilling use of gifts for those who participated. The church was reaching out, but not effectively. Once the event was over, there were no lasting relationships or a sense of shared purpose to take its place. The missional focus was skewed because it didn't invite people into a transforming journey.

The cultural dysfunction of the cloister is deeply ingrained in our society. The idea of adventure sells. The promise of the journey is filled with thrill, instant gratification, and enjoyment without engagement. Hit the road. Find a treasure. Return home without any necessity for real change. The empty promise of consumerism promises a rush without the price of a transforming, outwardly focused journey. An adventure sells individual happiness without all the messy work of sacrificial community, great risk, faithfulness to the cause, and uncertain destination. The lie is an attractive one.

As we've talked about in earlier chapters, a good deal of contemporary church strategy is premised on religious consumerism: the production of the most innovative products to attract people into community. Craig stated the premise well: "If we build it, they will come." And it doesn't matter what *it* is. For Craig and Grace, *it* was the idea of spectacular events involving art. For others, *it* is strict adherence to denominational traditions and rituals. For others, it is cutting-edge worship or children's ministry or youth ministry. For others, mystery. For others, the liturgy itself. In any case, the missional focus is linked to production of the right products.

Now, there is nothing wrong with either innovation or tradition, and certainly nothing is wrong with creativity. My point is that, when ministry becomes about the product or event, community gets pushed to the side and the mission remains rootless. The idea that creativity can flourish for long without a missional community is sorely mistaken.

The Gap between I and We

As I was editing this chapter, I received a phone call from the pastors of a church in Illinois who had just completed the Transforming Church Index and wanted to discuss the results. They had recently finished a three-year strategic planning process and were planning to build a new building—a "creative" act. But they were experiencing a lot of resistance, and the leadership couldn't figure out why. So we opened up their sixty-six-page TCIndex report to the executive summary, which includes the ten survey questions that scored the highest and the ten questions that scored the lowest.

The church received positive responses, compared to the national norm, to the following statements:

- When a problem repeats itself in our church, it is because most people in the church contribute to that problem.
- I am aware of our church's financial condition.
- I have a clear sense of how decisions are made in the church.
- I am cooperative around here.
- My church has encouraged me to be involved in a ministry (either inside or outside the church).
- There are plenty of opportunities for average people to be involved in leadership at the church.
- I have received training from this church in some form of outreach, evangelism, or missions work.
- I am trusted around here.
- This church has helped me grow spiritually.
- There is faith in me around here.

The church received low scores, compared to the national norm, to the following statements:

- Our church effectively meets goals (deadlines, results, and budgets).
- Our church's programs and ministries are effectively promoted in our community.
- Our church keeps up with the changing needs of our community.
- Our ministries and programs reflect the felt needs of our community.

- This church retains its members.
- If our church were to close down, our contribution to the community would be sorely missed.
- This church's buildings and facilities are effective in supporting our ministries.
- This church has clearly differentiated itself from other churches in effective ways.
- Our church effectively manages its financial resources.
- This church has a clear statement of faith.

I noticed an interesting trend in these results—the use of the personal pronoun. All of the strengths involved an *I* (or an implied one), and all of the weaknesses involved an *our*. People had a general sense of their individual importance to the church, which is a good thing, but little sense of connection—either to others in the church or in mission to the community.

Both types of connections—internal relationships in community and the external outworking through creative mission—are necessary for a sustained and loving missional focus. This church was lacking both types. As a result, the building project wasn't connecting to people either. It was just a building. There was very little sense of unifying purpose.

The Temptation of Community

Norman was a longtime member of Walnut Creek, a traditional church in a rural area of Ohio. Norman's parents, his children, and his first grandchild attended. His doctor, his best friend, and his brother were elders. Following the retirement of the pastor, who had faithfully served for more than thirty years, Norman expressed an interest in the ideas of the new pastor—a young man with a head full of ideas about how to "reach the community."

Norman realized that Walnut Creek had drifted into isolation from its community. He had to admit it: He was reluctant to invite an unbelieving friend to church because he was afraid he might drift off into one of his back-pew naps. Certainly, the church could use more vibrancy, some new blood. A little change might do them all some good.

Within a couple of months of his arrival, the pastor called for a church "town hall" meeting. There, he laid out his vision for "reaching out to a broken world" with the love of God. Citing the desperate need to reach beyond the walls of the church, he invited the people to help accomplish his vision. Over time, the church began to grow. Although Norman began to feel uncomfortable with some of the changes, he was willing to make sacrifices so that the gospel would have a wider audience.

In a continuing effort to make the church more attractive to unbelievers, the pastor formed a group of people to brainstorm a second, more contemporary service. To make time for a second service, Sunday school would have to be sacrificed, and the people were invited to join small groups that met at other times, which the pastor promised would develop community. Although Norman was somewhat troubled by the fact that most of the people on the team were relative newcomers to Walnut Creek, he was willing to entertain other possibilities.

During church one Sunday, a date was announced for a trial run of the second service. After the trial service, members would be invited into a focus group to give feedback.

The contemporary service shocked Norman. He was unprepared for a drama featuring two dysfunctional families competing on the game show *Family Feud*. He wondered why there was no prayer for members of the church from the pulpit or, for that matter, no pulpit. He really doubted that Jesus liked the electric guitar. But most of all, from the deepest part of his soul, he wondered where he might fit in if the church continued in this direction. During the focus-group time, Norman, speaking on behalf of many of the "old guard," expressed his outrage. "We have sacrificed a great deal, but this is too much to ask," he said. "This is *our* church."

The contemporary service was voted down, and the impetus for an increased outreach stalled. The cloister survived.

The Paradox of Change

The connection between the realities of "creative" and "community" is much the same as the relationship between proton and electron: Split it and you've got a world of trouble. Just as Craig learned that creativity without community is impossible, Norman's retreat to a back-pew nap demonstrates that community without creativity is lifeless. The consumer mentality of "me first" inevitably yields to burnout; the community notion of "us first" leads to exclusion and apathy. When the balance of creative community fails in either direction, the journey of change will always stall or become circular. Rather than becoming a transforming journey, it will become a "there and back again" adventure.

In Norman's church—and in so many others I have consulted with—the emphasis on community without creative outreach leads to isolation and a dangerous mentality of "us and them." Perhaps a metaphor again illustrates it best.

Bridges Change Everything

In the mid-1990s, a bitter and divisive referendum was up for vote by the residents of Prince Edward Island. At issue: Should the Canadian government build a nine-mile bridge connecting the island to the mainland? The fulfillment of a 132-year-old promise would come with a $1-billion price tag. Many islanders felt the real cost would be much more.

Over time and generations, living on the island had shaped the way the residents perceived reality. Isolation makes a difference. By definition, it sets you apart, highlights the distance of here and there, us and them. People choose to live on an island. On Prince Edward Island, life was a cultivated peace, undisturbed, serene, and largely disconnected from the greater span of the real world—what one resident described as "two huge beaches separated by potato fields." From the soil of such idyllic shores, in fact, sprang the fiction of Anne of Green Gables, a redheaded, pigtailed, freckled, and innocent character, who had come to be the powerful and defining symbol of the island's peaceful nature. For nearly half the island's residents, the bridge offered little but threat—both real and imagined. The completion of a bridge would mean only one certainty: Nothing would remain the same.

The stories of Walnut Creek and Grace Community are representative of how churches get stuck on the journey of change and stand paralyzed at the edge of a bridgeless gap. In both cases, the real problem is rooted in the loss of creative community and the inevitable separation from the church's real mission of transforming journey. Where there is no bridge, you will find the cloister.

The Paradox of Purpose

The purpose of life, the work of God's creative community, is posed by Jesus as a paradox: "Anyone who does not take his cross and follow me is not worthy of me. Whoever finds his life will lose it, and whoever loses his life for my sake will find it" (Matt. 10:38–39).

The cross is a hard sell. As translated in *The Message*, the words of 1 Corinthians 13 are full of mystery, inconvenience, and unwavering focus away from a center of self.

Love never gives up.
Love cares more for others than for self.
Love doesn't want what it doesn't have.
Love doesn't strut,
Doesn't have a swelled head,
Doesn't force itself on others,
Isn't always "me first,"
Doesn't fly off the handle,
Doesn't keep score of the sins of others,
Doesn't revel when others grovel,
Takes pleasure in the flowering of truth,
Puts up with anything,
Trusts God always,

Always looks for the best,

Never looks back,

But keeps going to the end.

Love itself is a transforming journey.

In our culture centered on self-gratification, is it any wonder why churches find it so hard to develop, sustain, and expand a missional focus? Given the embedded tendency toward either consumerism or cloister, how can a local church maintain the necessary tension inherent in creative community?

Understanding the Threat

When our oldest daughter, Anabel, was a three-year-old, she was always active and eager to venture out. She routinely went to the basement to play with her toys or ran to the backyard to meet her friends on the swing set and slide. She was always in motion, engaged by curiosity and exploring with great delight everything within her boundaries (and sometimes without). But then her baby sister, Leighton, was born. Suddenly, Anabel stopped venturing out on her own. She greeted the arrival of her sister with a confounding inwardness. She no longer felt safe and loved. My relationship with Anabel was altered. Within three weeks of Leighton's birth, Anabel's behavior changed. She wanted—demanded—to be as close to me as she could. During the day, she desired to be in my lap. At night, she wanted to crawl into bed with her mother and me. Anabel was fearful the love of her father would diminish.

There are many reasons churches are not missional, but many of the critical factors are the same ones that stopped my daughter from exploring her world. The reasons all revolved around fear, perhaps the best antonym for love. In our consulting work, we have identified three expressions of fear that are the most common causes of inward focus. They are perceived feelings of …

- Insecurity
- Incompetence
- Insignificance

Insecurity

Leaders can make followers feel insecure without being aware that they are doing so. As I discussed in previous chapters, when leadership is equated with power, people suffer outright abuse. They are valued only for their role as cogs in the spiritual machinery or as facilitators of the pastor's vision. Although I have seen blatant examples of this kind of church formula, my experience is that the abuse is usually more subtle, less intentional.

In Norman's church, for example, the pastor did not seem to value the input from the old guard and, with the best of intentions to become missional, did not protect voices of dissent. In so doing, he excluded critical members of the church, created separation, and in the end, eliminated the very possibility of reaching out for the sake of the gospel. Seeking to tear down walls, he simply built more. Effective leaders will always protect voices of dissent, even if doing so leads to unpopular decisions.

For Craig, the drive toward excellence in the building of artistic bridges to the community was seeded in his own insecurity. Hired with no formal background in either art or theology, Craig's red-zone issue of competence motivated him to excel as a way of compensating for his lack of credentials. This insecurity caused him to do ministry in such a way that most others were excluded. As a result, they felt they were not trusted, and this bred their own insecurity. It was a vicious cycle.

Incompetence

Many pastors I have consulted with make the mistake of believing that part of their job is to protect people from pain—most often by minimizing conflict. In seeking to protect their members from the messiness and stress of ministry, a pastor usually acts with a good and kind heart. However, the people of the church, longing to be connected, don't see it the same way.

Like a child who is overprotected, the interpretation is often expressed in feelings of incompetence such as, "The leaders don't trust me or feel that I'm gifted enough to engage in big issues."

Often, incompetence simply involves misdirected resources. Craig desired to engage others in the work of the ministry, but because of the pressing nature of the next bigger and better event, he simply did not possess the time or energy to connect others. Those excluded often assumed the church already had enough competent help and did not feel welcomed into ministry. In Norman's church, a long and deep sense of community was threatened by a disconnection with the pastor's new vision for the church. The old guard, feeling that their opinions no longer mattered, sensed a deep displacement and a sudden onrush of incompetence. A long-standing trust between leadership and core members was violated. The result was an insurrection against needed change.

Sometimes the message of incompetence is sent subconsciously. I recently consulted with a church that scored very high on "member satisfaction" in our survey and very low on "member input." Essentially, this was a group of people who loved the programs but felt like they had nothing to contribute. As I talked with the pastor, I learned the church had gone through a critical values shift a few years previously. The transition from a church model where staff did most of the ministry to empowering and equipping laypeople was difficult. Many of the previous staff, whose gifts and passions no longer lined up with their new job descriptions, either resigned or were fired to make room for more qualified staff. The pastor was baffled that the change hadn't brought about a higher level of member involvement. When I asked the members about the staff turnover, however, I discovered that none of them knew why the staff had left. They knew that there was a major adaptive issue involved at some level, but church leadership had chosen to keep the issue very hush-hush. What the leaders failed to recognize was that by not including the membership in the discussion about the values shift, they essentially sent the members a message: You are not competent to deal with these kinds of issues. Despite the leaders' honest intentions of moving to more of a lay ministry model, the members continued to show up for great programs but never felt like partners in the mission of the church.

Insignificance

When people feel disconnected from a shared sense of mission, a church's overriding sense of purpose—to participate locally in God's redemptive work in the world—largely disappears. Without a compelling missional focus, open doors are shut, windows turn into mirrors, and the people are left with little more than a reflection of their own faces. They cloister. Reduced to the space between four walls, purpose often shrinks to advancing a personal agenda or guarding a piece of turf.

The systemic nature of being a cloister morphs into a set of new problems. Conflict shifts from the mission of the church to personal needs. The issues that disconnected a person from an overriding purpose—feelings of insecurity, incompetence, or insignificance—attach to their own red-zone issues and set up a series of unsolvable problems. Without anything greater to focus on, a church member's energy is spent trying to fix the person standing next to him or her, without understanding his or her own unresolved issues. In a church disconnected from a missional focus, a culture of internal personalized conflict takes root, which leads to further separation from one another, the church's shared mission, and a dying world.

Adaptive Change

The love of God is expansive. Imagine a wave of sound or light or water. Its natural tendency is to move outward. As God's love touches each of our lives, our hearts are transformed and our capacity to love is expanded. Fear presents resistance—the breaker against the wave, the wall to the light, the blanket to the sound. Fear promotes a tendency toward exclusion, the opposite of a transforming missional focus. Leadership must model and present a kind of love that casts out fear.

The differing directions of Grace Community Church and Walnut

Creek were largely determined by an act of courage. Despite the appearance of success, Craig Lotz insisted on change. He stopped the endless cycle of event-productions and faced his own unresolved issues with competence. "As I began more and more to find my identity in Christ," Craig says, "I was able to slow down the pace of events." At one point, Craig had produced more than eight major events a year in addition to his responsibilities for artistic efforts in weekend services. For the new ministry year, he decided on just two events and shifted the focus to building leaders—actors, musicians, writers, photographers, filmmakers, dancers, and visual and graphic artists. He started a Bible study with the leaders of each team. He invited people into community and shifted resources to help equip and engage volunteers. He sought input into strategy and mission. In the end, what he discovered was both radical and familiar to him: In terms of being missional, who we *are* is as important as what we *do*.

To be creative outside the context of a meaningful community is to miss the entire point. The focus of the art moved from performance to response. As the artists began to understand the love of God, fleshed out in the relationships around them, they created together to develop acts of worship rather than to secure a sense of worth. Although the strategy is still new and largely untested, Craig says he has already seen some positive changes. The art, while organic and unpredictable, is also more collective—a reflection of a vision springing from the heart of "us" instead of his mind alone. And while there are fewer events to attract people from the surrounding area, those who do come are more willing to be drawn from the sidelines by the appeal of a sustaining, motivating, and loving community. And Grace Church stands poised, once again, to build bridges outward to the world around them.

Norman, on the other hand, returned to his back pew, where he consistently takes naps on Sunday mornings. He has yet to invite any of his friends to church. When the most recent pastor speaks of outreach, if he does so at all, he directs people to the map in the foyer—the one with all the strings of red yarn running to various pins throughout the world. The only transforming journeys in Norman's church are the ones taken vicariously.

9

CLOISTER/MISSIONAL, PART 2

The Exponential Power of One

Then Jesus came to them and said, "All authority in heaven and on earth has been given to me. Therefore go and make disciples of all nations, baptizing them in the name of the Father and of the Son and of the Holy Spirit, and teaching them to obey everything I have commanded you. And surely I am with you always, to the very end of the age."
—Matthew 28:18–20

On December 1, 2005, World AIDS Day, a PBS affiliate in Indianapolis aired a full-length documentary on the sweeping effects of the AIDS epidemic in Kenya. Focused on medical clinics, villages, and homes in the Rift Valley, the film showed the devastation firsthand by telling stories of what it was like to live with—and die from—AIDS.

The statistics were horrifying: 2 million people had died the previous year in Africa from the terrible disease; more than 7,000 a day were infected with the virus; there were currently more than 12 million orphans, and with the virus unchecked, as many as 20 million orphans were expected by 2010. But the stories told were even more shocking: widowed women infected with the disease, ostracized from society; tiny children with the HIV death sentence; doctors forced to deliver the deadly diagnosis; bodies discovered in the woods.

The theme of the documentary—that one person can make a difference—centered around how certain individuals in Africa were dealing with the tragedy with courage, ingenuity, and hope against all odds. At the same time, the documentary reminded viewers that each person possesses the power and opportunity to help. The filmmakers—a group of eleven volunteers and one part-time staff member of a church in Indianapolis—had come to know the theme by heart. Making the film had been a living laboratory for experiencing the power of a few to make a difference.

Questions of Significance

For months, Robin Howard had a sick feeling in the pit of her stomach every time she thought about leaving for a three-week trip to Kenya. Questions kept her awake at night:

> Where would the money come from for vaccinations she had to take before she went?
>
> How could she, a newlywed, leave her husband for so long?
>
> Could she afford to take that many weeks off work?
>
> How could an introvert like her interact with people she didn't even know?
>
> What business did a group of church volunteers have making a documentary?
>
> Where, exactly, would their plane land?
>
> And most troubling of all, how could she possibly play a role of any significance?

"For me," Robin says, "going with the Power of One team involved one leap of faith after another—like walking across a stream on tiny, slippery rocks. But through it all, I felt there was a reason I had to go."

Most of us want to make a difference, to be caught up in something bigger than we are. This inevitably requires risk. Producing *The Power of One* documentary involved no small risk for The Garden, a unique church located in Indianapolis. From its inception in 1995, The Garden has colored outside the lines and pushed the limits of what church means. Despite significant success along the way, it has continually resisted the tendency to become a cloister.

"I saw a spark in someone," says Pastor Linda McCoy about the time she was first approached about the idea of a documentary. "And my job is to fan the spark and see if it bursts into full flame. One of the core values of our church has always been that each one of us can make a difference in the world. At The Garden we approach ministry by finding something that brings a person alive and knowing there are other people who are brought alive by the same thing. We had already been reaching out in this fashion in our local community. This was just the next step."

The documentary told a powerful story. But the making of the documentary told an equally powerful story: a story about a church plant meeting in the Beef & Boards Dinner Theatre in order to attract people who would never attend a typical church. A story about a church determined to unleash the creativity of its people so that God's unconditional and transforming love would change the surrounding community.

Laserlike Focus

In my years of consulting, I have never run into a church quite like The Garden. Because its purpose involves a laserlike missional focus—even to the exclusion of more traditional elements such as small groups and youth programs—it has been able to succeed in reaching out in ways many other churches cannot duplicate. Pastor Linda McCoy believes the church is called to play a unique and specific role within the greater context of the church at large.

"We decided from the start we wanted to be all about being missional," Linda says. "Because of this focus, we knew the church would look different. We knew it wouldn't please everyone, but we were going to try to reach the people who weren't being reached by the church. In Indianapolis, that is more than one-half of the population."

The nature of The Garden's evangelism is unique. What is universal is that every church must find its own way of facing outward. Traditionally, this effort gets labeled "outreach" or "missions," which makes it one of the things we do more than a defining characteristic of who we are. Doing outreach is not enough. So what is?

Being missional is simply unleashing the collective passions of the church—its code—into the world. What makes the task difficult is the enormous emphasis on self that leaks from our culture into the church. Our default mode is to think of the church in terms of how it meets each of our or our family's needs. In moving people's focus outward, away from self, the church faces enormous obstacles and embedded cultural dysfunction. Transforming churches are figuring out how to overcome these obstacles and unleash the power of passion into their surrounding communities. In fact, according to our research, local outreach is a greater indicator of church health than global outreach. Paradoxically, the turn away from self makes people more content and energized in their churches.

In every church with a healthy focus on those who are outside, there is a strategy to move people from …

- attendance to commitment
- consumption to community
- entitlement to entrustment
- insignificance to impact

The Option of a Different Ministry

Before The Garden, Robin Howard's experience with church had been traumatic. As a child, she was forced to go three times a week, taught that smokers and drinkers went to hell, and encouraged to draw Crayola art of flames in Sunday school. In her child's vivid imagination, she drew a picture of God the punisher. As a young adult, she walked so far away from her religion she eventually started to think of herself as an atheist. "The real problem," she says she now understands, "was I could not reconcile God with the church." While in college, she went to church one Sunday at the request of someone she was dating. As she walked into the building, she had a panic attack. It was years before she tried again.

Although Linda McCoy had never met Robin Howard, she had people just like her in mind even before The Garden was started. Prior to the church's launch, Linda had been through a profound time of wrestling with the future direction of her ministry. "I didn't know what I wanted to do, just that it would be different," Linda says.

On an airplane trip from Indianapolis to Denver in 1994, Linda was considering her options. Linda had served for a number of years as part of the pastoral team at St. Luke's United Methodist Church in Indianapolis, and her world was rocked by the senior pastor's retirement after twenty-six years of service. While the new pastor was gifted and competent, it was soon clear that things would need to change for Linda to continue working there. She had considered other options—the chaplaincy of a nursing home and the pastorate of a floundering church start among them—but nothing seemed to fit. She was flying to Denver to continue work on her doctorate. Linda had no clear idea of what was next, but she had several values that were important to her, including that her ministry setting involve collaboration, emphasize inclusion, and be missional.

In her fourteen years of ministry at St. Luke's, one of the largest Methodist churches in the country, Linda had grown accustomed to working in teams. The six clergy on the St. Luke's staff, while each overseeing a specific area of ministry, developed vision and made decisions together. She knew she wanted to do ministry with a team and wanted to focus that ministry on those who had previously felt excluded from church. Now she just needed an open door. But she couldn't see any around her.

So great was her confusion, she was considering leaving ministry altogether. On the plane, she was reading a book by a management guru titled *The Tom Peters Seminar: Crazy Times Call for Crazy Organizations*. She was struck by the story of a Japanese businessman who went to his boss with a simple question: "What do you want me to do? What do you want me to make?" Just after Linda read the boss's response—"Make something great"—she fell into a deep sleep. She can't remember the specifics of the dream, only that she awoke feeling the struggle and turmoil replaced by peace and confidence. From that time forward, she understood her future to be a God thing.

Understand Who You Are

When leading a church toward becoming missional, you must first understand who *you* are as a leader. Like many pastors, Linda knew her gifts, passion, skills, and preferences and took those into account before she began any ministry. But the church is more than a collection of people with gifts, passions, and skills. A missional church must have a clear sense of itself as a living organism. For an established church, this starts with an understanding of its code—its unique DNA and shared experiences. Discovering the common ground through a clear and defining code allows a church to have a specific focus. It understands that, functioning within the larger body of Christ, it doesn't have to be everything for everyone.

As I discussed previously, healthy churches have a clearly defined set of core values and a compelling mission statement. They express the code of the church in written form. Too often, a committee will sit in a conference room with a flip chart and determine values that don't communicate any sense of identity or personality. Plain-vanilla values like caring, respect, and service are nice ideals for a church, but they fail to communicate the church's unique code. When a church understands who it is and communicates its code with clarity, people are more likely to start the process of involvement—giving financially and attending regularly. Most important, people begin exploring options for ministry.

Involve Others

Eventually Linda McCoy settled on the idea of creating a "new thing." Her first instinct was to involve others in her decision. She sought input from the new pastor at St. Luke's, Kent Millard. His response was simple and direct: "If this is from God, I want to be on God's side." Although Linda did not believe she could serve on the staff of St. Luke's anymore, she was wise enough to seek their support. The language used to describe The Garden's relationship with St. Luke's—as a "blossom"—was true on more than just a pragmatic level. The Garden shared much of the same code as St. Luke's; they just expressed it differently.

Linda's quest to involve others did not stop with a promise of support from St. Luke's. For Linda, team ministry was not an option but a necessity. She knew she would never succeed alone. Meeting with a handful of others, many of whom she had worked with in her previous ministry, she developed a concise purpose statement. She understood that mission activities sprout from mission statements.

She simultaneously opened conversations on two fronts: with those who were excited about the church's potential and with those who had reservations. At the same time she recruited potential partners, she protected dissenting voices. She initiated conversations between those who were with her and those who might be against her, and she listened. But she never put the issue of a new start-up for debate. "We never asked for a vote of approval or for specific input on what this was going to be," Linda says. "We just said, 'This is what we'd like to do; what do you think?'" Linda then issued a general invitation to the congregation at St. Luke's: "If you are interested in this kind of ministry, give us a year of your time to get it launched."

Although Linda was involved in starting a new work, her strategy of involving others is necessary in all adaptive change. An already established church seeking to change its orientation from inward to outward is faced with an equally—if not more—daunting challenge. There are no quick fixes. Too often, leaders doom the efforts with initial decisions. They either try to resolve the problem without engaging others, or they fail to raise the adaptive issues.

As I was working on this chapter, I received a call from a pastor in Cincinnati who was extremely confused. "Kevin, we outgrew our space and property three years ago. On a Sunday morning back then, I announced that we were considering relocating and that we wanted members' input. We ended up with a mini-riot on our hands! A week later, over one hundred people left the church. Kevin, what happened? As leaders, we didn't say that we were relocating. We just said we were considering it!"

Even though he thought he was engaging people in the process, this pastor made the mistake of starting with a solution. His Sunday-morning announcement immediately created a polarity in the church despite the fact that he said he wanted member input. He would have been wiser to raise the problem—we're out of space—and engage the membership in discussing the problem before suggesting any possible solutions.

From Linda's example, we learn critical lessons about the nature of effective leadership:

- Engage others in discussing the problems and opportunities (not as a pretense but with open ears)
- Protect—and learn from—dissenting voices
- Raise important issues (orchestrate conflict) and provide perspective on varying points of view
- Make the mission statement the reference point for debate and conflict

Learn, but Do Not Imitate

Linda understood the difference between imitation and ingenuity—one mimics where the other adapts. After identifying key people who would play a major role in the church plant, Linda began to travel with groups to visit other innovative churches with a strong missional focus. Not only was it a time of discovery, it was also a great way to build community and ownership. "We visited a lot of different places that were doing nontraditional things to reach the community. We took a lot of road trips, and afterward we would sit around and say, 'Does that feel right for us?' We picked up some things, and we discarded some things. We weren't interested in churches giving us all the answers so much as seeking out those that were asking the right questions."

At the same time, Linda began to form her teams—leadership, worship design, hospitality, and others. As they were sorting through creative options for outreach, they also researched the specific community within Indianapolis where they had decided to plant the church. They dug deep into the culture by identifying what kind of music people listened to, how many people attended church, what they were watching on television and at the movies, and what kind of social services were present. "We were intentional about getting to know the community and being involved." Again, the key theme was in creating partnerships. "We wanted to be part of the community—not something working outside of it," Linda says.

An Intentional Missional Focus

The first time Robin Howard stepped inside The Garden, she felt at home. "I loved it right away. The first time I came to The Garden, I felt like I had found a group of nonjudgmental people with all kinds of life experiences and backgrounds, who sometimes played Foo Fighters in church. For the first time in my life, I felt myself in the presence of a loving and compassionate God, who was speaking my language and meeting me exactly where I was."

For four years, Robin Howard did not really get involved at The Garden. Part of her reluctance stemmed from her childhood experience of church, where people served more out of a sense of duty than from a caring heart. Part of it sprang from the fact that she was highly introverted. But most of it arose from deep feelings of insignificance. She desperately wanted to make a difference, but she didn't know how.

A few years before coming to The Garden, at the age of twenty-seven, she had quit her job as vice president of marketing at a tech company. She wanted to pursue art as well as the meaning of life. More than anything, she decided she wanted to help people. "I knew I had some artistic skills, but it's not easy figuring out how to help people with that. I was in deep despair with what I had to offer." She remembers praying: "Lord, I don't have much to offer You, but if there is a way to use an artist—then send me."

Being missional must be intentional. There are too many powerful forces at work, both culturally and universally, to believe being missional will simply evolve over time. In a fallen world, with broken hearts, learning to love others is difficult. Over time, a church will naturally gravitate toward the cloister—separation, isolation, and exclusion. Like Linda, we must seek to understand. Once again, we see a healthy pattern of energetic and shared exploration in Linda's strategy:

- Innovative methods to reach out in love to those outside our immediate circles
- Concentrated efforts to discern and participate in the unique makeup of a local community
- Risky steps outside of comfort zones or traditional bounds

Such risk taking can produce much anxiety. To understand how to reach a community best, you have to become a part of it. For example, in The Garden's immediate community, there are a number of twelve-step rehabilitation programs—for alcohol, drug, sex, and many other addictions. The church soon partnered with many of them, encouraging their members to get involved.

Often, stepping out into the community mandates a high level of discomfort and stress. One of my partners at TAG Consulting is a psychologist. Over the years, he has dealt with people who suffer from various conditions, often because they are inwardly focused. To help them shift their orientation from self to others, he routinely places them in uncomfortable situations. He gives them "assignments" to volunteer in a nursing home, an after-school program, or some other community service. At first, he nearly always encounters great resistance and fear. But over time, when they begin to experience the plight of others and see they can actually help make an impact, they begin to work through their own issues. Likewise, the church must learn that, when developing a missional focus, leadership must often seek to place their people in uncomfortable situations "out there." Frequently it is the only way to assure people—contrary to their initial thinking—that they can feel safe, competent, and significant.

The Primacy of Mission

Having researched and engaged the community, The Garden intentionally narrowed its mission statement to a few words: "To engage all in the quest to know and to share the unconditional love of God." As the core members prepared to launch the first service, it was more than simply a marketing slogan. Rather, it served as a filter for what The Garden would and would not do. While core values express the personality of a church, mission focuses its activity. Through the perspective of its mission statement, all the critical questions were addressed:

- What is our primary purpose for existence?
- What is our unique role within the greater body?
- What contribution can our church make to the church of the future?
- What should we do differently from the church of the past?
- What ministries or needs are necessary outside of this unique scope?
- What things don't we focus on?
- What results do we intend?
- Who are the primary beneficiaries of our ministry?

In essence, a good mission statement should contain a reason for existence, an intended outcome, and a primary beneficiary. Many mission statements are far too vague to create focus. Other mission statements fit the formula but fail to tap people's passions. The final test of a mission statement is: Does it move us outward and onward?

Seeing the Vision

From The Garden's mission statement, Linda was careful not to "hand down" a vision. Rather, in the various teams, she phrased a simple question: "Okay, this is what we would like to do. What might that look like?" By inviting others into leadership, the vision was shared. That in turn created ownership of ministry, which inspired a movement away from self-interest to accomplish the mission.

Vision is the picture of a church's desired future, and it provides direction to that end. Vision is the answer to the question: If we were to accomplish our mission, what would this church and our community look like? Vision emerges from mission. Once a church has a clear, compelling mission and a picture of the future, it can then develop a handful of focused strategies to begin moving toward the vision.

Too often, pastors feel they need to be the ones who come up with the vision. Solomon never said, "Where there is no vision, *the pastor* perishes." Vision is most compelling when it is shared. In creating a missional focus, the leader's task is to ensure there is a shared vision, not to hand it down to the people. Sure, some leaders are natural visionaries. But that is not a requisite for leadership. If the leader keeps the people focused on the mission, the vision will begin to emerge. When it does, people will have a greater sense of ownership than if it had been handed down to them.

Focused Strategy

Transforming churches, over time, develop a coherent strategic architecture—clear values, mission, vision, and strategy. Strategy tells us how we will fulfill our mission and achieve our vision within the boundaries of our values, often with a five- to ten-year window. Strategy can and should change as our context, needs, and resources change. Typically, a church should focus on three or four primary areas of strategy. Too often, churches attempt to do everything. Remember the old adage "Do a few things well"? That is a great definition of strategy. Can you name the three or four things that your church does extremely well? Can you identify the ministries or programs that are most helpful in fulfilling your mission?

The Garden's strategy took into account these unique congregational factors:

- context (needs and issues within the local community)
- capabilities (the talents and resources of its membership)
- creativity (ability to launch new ministries and programs)
- code (ways to preserve the church's identity and values)

The Garden's leadership paid special attention to removing barriers that prevented people from understanding the unconditional love of God. In Linda's words: "So often, we make people jump through certain hoops or know the secret handshake or recite certain formulas before they can get into the inner circle. Because we believe God's love is inclusive, we needed to be very careful not to exclude people by what we did or how we did it."

Barriers were identified, which included …

- use of religious jargon
- judgmental stances
- insider music
- pleas for money
- long and didactic preaching

In addition to identifying and eliminating potential barriers, The Garden's leadership also sought to orchestrate communication in "the language of the culture." Each service would feature …

- synergy (a central theme communicated through a variety of media)
- popular music only (no religious songs)
- visual imagery (television or movie clips, photography)
- short messages (ten to fifteen minutes long)

When I visited The Garden to conduct focus groups in 2002, I was amazed to find several atheists in the focus groups. They were interested and asking questions, and felt as if The Garden was a place where they could get their feet wet. "No experience necessary" read one of the church's slogans. Anyone, with or without a spiritual background, could come and take part.

Reimagining Church

Since The Garden's first service on September 10, 1995, the missional focus has continued. During one recent Sunday, the theme centered on interdependence and how it is often harder to receive help than to give it. A version of the Beatles' "Help" kicked off the service, followed by other songs such as the Eagles' "Desperado" and Three Dog Night's "One." Threaded through the fifty-minute service was a series of video clips from the television show *Joan of Arcadia*, focused on the interaction between a grandmother who was growing senile and her grandson, who had been paralyzed a few years earlier. Images of the Marlboro Man, an icon of self-sufficiency, flashed on large screens. "Sometimes," Pastor Linda McCoy said during her twelve-minute sermon, "it's hard to depend on others. But we all need one another."

Not many churches will—or should—be like The Garden. That church lives out an intentionally specific calling to reach those whom other churches don't, with a natural affinity for baby boomers living in Indianapolis. Your church will not be like The Garden. And that's part of the point. The takeaway from The Garden is that your church must also work hard to develop a missional focus relevant for your particular community. And as your leaders give the work away to the people, highlighting adaptive issues and sharing the responsibility, the missional focus will radiate from a creative community, a transforming church.

The Power of One Multiplied

Imagine a rock dropped in the middle of a pond. The ripples start right where the rock fell into the water, but they inevitably move outward. As The Garden connected with its local culture, partnering in ministry both within the church and community, its own mission expanded.

The Power of One documentary, chronicling the AIDS epidemic in

Africa, was seeded in the heart of Indianapolis—in the mayor's office. When Stan Abell, a part-time pastor at The Garden and a huge U2 fan, found out that U2's lead singer, Bono, was to speak in Indianapolis, he was connected well enough through ministry in the city to get a private audience with the group's leader, singer, and founder of DATA (Debt, AIDS, Trade, Africa).

The meeting made a profound impression on Stan. He was convinced that the church had to be involved, directly and personally. Further, he believed that The Garden could lead other churches in the city into concerted involvement and impact. Stan discussed his vision with Linda McCoy, who decided to devote a service to the catastrophe of AIDS in Africa.

Along with Suzanne Stark, who led the worship design team, they began to put together the broad strokes for the service—clips from an MTV documentary featuring Bono and Chris Tucker, a cut of Bono speaking at Stan's former high school, two U2 songs, a centerpiece work of art, and music from Pink Floyd. Video clips, songs, and a short message worked together in synergy. The service was one of the most powerful in The Garden's history. When Suzanne and Stan came together afterward, their response was the same, spoken in unison: "We've got to get this out. We've got to take it on the road. We've got to get into the schools and into the community."

There was one small problem: The MTV video was copyrighted. They couldn't use it. That's when Stan posed the question, "Why don't we do our own documentary?" It was, he says, a naive suggestion.

That's what Stan told Robin Howard, who was volunteering her writing talents to St. Luke's, The Garden's mother church. Robin had been assigned to do a story on Stan. "I had never met Stan," Robin says, "and I only knew a couple of things—that he was a huge U2 fan and that he was going to Africa for some reason or other." After bonding over spiritual themes in the music of Bono, Red Hot Chili Peppers, and Audioslave, Robin was shocked when the words burst out of her mouth: "I want to go." As it turned out, Stan was in need of a writer and an artist to come on the trip to Africa. For the next few months, Robin had occasional nightmares of a plane crashing and of her failure to make a difference.

Stepping Out

Stepping out is a matter of taking one small step at a time. Although Stan's idea contained an element of naïveté, the distance between Indianapolis and Kenya was not as great as you might first imagine. The expanding outreach of The Garden illustrates critical points about the nature of being missional:

- It builds upon previous concrete steps.
- It is empowered through the development of a culture of trust, calculated risk, managed conflict, and partnerships within the church and community.
- By unleashing passions, it moves people to ever-greater commitments away from self and into service.
- It starts locally and expands outward.

The Power of One didn't happen by accident. The foundational steps for such a project were already in place because of a missional focus within the city of Indianapolis. The Garden had already produced video for services—music trailers, narratives, and short documentaries featuring the work of local charitable organizations. Led by Mike Jensen, a professional videographer who left a CBS news affiliate to start his own business, some significant gifts and passions already were in play. Without such traditional programs as Sunday school or small groups or youth programs to support, The Garden's philosophy was to devote resources to unleash and equip teams of people with specific gifts and passion. A trip to Africa, in that sense, was simply the next logical step—a big step, certainly, but hardly impossible or unimaginable.

The next Sunday, Stan approached Mike about the possibility of going to Africa to film a documentary on the AIDS epidemic. Mike loved the idea; in fact, he was looking for a project just like that. As word got out, others at The Garden expressed an interest in going. First, Mike's assistant, Joleen House, a visual and technical guru who had grown in ministry, asked to be included. Soon there was a long list of gifted people interested in donating their time and talents—a professional photographer, a second videographer, a nurse, a schoolteacher, an artist, and a writer, to name a few of the twelve people who eventually formed the team. It was a creative community within a creative community.

The next step also built upon previous local ministry. The Garden had often worked in partnership with local institutions. Stan began to encourage Indiana University and Moi University School of Medicine in Eldoret, Kenya, to join together to help do something about the epidemic in Kenya. Started in 1990 as a student exchange program between students of Indiana University and Kenyan medical schools, the partnership became focused on AIDS shortly after the pandemic erupted in the mid-1990s. They agreed to begin working together. A challenge to raise $50,000 within the congregations of The Garden and St. Luke's was met with a matching grant.

Still, Stan harbored reservations about sending a team of twelve artists to Africa to film a documentary. At $1,400 a pop, Stan calculated the risk. There might be a difference, he feared, between thinking outside the box and being out of your mind. Although a couple of people stepped forward with large donations, the team ended up raising the majority of support mostly through ten-, twenty-, and fifty-dollar donations. The professional photographer took portraits for twenty dollars apiece. One of the major players in health care in Indianapolis contributed money to purchase video editing equipment. In the end, enough support was raised to buy three Sony ProCams, plane tickets, and all the other necessary equipment.

Into Africa

The business manager of the IU/Kenya partnership agreed to go along on the trip, which was centered on the medical care surrounding the town of

Eldoret, Kenya—about five hours outside of the capital, Nairobi, in the fertile Rift Valley. When they arrived in August 2004, they met with Dr. Joe Manlon, who headed the medical program in Eldoret. After they explained the purpose of their trip—to honestly chronicle the catastrophe through human relationships—they received access to film everywhere: the various clinics, homes, examining rooms, and hospital rooms.

Robin Howard set off on the first day full of apprehension. Knuckles still white from the plane trip, she was tagging along with the film team and the familiar voices were speaking inside of her head: *Who? Little ol' you? A self-taught artist? Making a difference?* It didn't help when the leader of the crew asked her to fetch a meal. As the team gathered for an important meeting with Dr. Manlon, Robin felt overwhelmingly insignificant. But as Joe was speaking, a few of his words caught her attention: "Fighting AIDS means so much more than medicine. These people need an income. Look at all this papyrus." He gestured to their surroundings and continued, "Well, if we had a papermaker we could teach them to make paper and then export it." Robin just happened to know a papermaker. As part of her art training, she herself had learned the craft. "I'm a papermaker," she said to Joe. "I can teach them." And Joe, half-stunned, wondering if she was joking, responded: "Really? Great. Do it!"

For The Garden, the payback exceeded the risk. Even before the documentary aired on PBS, it had more than paid for itself. "Our investment was returned ten times over," Stan said. "And it's an investment that continues to return dividends far beyond anything we could have imagined. We have now received our papers making us a 501(c)(3) nonprofit organization, which means we can show this documentary anywhere we like. But for me, that's not the real power or potential."

For Stan, the real power is in the ever-expanding movement of being missional. "The original mission of The Garden is to share the unconditional love of God with all people," he says. "There is nothing more consistent with that mission than this. In fact, it is the furthering of the mission from our missional focus. Linda helped create a church that does church differently, and my vision is an extension of that—to create missions that do missions differently. You put those two together, and I see a ton of potential. On the plane over to Eldoret, my vision for this project was very limited. I thought we could raise some money for a very worthy cause. But on the plane ride home, my vision really exploded. I thought, *My goodness, look at the power of what this team—and other teams like it—can do. Not just in this place but around the world, around the country, through this powerful medium.* My vision is to be the eyes and ears of mission outreach with The Garden and St. Luke's."

For Linda, for Stan, and for all of those who have participated in the ministry of The Garden, it's just more proof of the unconditional love of God expanding outward through *The Power of One*, multiplied over and over again.

Following a week of preparation, which included harvesting papyrus from water filled with pythons and searching miles for a blender, Robin Howard taught a group of women—many of them widowed, HIV positive, outcasts, and desperate to feed their families—the skill of papermaking. In a journal, she recorded the moment this way:

August 6th, Eldoret

Today the film crew goes off without me, and I teach papermaking at the workshop. Women have come from very far away to learn to make paper with me today. I pray to not muck it up. I speak to them in as much Swahili as I can, and I have an interpreter who helps me. The women get it immediately and knock me out of the way to do it themselves. By the time I leave, there is paper drying everywhere. They elect the oldest woman in the group to speak for them. She tells me they are honored that I came and thank me for teaching them. They have no idea that the honor is forever all mine.

CLOISTER/MISSIONAL SPEED BUMP

Transforming Church Checkup

1. Would the neighbors around your church say, "We're glad this church is here," even if they don't attend?

2. If your church relocated, would anyone in your community care?

3. Are your members actively reaching out to their friends, neighbors, and coworkers?

4. Do your members show genuine concern for those who don't know Christ?

5. Do your outreach efforts generate a personal investment that goes beyond a financial contribution?

If you answered no to any of these questions, your church may have an inward focus that needs urgent attention.

Travel Tips

1. A church will resist change unless it has a compelling external focus that is shared by a large number of members.

2. Redefine your mission statement to target people on the outside.

3. Focus your evangelism and missions efforts largely on your own local community.

4. Help people connect to your outreach efforts.

5. Resist the temptation to be all things to all people.

6. Take time to build relationships with leaders and organizations within your own community.

7. Discover the needs of people in your community.

8. Take time to develop a strategic plan that bridges your church's passions and strengths with the needs of people in your community.

9. Engage a large percentage of your membership in the process of discovering your community and developing your strategic plan.

Reflections

1. In what ways does your church have impact beyond its own walls? Does your answer to this question give you satisfaction or concern?

2. What kinds of creative outreach does your church conduct? Are these efforts aimed at the surrounding community or elsewhere? How much does this push members outside their comfort zones?

3. If your church disappeared tomorrow, what would the impact be on the local community?

4. What is your church's compelling reason for existence?

10

INERTIA/REINVENTION, PART 1

Dead Ends

Therefore, if anyone is in Christ, he is a new creation;
the old has gone, the new has come!
—2 Corinthians 5:17

During the first service in Fairfax Community Church's new facility, Rod Stafford spoke about Joshua, a man who, like himself, was familiar with dead ends.

Despite the fact that thousands of years separated their ministry stories, the parallels were remarkable. Long before Israel finally crossed over to claim the Promised Land, Joshua had stood by the Jordan River, looking and longing. Of the twelve Israelite spies sent to observe the Promised Land, only he and his friend Caleb wanted to cross over and take possession. The Israelites, listening to the majority report, chose to play it safe, over the objections of their leaders. They wanted to go back to Egypt, and as a result, God extended their wanderings in the wilderness by another forty years.

Thirty-nine years before the day Rod preached in the new facility, Fairfax Community had reached a similar dead end. As they were poised to move from their forty-year-old church home, which was literally on a dead-end street, phone calls from lawyers revealed that deed restrictions on their Hunt Road property made it virtually impossible to sell the building. The news was a blow. Their intended moving site was located off a major highway in one of the fastest-growing counties in the United States—a perfect location. But they were lawyers, after all, and the majority agreed that what was, simply was. That was 1966.

The point Rod makes in his sermon on this day: Don't listen to the majority report. That's what it means to play it safe.

Hardly a Laughing Matter

I hadn't said anything funny, at least not intentionally. So why were they chuckling? Gathered with a focus group of twenty-something members from a congregation in Indianapolis, I had simply asked them to react to one of the statements from an abbreviated version of the Transforming Church Index each one of us was holding: "Our church effectively closes down programs or ministries that are no longer effective."

One member turned to me and said, "This church hasn't closed down anything in 150 years from what I can tell!" Chuckles turned to snickers. Smiling, I moved on to the next statement: "Each individual member feels connected to the big picture of what the church is trying to accomplish."

This time, guffaws. Soon each of the members, tracing a finger down the survey, shouted out the statements, one after the other, along with various editorial comments:

"Everyone is motivated by the church's vision for the future"?

"You can't be serious, Kevin. What future?"

"Our church keeps up with the changing needs of our community"?

"This church is like a very well-preserved 1956 Ford Crown Vic. It looks good on the outside and even runs fairly well. But it's not an everyday car you drive in the neighborhood."

Loud laughter and claps, some mine. And finally came the greatest punch line: "Changes are readily embraced by our congregation."

That statement had them in tears.

It's really not a laughing matter. The story of this church is like so many others I have consulted with—a once-flourishing local body that had great impact but is now reduced to irrelevance. Back in the 1950s, the church had 2,000 active members, but now worship attendance hovered around 125.

The focus group's reaction to the statements from the TCIndex didn't surprise me. Nationally, the lowest TCIndex scores are in this cluster of questions, which measures a church's ability to change. When I sit down with church leaders to tell them the poor results, they often scratch their heads and say, "Yeah, why is it that people don't want to change?" And my response is always the same. I tell them I have never heard a person say, "I am unwilling to change."

Then I add that I frequently hear, "Just don't ask me to give up things that are important to me."

Fundamental Laws

A fundamental law from a broken world: Inertia happens. Inertia, Newton's first law of motion, is the tendency of a body at rest to remain at rest or of a body in motion to remain in motion in a straight line unless disturbed by an outside force. On levels far beyond the physical, inertia is at work—even in churches. Love fades. Lust breeds. Enthusiasm builds. Status quo reigns. Athletes grow old. Wars emerge. Leaders grow tired. Momentum builds. Dead traditions take root. Reflected in the fundamental laws of physics, sociology, theology, philosophy, or the living out of a life, we stumble again and again on the same thing: the reality and mystery of inertia. An object at rest tends to stay at rest; an object in motion tends to stay in motion.

People are willing to change, but they do resist change. The nature of the resistance then becomes our teacher. The thing to focus on is not the *state* of the body—whether at motion or at rest—but rather the "outside force" that can overcome the resistance. People resist change due to disproportionate levels of anxiety. Understanding and regulating anxiety are critical to creating the right environment for change. People *resist* change when:

- They feel it is imposed upon them. (They become frightened.)
- They sense too much anxiety or fear. (They become paralyzed.)
- They experience no sense of urgency. (They become complacent.)

Full Sail on the Sea of Change

For the first few years of his ministry, Rod Stafford navigated the sea of change with very few ripples. Leading a church at the cutting edge, he had come to believe, didn't mean you were supposed to bleed. After arriving at Fairfax Community Church in 1986, his first few years of leading change were remarkably absent of any real conflict. So much so, he says, that he began to mix "naïveté with arrogance." He came to believe that the reason so many churches experienced conflict was because the leaders didn't really know how to handle change. The absence of conflict, in fact, was how he measured healthy change. He was a fervent disciple of the win-win proposition.

Rod had reasons for confidence. In his first five years at Fairfax Community Church, the church had more than doubled in size—from fewer than one hundred to over two hundred. He had steered the church through some difficult transitions with very few scars to show for it. He was smooth and fast and efficient, eluding the naysayers. And—best of all—there were no losers. Among the changes:

- moving from a lay-led model to a staff-led model with the hiring of the church's first associate pastor for youth;
- changing the congregation's perspective of the staff's primary purpose—from actually *doing* the ministry to equipping and empowering others to do the ministry;
- launching a contemporary service, which was strategically focused on reaching the next generation of believers;
- inspiring people to see beyond the dead-end sign on the street where they were located and envision a great impact on their community, and even the world.

The strain of two services and the confines of a small traditional building would soon be a thing of the past for Fairfax Community Church. Rod believed 1993 would be a significant mile marker, a critical point when an unlimited future opened up. Without even so much as a carpet burn or a twisted ankle, FCC was poised to shake the world.

From his office on Hunt Road, Rod looked beyond. "I looked past our dead-end street. I looked at the area. In a fast-growing suburb of Washington DC, I viewed ministry as a profound opportunity to penetrate the culture. People reached in this area would make a significant impact. People who live here are very transient, moving every three to four years, going to places all over the world. The impact church has on their lives could impact the whole world. I sensed that immediately."

Objects in Motion

A body in motion tends to remain in motion in a straight line unless disturbed by an outside force.

Here is the idea reframed for the church leader: Success tends to breed resistance to change. Like many pastors on a roll, Rod assumed that real change does not involve pain. A church with momentum—the body in motion—can lose sight of the necessity for change.

In his groundbreaking book *Leading Change,* John Kotter writes, "Too much past success, a lack of visible crises, low performance standards, insufficient feedback from external constituencies, and more all add up to: 'Yes, we have our problems, but they aren't that terrible and I'm doing my job just fine,' or 'Sure we have big problems, and they are all over there.' Without a sense of urgency, people won't give that extra effort that is often essential. They won't make needed sacrifices. Instead they cling to the status quo and resist initiatives."[23]

As a consultant, I have observed that the greatest resistance to change occurs when a church is at its peak—precisely the point when change is needed the most. Charles Handy, a British business writer, frames this reality as the Sigmoid Curve (see following graphic). An organization goes through four basic transitions in its life cycle: development, growth, maturity, and decline. The organization must go through continuing transformational change if it is to survive. The optimum time for a church to change is during the early part of the maturity phase, because it has resources available to launch a new Sigmoid Curve. But the resistance to change—the forward momentum of success—reaches its peak at the same time.

The Sigmoid Curve

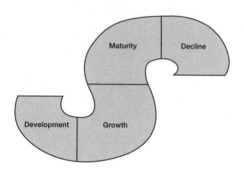

A Split Personality

Rod Stafford first sensed the splitting of the church's personality—the disconnection with its code—when leadership decided to move to two different styles of worship. At the time, Rod was a firm believer in the majority report: They were all for change as long as it happened without conflict. "When I look back on it," says Rod, "the reason we wanted to do the two services in the first place was that it would be the best way to promote change without anyone feeling hurt."

From all outward appearances, the move to two different services was another victory. During the first year of the change, the church experienced its largest jump in attendance—up 24 percent. So far, so good. But something was troubling Rod, something he couldn't quite put his finger on. "The congregation wasn't sensing anything at all. But I experienced something that kept me awake at night." At about the same time, Rod also became concerned about the day-care program at the church. "It seemed to me it was the tail wagging the dog. A disproportionate amount of resources seemed to be going into it."

For a long time, Rod attempted to put a name to his discomfort.

Early on, he had correctly intuited the church's code: building community, reaching the next generation, impacting the culture. On the surface, preserving the traditional service (where community had been built) and the day-care program (representing outreach) seemed congruent with the church's code. But they weren't effective anymore.

Although Rod never could have put it in words then, he intuited the often-paradoxical nature of change: *To preserve the code, you often have to crush former expressions of code that are mutating into mere symbols. Relevance is about rediscovering code and applying it in new ways and forms.* To Rod, it seemed clear that neither the traditional service nor the day-care program was serving the third critical element of the code: reaching the next generation of church members.

But if he replaced the traditional service and slowly phased out the day-care program, Rod understood the inevitable fallout. The majority report could no longer rule.

The Need to Change

The mantra of corporate America is a nice little phrase: "Change or die." It's catchy. "Change or die." It helps consultants earn a living. Everybody nods in agreement when they hear it. "Change or die." Investors rally behind the enthusiasm. So why does the mantra so often fail to inspire true transformation? In my work with businesses and churches, I see well-intentioned change initiatives fail time and again.

- Federal government employees roll their eyes when the new administrator announces the reorganization. "What are they going to call it this time?" ask the cynical employees.
- Middle managers participate in strategic planning sessions but know in their guts that nothing will change.
- Long-term church members know that they were here long before the new pastor, and they will be here long after he's gone.

In our desire to create transforming churches, we start with two interconnected realities: Change is necessary to stay relevant, and change is painful. Again, inertia refers to the tendency of a body at rest to remain at rest or of a body in motion to stay in motion in a straight line unless disturbed by an outside force. And who really wants to be disturbed? At the same time, the church must learn that when it comes to the problem of inertia, the key is regulating resistance—not eliminating it. A church must learn to live out its core values and mission in an ever-changing context. If it doesn't, it dies or falls into irrelevance.

Although some churches insist on "sticking to the tried and true," most church leaders will tell you change is a necessity. But like the younger Rod, they believe they can—and should—navigate change without conflict. From a very early age, churchgoers are often taught that "healthy conflict" is an oxymoron. For Christians committed to love and peace, it seems disagreeable to disagree. After all, Jesus told us to turn the other cheek, to be meek and humble, and to do to others as we would have them do to us. So we come to believe that a healthy ministry environment features little or no conflict. But when a church discourages conflict, it fails to make the kinds of changes necessary for ongoing health and relevance.

By conflict, we're not talking about personalized or politicized confrontations! Rather, healthy conflict is an honest debate—sometimes heated—over competing values. Healthy conflict focuses on how best to accomplish our mission and what is in the best interest of the greater good. It requires kingdom thinking. We often forget how much healthy conflict Jesus encouraged. He constantly challenged the religious elitism of His day. He challenged racism and sexism. He raised adaptive issues with His disciples on a regular basis. Jesus never minimized or avoided conflict.

A Red-Sweatshirt Day

Rod Stafford is not sure, but he believes the meeting with Norma, the church organist, marked the first of his many red-sweatshirt days. He remembers his palms sweating and his mouth so dry he could hardly speak the first words: "Norma, I'm afraid I have bad news."

Norma had served faithfully and joyfully for twenty years. And now her pastor was saying they would no longer be using the organ much.

And the traditional quartets and trios—these were also fading out. And by the way, thanks for all of your wonderful years of service. "I remember looking into the eyes of this incredibly gracious woman who had served the church so well and for so long and seeing the sadness and hurt."

Following the meeting, he drove home and started a new tradition: the red-sweatshirt day. Leave the church after the service. Drive home. Walk upstairs and pull the sweatshirt from the closet. Draw the hood tight. Go back downstairs. Sit, alone, watching TV until the wee hours of the morning.

A conversation with Marvin, former church soloist. Red-sweatshirt day.

A conversation with Lucille, former choir director. Red-sweatshirt day.

Mary, member of a singing ensemble. Yep.

And when a group of former musicians, many of them core members of Fairfax Community, decided to leave together to find another church, the number of consecutive reruns Rod viewed lasted for days.

Painful Realities

Despite the pain, Rod says, the conflict was necessary, even pivotal. "It was a huge transition philosophically," says Rod. "Increasingly it gave me—and the staff—permission to say, 'This is who we are, and this is how we should go about ministry.' If we truly believe it's one big church out there, and we are one little piece of it, then it's okay to say, 'This might float your boat, and then again, it might not.' The church is full of different expressions and flavors of faith, and this may or may not be yours."

In a deeper sense, the realization did not make it any easier for Rod. While he may have given the church permission to change, he personally continued to wrestle with the pain of conflict. The organist, as well as much of her family—extended and musical—ended up leaving the church. Other core people followed. The people who served in the day-care program were also disgruntled with dwindling resources. For the first time since Rod arrived, the church failed to grow.

"It was very difficult for me," Rod explains. "I really cared a lot about how people thought about and viewed me. I don't like to hurt people." The conflicts exposed Rod's red-zone issues. "I'm probably not clinically manic-depressive, but the swings are certainly there. When there are conflicts in the church and people aren't happy, I carry that unhappiness personally and very heavily."

In ways beyond his conscious awareness, Rod Stafford was changing. Like many pastors, Rod has a desire to please the people he leads and to move the ministry forward for the sake of the church. He is caring and highly relational—a really likable guy. But when he is twisted slightly by any self-doubt, the need to please people and be the problem solver becomes an overwhelming focus.

"I have learned that when the church is in conflict, my tendency is to process my way through it. I'm very strategic in my thinking, and I used to feel that if I could dwell on a problem long enough and work through a process from different angles, I could come up with a solution that would fix it. In fact, that's what I thought a good leader did."

He hated the idea of something remaining broken, especially a relationship. Conflict was something that needed to be resolved. And—as a leader and pastor—it was mostly his job to make sure the work was done. Not only did he fear the pain of conflict, he also was appalled by its messiness. With each person who left—many of them dear friends—he was newly horrified by the fact that he had failed to please everyone. The red hooded sweatshirt, pulled tightly around his nose and eyes, was mostly a red flag. The desire to please bordered on a demand to be respected. A desire to care often camouflaged the fear of failure.

"I don't like it when people are unhappy with me," Rod says. "I want people to respond well to me and what the church is doing. No one really *likes* to be criticized. I always thought if I could just get to a certain level of success, everyone would begin to trust and not be unhappy with me. So, I worked that much harder to succeed."

Changing Our Ideas about Change

We need to change our understanding of change. As Fairfax Community lost momentum and attendance began to dwindle, Rod began to buy into a common illusion: *People don't really want to change.* And who could blame him? Faced with painful conflict and disappointed people, who hasn't concluded the same thing? If you are a pastor or church leader, *you* have thought the same thing. Good chance you are thinking it right now.

People fail to change because the environment is not conducive to change. It is either too demanding, too intimidating, or too complacent. In order to promote healthy change, I believe we must first modify our ideas about it. Real transforming change is not …

- Sanitary
- Dictated
- Momentary
- Linear

Not sanitary. As Rod discovered, change is not tidy. Messy, complex, maddening, multidimensional, uncertain, elusive, and often dirty, but never tidy. Real transformation reflects real life in a broken world. It is not for the faint of heart.

Not dictated. Of course, we have all experienced change that is demanded of us. The boss or the spouse or the doctor tells us to do this or else. And most of the time, the job gets done. Like a doctor prescribing medication, change can be dictated for technical problems. But transformation, or adaptive change, can never be dictated. Dictators can rarely instigate adaptive change. Because there is no internal motivation for change—in fact, continual demands breed distrust—a dictator (or control freak) has little chance of stimulating change as a long-term strategy. Many times when pastors get frustrated, they resort to using power to demand change instead of creating an environment where people can find the courage to embrace change.

Not momentary. Great change does not happen at one point in time. This is the great lie of our culture. This pill will take care of this problem. This product will give you this feeling. Reading this book will transform your thinking. The philosophy of consumerism is bent around the idea that, once you reach a certain point, life will finally make sense and things will *work.* Churches fall to the same temptation. "We moved from traditional to contemporary ten years ago, and now we're finished changing."

Not linear. Another misconception about change is that it follows a predictable path. In fact, true change occurs near the edge of chaos, and in unexpected ways. But we all want the "five steps" to building the perfect church, the perfect marriage, or the perfect body. In some ways, this book has been difficult to write because it is about change and change is, by definition, nonlinear. In fact, even putting these chapters in any kind of sequential order is potentially, though unintentionally, misleading. The process of real change is hard to separate into chapters or reduce into steps.

When leaders experience resistance, they know that they are actually exercising leadership. Through this resistance, competing values surface. When the church works together to reorder priorities in the context of the church's code, new levels of health are achieved. To reach this point, leaders must understand the reasons behind the resistance to help people move through it.

Resistance Movements

When leading transformation, anticipate that pain will come prior to the reward. Of course, this is how life works: childbirth before we can hold the newborn; darkness before dawn; discipline before high grades; and the cross before the resurrection. As Rod endured the pain, the red hooded sweatshirt pulled tightly around his eyes and nose, the church eventually reaped the rewards. By doing the difficult, ongoing, and messy work of aligning codes, both on a personal and a collective level, Rod Stafford led healthy change at the church.

Small groups emerged as a new expression of community. Vibrant children's and youth ministries exploded with new growth. Worship services retained older members but were unashamedly in sync with the heartbeat, and the drumbeat, of the next generation. The code was preserved, but the expression of the code had changed dramatically and was much more relevant to the new growth occurring in Fairfax County.

Eventually, a new Sigmoid Curve was in full swing. By focusing the church on its unique identity in the context of a rapidly changing community, the church became more in sync with its own code. New people attracted to the vision replaced the disgruntled who left. And the good-byes, although never easy, became more gracious and celebratory in nature. "When a pastor leaves or feels another call, people are usually good at showing him grace and encouragement," Rod says. "It's not always true when laypeople feel the need to leave. They are often treated as people abandoning the ship or as traitors. I worked very hard to say good-bye gracefully, to thank people for their involvement, and to wish them well at their new church."

By helping the church rediscover its unique code, Rod felt the freedom not only to say what the church should be doing but also what it should *not* be doing. "What we were trying to do is create a place for passionate and authentic worship, where God's Word was taught, where community was taking place, where people were being equipped for ministry and looking outside of the church. I think we began to do those things very well—and they all sprang from an understanding of who we now understood our church to be."

Regulated Emotions

Remember the principle of inertia: *the tendency of a body at rest to remain at rest or of a body in motion to remain in motion in a straight line.* This is a law that cannot be changed. But there is a second part to the law: *unless disturbed by an outside force*. This outside force can truly be something on the outside of a church (changing demographics, zoning issues, political realities) or something orchestrated by effective leaders.

Transforming leaders are focused more on the process of change than on the results. Good leaders regulate energy and stress. If the church is complacent due to maturity or "success," an effective leader will introduce energy and stress to make sure the anxiety is raised to an appropriate level. People learn and grow the most when they are emotional. Emotions that lead to change can include anxiety, thrill, joy, sadness, frustration … or even anger. Effective leaders know how to raise the emotional levels of the congregation to moderate, not disproportionate, levels.

An effective leader may have to orchestrate conflict, introduce competing values, or close down a "good thing" in order to raise the temperature. If the resistance is too great because people fear loss, the leaders will narrow the dialogue to a specific issue so the pace of change is more realistic.

Think about how this flies in the face of what we read in many leadership books or hear at conferences. I have found that effective leaders rarely know what made them effective, but they think they do. They think it was a model that made them effective. Or they think it was a certain set of talents, gifts, or attributes. The danger is that these leaders often write and teach about leadership, and completely miss the boat. Why? Because they don't really understand what made them effective in the first place. And then other pastors read the books and attend the conferences and try to "do what they did" and fail miserably. The answer is not the model. The answer is the process that is often below the radar of these effective leaders—outside their own awareness.

Go to a megachurch conference or read a top-selling church strategy book, and you'll get some good information. But notice the lack of awareness around the process and the overemphasis on the model. The model is the end result of the process, but every process is unique. By definition, a model is difficult to replicate from one place to another.

I have a friend who is a well-known pastor. He spent years developing a discipleship approach at his church. The process began within a nearly dead church. Slowly, over time, he tried different approaches to develop spiritual maturity throughout the congregation. Some things worked well. Others failed miserably. Through the highs and lows, the congregation was eventually transformed into a vibrant, mature community, and the end result became a discipleship "model."

My friend then published the concepts, developed training materials, and set up satellite churches throughout the world. After several years, he is now quite frustrated that the discipleship model isn't generally taking root or working in other settings. What he has failed to recognize is that the process of developing the discipleship model was much more important than the model itself. He is still looking for the answer to his frustration. The answer is really found in the concept of inertia. What is the process by which we create an outside force that will either stop an object in motion or jump-start an object at rest? Leaders function like thermostats, keeping people warm enough to be slightly uncomfortable, but cool enough that they don't leave.

Transformation, then, in a fundamental sense, means conflict. There is no way around it. I like to think of the process of change as a dance. Change follows conflict and conflict follows change. One leads and the other follows, and then they switch roles. It continuously baffles me why so little is written about this dance. You can't have one without the other. Resistance and change go hand in hand.

The Majority Report

No one—not even Rod—questioned the majority report. So deeply was the rumor embedded in church lore, it was simply accepted as fact: Their property on the dead-end street could not be sold. Not perceiving any other options, the leadership decided to move into a rented high school to allow space for the ongoing growth. For Rod, Fairfax High School proved to be the wrong environment for change. And it was an unconscious yet vicious assault on the church's code. The misstep was nearly fatal. Why?

- Despite doubled attendance for that first service at the high school, forty of their own people chose not to make the move—the largest exodus in the church's history.
- In the span of one week, the church had removed itself from its home since 1941 to a sterile, lifeless auditorium where they had to be out by 1:00 p.m. every Sunday.
- Many of the members did not actually attend the service because they had to serve in other ministries for children, youth, or hospitality. Ironically, moving from two services to one created even more separation.
- Casual conversations in the narthex between services were lost, dampening any sense of community and putting too much pressure on small groups as the sole vehicle for fellowship.

The church was paralyzed. Unresolved competing values—building community and having an impact on the surrounding culture—created a stalemate of sorts. And the members were the losers. Because of a situation largely out of Rod's control, the stress was simply too great for church members to endure.

"I was asking people to give up more than they were capable of giving," Rod says. For the next two years, the church, as well as Rod personally, went through some "very dark days." Each week, attendance continued to drop. "When you have 1,200 seats and 200 people attending, what you see are the empty seats. Over time, it's disheartening. It's like the Montreal Expos in their last years, with one fan sitting in Section D and another fan sitting in Section E. It creates an environment where it's hard to cheer. We all began to feel defeated to some degree—I guess the thing that amazes me now is that we didn't feel it more."

To make matters far worse, Rod's staff was riddled with disharmony.

Rod, a highly relational person, was accustomed to a close-knit staff team. But this one eventually fell apart, with two key players leaving within six months of each other. The sense of darkness—of failure at nearly every level—was often overwhelming. "We had set out to fill up this auditorium and make an impact on our new community. And each week somebody roped off another section so people couldn't sit there. Every Sunday, the words *critical mass* took on new meaning."

Curiously, Rod says he received more job offers from other churches during those years than he has before or after—even though he wasn't even considering leaving Fairfax Community Church. "I think to survive emotionally, for a portion of that time, I was in denial of what was happening. I just believed that somehow, some way, if I just worked at it hard enough, I could will it to be different."

Arising

On another dismal Sunday, with another rope hung to partition off another section of auditorium seats, Rod came home to his usual after-church ritual: climb the stairs to his bedroom and pull out—from his growing collection—a red hooded sweatshirt. As he was tightening the drawstrings, one of them snapped. Instead of picking out another, Rod decided he would go out for a drive. On the spur of the moment, he remembered: The family lizard needed to be fed.

11

INERTIA/REINVENTION, PART 2

Transforming Church

See, I am doing a new thing! Now it springs up;
do you not perceive it? I am making a way in the
desert and streams in the wasteland.
—Isaiah 43:19

Silent film star Charlie Chaplin's world was shaken with the 1927 release of *The Jazz Singer*, the first "talking picture." Four years later, slow to grasp the meaning of adding sound to movies, he predicted the "fad" would quickly pass. "I give the talkies six months more," he said in an interview. In 1977, Ken Olsen, the cofounder and CEO of Digital Equipment Corporation, a computer manufacturer, said, "There is no reason for any individual to have a computer in his home." Around the same time, Bill Gates began sharing his vision of a PC in every home by the year 2000. A quick question: When was the last time a silent movie was produced for the masses? If you don't know, you can always Google on your home computer.

My point is this: Our habits of thought can either lead us to get buried in the past or drive us to reinvent ourselves for continuing relevance. "The chains of habit," wrote Samuel Johnson, "are too weak to be felt until they are too strong to be broken." St. Augustine said that "habit, if not resisted, soon becomes necessity." And John Dryden said, "We first make our habits, and then our habits make us."

I wonder: Is it our habit to change?

The Cricket Vision

Leaders of transforming churches persevere in the journey of change. But as Rod Stafford discovered, that is easier said than done. For Fairfax Community Church, the growing majority report, with each passing week, was that the ship was going down. Attendance dwindled, enthusiasm deflated, and Rod, having worn out a string of red hooded sweatshirts, experienced a vision from God. The church would later name it Rod's "cricket vision" because he was buying crickets for his family's pet lizard when God spoke to him. He is not really sure it was a vision. It was more like a few well-chosen words or the seed of an idea. But whatever it was, Rod had no doubt about it: He knew what God wanted him to do.

You have to understand that Rod is, by design, a man who keeps two feet on the ground, two oars in the water, and one eye behind him. His first response to a burning bush would be to call the fire department. So when he understood the clear voice of God, he was more surprised than alarmed. "It was as if God opened up the top of my head and poured in this vision of what we needed to do as a church," Rod says. "And not only that, but the specific steps we needed to take along the way. It all happened in a very short time—probably less than a minute or two. I just kind of went, 'Wow.'"

Rod went home and told Donna, his wife, "I know what we are supposed to do." The next Sunday, speaking in a nearly empty auditorium, he outlined the plan: They were to return to the church on the dead-end street. Rod admitted that he should have been depressed. The Sunday the church returned to the small facility on Hunt Road should have made Waterloo or the Alamo seem like a victory. After two years of meeting at Fairfax High, determined to transform the community, the church was forced to return home—a circular journey marking a sense of failure, wandering, and misdirection. That was the logical read. But the reality was different.

"When we returned, it was the oddest feeling. I won't deny that it was incredibly discouraging and humbling for all of us—we almost literally went back to our old church crawling on our hands and knees. At the same time, many of us experienced a kind of quiet confidence at work. It was sort of unspoken, but the feeling was if we could survive the years we had just been through, then we could survive just about anything. Most pastors don't survive such an ordeal, and if they do, it takes forever to rebuild broken trust. But the thing that was amazing to me is that we trusted each other even more having been through this."

For Rod, the return was paradoxical: humbling and empowering, crippling and freeing, dangerous and energizing, a pathetic return and the start of a bold new journey.

I wonder how many church leaders have developed a similar commitment to continuous change. Are we focused on the future or the past? Do the prophetic voices of our churches sound more like Bill Gates or Charlie Chaplin?

Great Opportunities

In a rapidly changing world, the church possesses great power to help shape the future. As the modern era's emphasis on materialism, reason, and individualism continues to fade, our culture hungers for community, meaning, and the quest for spirituality. The church has much to offer. But can we reinvent ourselves to remain relevant, navigating change with alacrity and agility while clinging firmly to our core principles? Those churches that do not manage change are doomed to be controlled by it—if not destroyed.

The Champion of Mistakes

But we fear change. The possibilities of pain and failure dog us. The majority report recommends we stay with the status quo, the safe and easy paths of adventure, and ignore the dangerous roads of quest.

As a Carolina Tar Heel, I loved watching Michael Jordan play ball. On one occasion, I even shot baskets with him in the university gymnasium. He has always impressed me as a man on a journey. In college, Jordan was good. By the time he won his last championship with the Chicago Bulls in the mid-1990s, he was, in my mind and many others', the greatest ever to play the game. During Jordan's heyday, I picked up a newspaper while I was visiting a client in Chicago. On the cover of the sports page was an interview with Michael Jordan that shocked me.

Instead of talking about his successes, Jordan spoke almost exclusively of his failures: the thousands of shots he had missed, the hundreds of games he had lost, the dozens of times he had had the ball at the end of the game and had come up short, and all the various and sundry other ways he had failed to deliver. Why would an athlete of his caliber speak almost exclusively of his failures? His conclusion was simple: "Those are the things that made me great." You can't change if you never risk failure and pain. But what MJ was implying went deeper than that. It is, in fact, the experience of failure and the crucible of adversity that shape us. Our culture does not honor failure—not even our church culture, where attendance and budget numbers provide a convenient way to keep score in the messy business of life transformation.

Transformation, in this life, never resolves itself. It is ongoing and messy. I love the line in the movie *Parenthood* delivered by Jason Robards to Steve Martin, who plays one of his sons. He says, "With parenting, you never cross the goal line." The same is true of ministry. While it is important to set goals and celebrate their achievement, the fact is that success in ministry cannot be equated with resolution of conflict or finishing transformation. In an unpredictable world, the goal is not fixing conflict, but rather navigating conflict in the process of change.

As Michael Jordan or Rod Stafford can tell you, there is nothing like mistakes to teach you the way to move forward. The experience of failure is an invaluable mentor.

Magnificent Defeats

Rod Stafford came to understand that if he was going to lead transformation, he first had to be transformed.

The journey from 1995 (leaving his church on a dead-end street) to 1997 (returning to his church on a dead-end street) seemed to mark a circular path. Two years of wasted time, effort, and resources. Literally and figuratively, he seemed to be back where he started—down a dead-end street. And Rod was tempted to see it that way. But even before the cricket vision, God was at work. As many times as Rod wondered why "people didn't want to change," God began to show him areas in his own life that were preventing change. These were his personal red-zone issues—his unresolved and unmet needs, his shadow side, his blind spots. As he struggled through the dark years of his ministry, God was at work in deep levels of his mind, heart, and soul.

Rod had the courage to avoid playing the role of hero—a man with all the answers. When the search committee or board hires someone to lead a church, that person is expected to do all the right things: fix the problems, create a vision, and execute a strategy. And for a long time, Rod tried to do all those things. But that is not the job of leadership. A good leader recognizes church as community and calls for a partnership of ministry—calling and equipping others to work together for healthy change. The leader must also recognize his red-zone issues and refuse to allow them to damage his role as a leader. Rod's red-zone issues were twofold and interconnected: First, he wanted to fix all problems, and second, he wanted to please people. He had a difficult time with continuing brokenness. In his mind, he harbored the idea that once he achieved "success," people would like him once and for all.

Once again, failure came to his rescue. The cricket vision, in fact, was preceded by two personal insights. The first came through a conversation he had with another pastor, who led a church of more than ten thousand people. The pastor confessed to Rod, "I always thought that when I achieved a certain level of success, criticism would die down and people would not be so upset with me. But you know what? There hasn't been a day go by when I don't have someone unhappy with me."

That was a revelation to Rod. "It became evident to me that a personal strategy based on trying to please people was ineffective." Rod began to understand that a pastor's role is to care for and empower his people, not be accepted by them. A "need" for acceptance, in fact, often blocked the capability for caring. His relational demeanor often camouflaged his ability to challenge people to discover their purpose.

The second understanding cut deeper. He didn't know what the church should do. He finally had to admit it: He was incapable. The darkest of the dark days at the high school taught him he had no control over many outcomes. "I got to the point where I was processing myself to death and losing a good deal of sleep. Finally, I got to the end of that, and I said, 'I cannot figure this one out.' It took me the longest time to get to the place where I had to admit I could not control how people responded to me or even if issues got resolved. It taught me to let go of things, which of course was very freeing."

Rod's red-zone issues are common for pastors. Church leaders are often men and women of great resolve, gifts, and desire to care for people. They don't understand that their determination to remove stress and pain in fact creates even more stress and pain.

The Release of Ministry

The journey toward becoming a transforming church requires leaders who are willing to undergo their own journey of transformation. As Rod traveled through his own dark days, he was finally able to let go of his need for clean resolution. As a result, Rod was more liberated to lead his people. "During those difficult times, there was something profoundly spiritual happening to me that I only later began to see affected my heart and my leadership. When I began to understand that I could release those things, I grasped we had no reason to be cautious. That's when I stood up and talked about the cricket vision to the congregation and articulated that we were going to be moving back to the old church. Even though it was a humbling time, it was also a realization that we were able to take risks. Both the church and I had already reached the end of the rope."

Encouraged by God to release control during the dark days at the high school, Fairfax actually experienced foundational change at the same time things seemed to be outwardly crumbling. On nearly every critical level of dysfunction, the church was moving toward health. Rod says now, "All of the progress the church has made in the last eight years can be traced back to changes that happened as a result of those very dark years." What were the primary areas that changed?

Community

From the start, Fairfax has always been about connecting people. In many ways, Rod led the church well—developing and encouraging small groups, empowering people in ministry teams, and creating places for relationships to develop. However, because of Rod's desire to "fix" ministry problems and relationships, he was often unwilling (or unable) to risk fully engaging others as partners—fellow leaders. Early on during the high school years, God was wrestling control from Rod. Because he did not have healthy relationships with staff, he worked with laypeople, who eventually became "more like staff than my own staff." He had to learn to let go.

The release of ministry involves trust, and when that happens, the trust is returned. When people trust, they are more likely to embrace the gap between what is and what could be, and work toward the necessary change.

Code

As we have already seen, through guidance from the Holy Spirit, Rod very early on intuited the code of Fairfax—people in connected relationships involved in reaching out to the next generation of believers. Even before he was able to clearly articulate values and mission arising from that code, he was in the process of reinventing the church, which is almost always more about rediscovery than discovery. During the dark years of the high school, while the church was dwindling in numbers, it was also building what Rod refers to as "critical mass." Those people who remained were rediscovering the code of the church in fresh new ways.

Missional

When a church goes through periods of failure, the greatest danger is allowing the failure to turn to disillusionment. Disillusionment leads to cynicism. Cynicism leads to self-centeredness. Self-centeredness then gives birth to more and more failure, and a vicious cycle breeds. The initial reason for Fairfax's move to the high school was its desire for great impact on the culture—perhaps even at the expense of building community. As the impetus of being missional fizzled, the church began to experience disillusionment. As they reopened the doors on the dead-end street on Hunt Road, Rod's primary concern was a return to a "deeper intimacy," both through the facility and their relationships with one another. "Perhaps," he heard people saying, "this was the church we were always meant to be."

Rod took great pains to continue raising the competing value of missional focus to avoid the natural tendency to cloister. Fortunately, Rod had at least two central realities in his favor. First, the people who remained behind were drawn together by the code, which involved building community and reaching out to the next generation. And second, despite his failures—or probably *because* of them—Rod was preparing to make a couple of bold moves in leadership.

Bold Moves: The Vision Emerges

The first thing Rod did after settling back into his church on a dead-end street was to clear the table. "In many respects, the move back to the church was bolder than the move to the high school," Rod says. "We wanted to create a blank slate and remove personal agendas from leadership." A good deal of failure at Fairfax could be traced back to the structure. Decision making was split between a board of trustees and a church council composed of people leading committees and ministries. One group was charged with vision, the other with financing. Both were invested in personal interests and turf protection. The result, more often than not, was a carefully balanced paralysis, a leadership stalemate. Because Rod's view of leadership had changed dramatically—from trying to fix problems and please people to engaging them in the problems and solutions—he sought the best leadership structure to release authority to the people.

Rod's desire was to create *one* advisory board to assist the pastors and staff in creating direction. Essentially, the proposal was designed to allow Rod to lead, so he could more effectively engage and equip the people of the church for ministry. The lessons from the high school years, however, prevented Rod from offering the idea as a "fix." He deeply desired and needed the input of the congregation. Without knowing he was following the 3-D Method—dialogue, discussion, and decision—Rod invited others' input on restructuring how decisions were made. "What we did," Rod says, "was to create a structure that facilitates and encourages change."

A single advisory board was formed, using people who didn't have a personal agenda at the church—people who were free to give advice without protecting self-interest. In doing so, Fairfax created a safe environment to engage, regulate, and pace change. And instead of the leader "fixing" the problem, the people were called to partner in ministry and work toward healthy growth. In a few months, Fairfax Community Church was once again threatening to burst the seams of the small traditional facility down a dead-end street.

During this time, Rod's other "bold move" of leadership was simply to question conventional wisdom. "When I arrived as senior pastor in 1986, the majority report on our property had almost risen to the level of canonized Scripture. So for the next ten years I just accepted it: The property could not be sold. All of the plans we made, all of the vision we communicated was built around the majority report. One day I simply decided to do something really stupid—to take the actual deed to a lawyer to look at. The next day he called me and said, 'You shouldn't have any problems selling the building.' Of course, I knew he must be wrong, so I took the deed to another lawyer, who told me the same thing. It was at that point that I realized the same thing that the Israelites eventually realized—the majority report had been wrong. So we began planning for a different future."

On May 8, 2005—thirty-nine years after the majority report was first received, preventing the church's intended move—Fairfax Community Church dedicated its new facility. Far from a dead-end street, the new location was on a major highway in the heart of the expanding community of Fairfax.

The Focus of Mission

In the four months immediately preceding Fairfax's move into a new facility, the church averaged 617 in weekend worship attendance. One year after moving into the new building, an average of 1,274 participate in weekend worship services. That represents an increase of 106 percent. By the time this book was written, Fairfax was already nearing 80 to 85 percent capacity in each of their two weekend services and had plans to launch a third service in the fall of 2006. But growth numbers aren't the only rising statistics. Participation in small groups has increased by 63 percent, financial giving has increased by 45 percent, and the number of people presently serving in an identifiable ministry position has increased by 34 percent. The church's visibility in the community has increased significantly. More people are inviting their friends to attend. The large lobby and coffee shop encourage people to hang out more before and after the services. Spontaneous community is happening. Numerous new ministries have started.

A healthy church will grow. But contrary to conventional church-growth strategy, that growth will be paced and natural rather than forced. When a church begins to grow rapidly, the greatest task of ministry, almost paradoxically, is to say no. As more people come with a passion for ministry, leadership must focus on staying true to the mission. Again, your code will be your guide. Rod says, "The pressure we face from many new members, especially those who were actively involved in another church before they came to Fairfax, is to start ministries that were a part of their previous church. Almost daily, our staff or ministry leaders receive suggestions concerning new ministries. I tell the staff that one of the most spiritual things we do as leaders is to say no to new ministries that may be good but are not strategic to our mission. We are not trying to become a 'full service' church. We want to remain focused on our primary mission to penetrate this culture with the gospel so that lost people become fully devoted followers of Christ."

Fairfax Community Church continues to change. But unlike the whiplash transitions experienced in its history, the pace of change has been incremental, regulated, and paced. "We really have had no major unexpected changes," Rod says. "Change has been more freely happening but at a slower and more consistent pace. Because the need and process for change have been built into the very fabric of the church, members do not resist it at nearly the same level members at other churches might. This is, in part, due to the fact that Fairfax has kept up with the changing needs of the community and its membership."

For example, worship services look a lot different now than they did ten years ago. But there was no single point in time when worship services changed. Chris Joyner, worship pastor, says, "I've never viewed our worship services as going through one major change. Because the changes are regular and incremental, the congregation seems to adjust well. They are very responsive to changes, without ever feeling overwhelmed by them. For us, change has been more of a journey, rather than a point in time. Change has become part of our code."

The steady and healthy growth of Fairfax Community Church is reflective of Rod's conviction that change is a long-term process that requires an ongoing investment. Change for the sake of change is never a good idea. But in order to stay relevant to an ever-changing context, change must become part of the fabric of how a church functions. This doesn't just include adding new things. Change includes abandoning things that are no longer valuable or relevant.

Peter Drucker, the late management guru, said, "Know the value of planned abandonment." A church must be able to close down programs or ministries that are no longer effective as readily as it empowers new and innovative ministries. When Fairfax moved into its new facility, for example, it did not even pursue a zoning request for a day-care program. That particular form of outreach was inconsistent with the church's code and so was discontinued.

The Ethos of Relationships

Transformation takes time.

"The code—or culture or ethos or whatever you want to call it—of a church all grows out of relationships," Rod says. "That is how kingdom work manifests itself. And that takes a long-term, consistent investment to change. I have come to believe the reason a lot of churches don't change is that they don't give it enough time. One of our friends bought a farm in southern Virginia and turned it into vineyards. And that is exactly what she has come to learn: Good vineyards are at least thirty years in the making. There is no way to shortchange the process. As I look back on this journey at Fairfax Community Church, our culture, our ethos is profoundly different now. And it wouldn't have been that way except for the entire journey."

From the beginning, Fairfax Community has been about connecting people. Rising out of the church's code was a high value of connecting people with God, one another, His Word, and the redemptive and transforming outreach of His love to the world. Rod's work has been to empower people to become partners rather than consumers in the mission of the church. Partnering means not just volunteering to accomplish tasks, or starting another ministry designed to meet only the needs of the faithful, or simply coming and sitting in a pew for a couple of hours every week. Rather, it's partnering in the mission of changed lives.

Once people get in touch with Jesus' paradox—when you lose your life for My sake, you will find it (Matt. 10:39)—church work does not become easier. Rather, it becomes possible. Rod says, "When you give the people the opportunity to be involved in life-changing, passionate work where they can exercise fully what God intended them to be, they really get motivated. It deeply touches the heart and gives them purpose."

The Servant Hero

Sam Gamgee is the least likely hero of *The Lord of the Rings*. We first meet Sam eavesdropping on a conversation between Frodo and Gandalf, the wizard. After being discovered, Sam is pulled through the window by his collar. "Confound it all, Samwise Gamgee," Gandalf snaps as he forcefully places him on a table, "have you been eavesdropping?"

Samwise, terrified and ashamed, sputters: "I haven't been dropping no eaves, sir, honest. I just been cutting the grass under the window there.... Don't hurt me. Don't turn me into anything ... unnatural." Gandalf, ever wise, decides to make better use of Sam. He dispatches him on the journey with Frodo. Sam is perhaps one of the most unlikely candidates for heroism in literary history. Bumbling, speaking with peasant grammar, as low as you can go on the social order, he begins the journey as an unquestioning servant, a tagalong. By nearly any measure, he is not wise or powerful. And, indeed, in many ways Sam fails in his mission—he cannot protect his master from the devastating pull of the Ring, and he often threatens to kill the creature Gollum, the only one who can guide them to their destination.

What saves Sam—indeed transforms him—is his faithfulness. He is unswervingly faithful to his master and to the quest. His servant's heart eventually makes him a hero. In what is perhaps *The Return of the King*'s most powerful scene, Sam carries Frodo up the face of Mount Doom. After crying over his exhausted and spent master, now almost completely under the spell of the Ring, Sam cries out: "Come, Mr. Frodo! I can't carry it [the Ring] for you, but I can carry you." Despite his own exhaustion, having nearly starved himself so that Frodo could eat, Sam carries his master with surprising ease.

What matters is faith—in the goodness of the journey and in one another. Issues of comfort, convenience, personal happiness, or even success become secondary to building a community bound together to serve the greater good.

Because *The Lord of the Rings* was set in a pre-Christian mythology, the connection between the Fellowship's journey and the will of God is rarely explicit. Rather, it is inferred in much the same manner as 1 John 3:14: "We know that we have passed from death to life, because we love our brothers. Anyone who does not love remains in death."

The quickening spirit of servanthood is what binds us together. For the Fellowship, as should be the case for each church, transformation happens in the context of ministry in shared community.

Servant Stories

Fairfax Community Church has hundreds of stories of people connecting in ministry, giving of themselves, and finding a deeper purpose and significance in the context of a transforming community. One story will suffice for now.

In the aftermath of Hurricane Katrina in August 2005, Durwood Anderson was one of twenty-five or more people from Fairfax who traveled to Louisiana to help in relief efforts. Durwood was especially touched by the plight of the Robert Garcia family. Robert, who experienced the loss of his wife prior to Hurricane Katrina, was completely wiped out. Not only were his house and fishing boat destroyed (he fished for a living), so were the homes of his adult children who lived nearby. Durwood was so moved by Robert's situation that he came back and took the initiative to raise funds from friends, family members, and former coworkers to help rebuild Robert's house. Durwood, an active man in his seventies, has traveled back to New Orleans for two personal visits with Robert and his family, and he is committed to maintaining a long-term relationship with them. Durwood has been an ambassador of Christ to Robert, who is not involved in any local church.

A Personal Epilogue

Rod Stafford still faces stress and discouragement. Old challenges are continually replaced by new ones. But here's what is different: Fairfax Community Church is focused on its code and mission, and the challenges no longer threaten to derail ministry.

As a result, Rod donated his red sweatshirts to Goodwill.

INERTIA/REINVENTION SPEED BUMP

Transforming Church Checkup

1. Has your church changed and adapted to the demographics of the community or culture around it?

2. Does your church keep ineffective programs on life support?

3. Is your church out of touch with the changing needs of your community?

4. Do you feel that your church is somehow "stuck"?

Travel Tips

1. Immerse yourself in your culture so you can understand the trends that are occurring.

2. Research changes in your local community.

3. Engage your members in the process of discovering how the world around you is changing.

4. Embrace failures and mistakes. That's the only way to really learn.

5. Make sure that change is introduced at the right pace—not too quickly or too slowly.

6. Assume that most issues are adaptive. That way, you'll avoid the quick fix.

7. Be careful when using the word *change*. That may create unnecessary resistance to the change itself.

8. Build an informal coalition of people to help support the change process.

9. Realize that the process you use to bring about change is more important than the change itself. If the process engages many people, the change will be embraced by many people.

10. Monitor your own urgency. If you are overly anxious, you are not allowing the members to have enough anxiety to change.

11. Embrace conflict and ambiguity. Change only occurs near the edge of chaos.

Reflections

1. Are you focused on the future or the past? What is your church's vision for the future? Could you state it in a few short sentences?

2. What programs has your church shut down that were no longer effective? What programs should you consider shutting down?

3. How comfortable are you with change and "orchestrating conflict"? What are you most afraid of in this process?

12

TRANSFORMING PEOPLE

It was he who gave some to be apostles, some to be prophets, some to be evangelists, and some to be pastors and teachers, to prepare God's people for works of service, so that the body of Christ may be built up until we all reach unity in the faith and in the knowledge of the Son of God and become mature, attaining to the whole measure of the fullness of Christ.
—Ephesians 4:11–13

While our survey asks over one hundred questions, only one really counts: Is God using your church to begin transforming people into His image? In this book, I've used five churches as primary examples of transforming churches: Community Church of Joy, Heritage Church, Tenth Avenue Church, The Garden, and Fairfax Community Church. Each is at a different stage in the journey. Some may fare well in years to come, others may not. Through the stories below, we'll take a look at how these churches answer the one question that really counts.

Kevin Summers

The cocaine lingering in his dream, Kevin Summers flailed his arms out against the darkness surrounding him. Slow-motion images of light and shadow and sound, bleeding together, began to paint for Kevin a clear picture of his future. Unless he kicked his habit, the direction of his life would soon be settled: sickness, jail, or death. His options were running out. As he punched the air—black and cold and heavy—the certainty of his fate weighed upon his chest.

He was still. He felt the silence. Then moving up from the bottom of a ladder, he climbed rung after rung after rung, until he was swallowed by the clouds' gray lining. Exhaustion had set in. He felt too far up to go back down and too far down to have any real hope of ever climbing out. He had the stop-motion feeling of a man walking up on an escalator moving down. This was his life—moving, yet lost in a wet fog of a dream that had somehow escaped him.

In a sudden transition, he found himself above the clouds. He instinctively knew what it would take to survive. Stepping off the ladder, he was not particularly surprised to find the clouds holding his weight. He shrugged his shoulders like a boxer dancing in his warm-up, put his hands on either side of his face, and lifted his head off. Carefully, with his eyes looking up at his amputated body, he guided it to a resting spot.

It took Kevin Summers forever to wake up from that nightmare.

For the longest time, he lived an existence without hope—one that mandated an essential disconnection with himself. Survival demanded as much.

✠

On a gray Los Angeles evening more than a decade ago, Kevin had reached the end. Along with his wife and three small children, he had lost everything—the high style of Los Angeles living, a manager's job, his home, his luxury cars. In the service of his addictive buzz, he had sold their furniture, piece by piece, robbed a convenience store for a pound of bologna, and moved into an efficiency apartment reeking of urine.

The nightmare of his life alerted him: He needed a plan. Without any luck, he had tried to get another job. He had missed joining the army by one question on the entrance exam. No options remaining, Kevin used the rest of their money to board his family onto a bus to Indianapolis, the city of his childhood. They left the cocaine in the apartment with the hope of starting clean. Kevin got a job at the fairgrounds, and his family lived in a warehouse. He managed for a few days, maybe even weeks, but then came a series of sleepless nights. One day after work, he followed his wife to her sister's home and joined them in the forgetful bliss of cocaine. Three days later, money and soul exhausted, his sister-in-law dropped him off under the streetlight of a busy street and told him to take a hike.

That was the lowest point of Kevin's life. He bummed three dollars and a ride to his mom's house. For the longest time, he cried in bed. And then he asked his mom to drive him to the hospital.

Having grown up religious, he cried out, "Lord, if You are there, help me." He checked himself into St. Vincent, a rehabilitation center. For the first time in years, inexplicably, he held out some small hope.

✠

One of the conditions of rehabilitation was to attend church. Next to the hospital, working in partnership with St. Vincent, was a church called The Garden. Kevin didn't mind going. After all, he had called out to the Lord for help. Without the drugs he felt the depth of his void. A chill wind was whistling down into his soul. He was open to anything but the religious echo of his childhood church. He didn't want to hear he had to get his life together before God would give him a second chance.

The Garden was different. The message was simple: *This is your life. What do you want to do with it?* No judgment. No guilt. No church experience required. Choices were presented. During the first service, a sense of peace descended into Kevin's void, giving him hope and persuading him to faith. He felt safe simply to be. He desired to explore the reality of God himself instead of having someone else tell him who He was.

In place of gray and blank nights, he began to dream again. A year into his sobriety, he climbed another ladder into the clouds. This time he kept his head and walked forward in faith. Reconnected to himself, Kevin felt God pulling him out of self. Addictions seemed confining, suddenly small. Only once was he seriously tempted back into drugs—the evening his wife, still into drugs, was shot three times in the back. After telling his three children, ages twelve, ten, and nine, that their mother was dead, he wrestled with the familiar and terrifying longing to be numb. To be half-awake and half-asleep. To be as close to nothing as possible.

His friends at The Garden didn't sugarcoat reality. They encouraged him into faith in the face of his terrible reality. For the first time, his children started coming to church with him.

Love moved Kevin forward. The people of The Garden never encouraged pity. Life is tough, they said, but with God's help, greater possibilities still exist. Faith is the belief that each person can make a difference. We can choose to lessen the pain, to explore the paths of purpose and joy, to connect each person with God and others. Over time, Kevin became a follower of Christ.

Having experienced life beyond hope, he eventually committed himself to extending it to others. Supported by the ministry and model of The Garden, Kevin started his own nonprofit business—Therapy Productions. Run by kids from his own neighborhood, including his own children, the company produces music videos. The Garden supplies lights, equipment, advice, and inspiration. Kevin provides the heart and soul. The void has been filled by the purposeful and mysterious movements of the Holy Spirit.

Evelyn Finley

Evelyn recalls attending Sunday school at the age of five at her grandparents' church. She was eager to know how you get to heaven. The teacher opened her eyes: "You have to believe in Jesus and that He died for us and was raised on the third day and that He is the Messiah, the Son of God."

Right away, because she is naturally given to questions, Evelyn asked what would happen if you didn't believe. The answer, she remembers vividly, was the opposite of heaven. For such a little girl, the response was troubling. Her father, she knew, believed in Jesus. Her mother, however, was Jewish. To her mom, Jesus was certainly not the Messiah, simply a good man. For the longest time Evelyn pondered each parent's ultimate fate and struggled with the answer she had been given in Sunday school.

Her parents handled their religious differences with equanimity. They simply taught their children the fundamentals of both faiths and let them choose. But it wasn't that simple for Evelyn. The choice of accepting Christ became the rejection of a parent. If her mother and father didn't believe in the same fundamentals, what was she to believe in?

During her teenage years, disconnected from any purpose or sense of self-worth, she disrespected not only her parents but also herself. She didn't have a strong sense of morals or values to guide her. At the same time, when it came to the most critical choice a person makes on the planet—what to believe—she felt handcuffed. Throughout college, she researched several different religions. She met with leaders from almost every denomination to discuss their belief system. Shortly before graduating, she began attending a Jewish temple.

In 1998, she decided to take an art history course in Europe, studying ancient religious symbols focused on salvation through Jesus. What she discovered pushed her further away from the idea of a Son of God: little facts like the first known artwork of Jesus was not created until at least two hundred years after His death. She wondered why, if Jesus did all the things in the Gospels, it took so long for them to be depicted in art. On one of her last nights in Europe, after discussing her spiritual journey with a classmate, she was given a cassette tape to listen to. She threw it into her luggage, returned to the States, and drifted further from the Christian faith.

Months later, while packing to move out of her parents' house, she found the tape. For a reason unknown to her, she grabbed her cassette player, set it down in the living room, and played the tape. It was the story of a Jewish man named Lon Solomon who had converted to Christianity. Evelyn resonated with the man's testimony—for its humor, charisma, and the shared wrestling and questioning of nearly everything. For the first time, she did not feel alone. She wasn't the only one who felt lost and clueless about how to make life meaningful.

Shortly afterward, Evelyn began attending McLean Bible Church, where Lon Solomon was senior pastor. As she listened, she began to see that her search had been obstructed by the demand for concrete facts. By looking through the eyes of faith, her heart could see the truth: Jesus completed her Jewish tradition. She did not have to choose one or the other, but the fulfillment of both. Her conversion was the easy part.

On many levels, Evelyn continued to struggle. She started to attend a very large Bible church in northern Virginia that was getting ready to expand but already felt uncomfortably large to Evelyn. Newly married, she and her husband desired to develop meaningful community and find a place where they could contribute. After taking the recommendation of a fellow employee, she decided to try Fairfax Community Church, which was located on a dead-end street named Hunt Road.

She immediately connected with Fairfax. The more contemporary music and the relevant messages of the pastor, Rod Stafford, made her feel at home. But more important, Evelyn felt the church to be a place where everyone was welcome. No judgments were cast at other denominations or religions. Instead, the church was simply a place to explore, discover, and be encouraged. The sense of belonging quickly led to involvement. Evelyn and her husband joined a small group—a safe place to learn and grow and challenge one another into deeper faith. Soon, Evelyn noticed an announcement in the church newsletter about a one-week missions trip to the Dominican Republic. She and her husband went, and it turned out to be one of the best experiences of both of their lives. Traveling with a church team of ten others, ranging in age from eighteen to seventy-three, she reveled in the shared community within such diversity.

Shortly after her arrival, the church down the dead-end street moved to a new facility. During her first visit to the new building, she walked slowly down the halls for children's education, which were creatively designed and decorated. She had a kind of a vision then—of her husband and herself dropping off their own children to hear the good news of the gospel while they listened to a sermon. That was what she had missed so deeply: a family sharing a common faith together.

Barb McCarty

From the time she moved into the high desert terrain surrounding Phoenix, Barb McCarty felt as if she were stuck in a lifeless wilderness. She had left behind a circle of close friends in Milwaukee to take up a new residence with her husband. Slowly, she had also disconnected from any guiding purpose or direction. She began to party with others whose souls were also vacant.

A lost child. Once again, that's the way she began to see herself.

At the age of thirty-eight, seven years after she had moved to Phoenix, she was on her bed, weeping. Her marriage, once vibrant, was filled with distance. For yet another night, she found herself alone and exhausted. For so long, she had carefully attempted to keep each of the threads from unraveling, but on this particular night, her life had come undone, and she possessed neither the energy nor the desire to pick up the pieces. Normally an upbeat person, Barb had fallen into a deep depression. Life seemed empty. The frequent trips to the Midwest to deal with a family illness had drained the family finances. Her father-in-law's slow and painful death from cancer had robbed them of any sense of a lasting life or everlasting love and mocked her own attempts to escape through alcohol. Each morning, without any overriding hope, she felt as if she were looking into a cruel mirror reflecting her own mortality. She knew she had to do something—but what?

She decided to pray. "God, please help. I need some friends who know You."

She had not prayed—a serious prayer, at least—since her childhood. She suspected God was there, but she could not imagine He cared. Growing up Catholic, Barb had once felt close to God. She talked to Him all the time. Before bed each night, she would pray with her dad, who would remind her that God was in charge and would take care of their family.

Then her parents got divorced.

Shortly after her mom remarried, Barb's stepfather was killed in a truck accident.

And Barb grew up feeling continually lost and directionless.

The morning after her wilderness prayer, having recovered at least some small part of a childlike faith, Barb McCarty received a phone call from one of her friends at work. Would she be interested in coming to a Women of Faith conference? Barb understood the call as an answer to prayer. What she heard at the conference surprised her: God loved her. The thought had never really occurred to her. A powerful God, a controlling God, a transcendent God—these were all certainly possibilities. But a loving God? It was not even on her spiritual radar.

Growing up in her church, she constantly questioned: *Why do we do these rituals and follow these rules? What is the significance of religion? What does God have to do with real life?* For Barb, the conference opened her eyes to a new kind of Christianity. She heard Christians speak of a deep desire to know God. Although she did not completely understand what that meant, the experience of worshipping with twenty thousand other women made a deep impact. In her desert, she cried again—this time tears of joy that a life of purpose might not be out of her reach.

Other remarkable answers to prayer followed. Barb's husband met a man who happened to be an alumnus of his college. He had just moved into the area and taken a job at the Community Church of Joy, a large church in the suburbs of Phoenix. A friendship between the families flourished. Soon the McCartys found themselves in a small group.

For the first time in her life, Barb experienced authentic and genuine community. She was learning the differences between faith and religion. Growing up, she had experienced two kinds of "believers": those who attended on Sunday but never let their belief affect the way they lived the rest of the week, and those who walked in robes and talked in a holy (and wholly foreign) language. What she saw at the Community Church of Joy—people focused on loving God and being loved by God—was attractive and, in some sense, intimidating to her at the same time.

Over time, the McCartys became involved in ministry and eventually joined a volunteer team overseeing missions and outreach at CCOJ. They worked with the homeless, supported missionaries, and came alongside an inner-city church. In the loving bond of deep community, Barb experienced several life-transforming moments. Through the real-life understanding of Jesus' paradox—you find your life when you lose it—Barb felt an intensifying sense of what, for so long, had been missing from her life: significance. She now felt as if her life had a purpose.

However, her past haunted her. Against the desperate, childlike hope that people really loved her for who she was, she harbored a dark secret. In the weeks before working to help open an orphanage for the church, she felt God whispering to her in a still, silent voice: *Trust Me.* In her other ear she heard the echo of her father's voice, right before his divorce: *God will take care of you.* She had to choose which God to believe—one of judgment or one of love. Just before the new ministry was launched, Barb gathered around her the community that had moved her out of the wilderness. She confessed her secret.

At the age of twenty, attempting to escape a troubled childhood, she had become pregnant out of wedlock and given birth to a child, whom she gave up to be adopted. As she shared her story, all the lonely and terrible feelings rushed upon her again. It was the first time she had told anyone other than her husband. As she awaited their responses, Barb wondered: Would she feel as lost as a child again?

Her community did not stop with telling Barb how much they loved her. They also assisted her in finding her birth child. A family of believers shared the reconciliation between mother and child. Another life transformed.

Seth and Linda Berl

It wasn't that Seth Berl didn't believe in God. He conceded the reality of a Supreme Being. Raised Jewish, and also having attended church on Easter and Christmas, he never really doubted that there was a greater power directing the universe. For him, the question of faith was much more practical: So what?

Seth always managed to get along okay without God. More than okay. He had the body to become a star athlete. He had the brain to become a doctor. He possessed the charm of one who seldom let life ruffle him. For Seth, life rolled along easily. Church was simply not necessary. He did not know what a transformed life meant. He had never met anyone who achieved one and, personally, possessed no desire to have one. Those few problems he could not overcome with natural ability, he simply chose to ignore. In the journey of life, he paid no particular attention to any one path because he felt most of them would probably do.

And then he and his wife separated. She believed he was, for the most part, checking out of their marriage. She told him sports had become his idol. Passivity was his chosen response, and glossy superficiality was his way to deflect the more difficult realities of life. Her admiration for a man with charm but no real roots had worn off. She desired more of him. At first, Seth responded the way he normally did—by ceding the points and walking away. At the same time, he chafed at the fact that his marriage was failing. Seth wasn't used to failing.

In his duties as a doctor, Seth worked part-time with recovering alcoholics. He had come to understand a fundamental reality: A life-shattering event is a necessary catalyst to lasting change. Seth determined that a separation from his wife would serve as that transition. Possibly for the first time in his life, he acknowledged his need for change. Love required him to be open to the greater possibilities.

A few weeks after getting back together with his wife, Seth took his son, Brian, to a church in Moultrie, Georgia, called Heritage. Brian, invited by friends, had taken a real interest in the church, and Seth had noticed his increasing maturity.

Even someone as uninterested in church as Seth understood Heritage was different. In a small Southern town like Moultrie, churches had bleached white steeples and manicured lawns, and those attending church wore dress ties, pressed pants, and measured, polite smiles. What mattered was the decorum, the right appearance. Heritage met in a corrugated warehouse. Worshippers danced and swayed and lifted their hands. They had drums onstage. Before picking up his son, Seth had a look around. The people he met were genuine, caring, and remarkably transparent. His curiosity led him back.

Soon Seth met Randy Benner, one of the founding elders at Heritage. They hit it off immediately. Instead of giving prepackaged answers, Randy encouraged Seth's inquisitive nature. Seth says the "first fifty times" they met, all he did was ask questions. Randy mostly listened. He did not have all the answers. As the relationship progressed, Seth began to open up about his separation from his wife, Linda. Seth soon understood that Randy loved him and wanted the best for him. That changed everything.

Linda also began to notice changes. She understood what kind of effects Heritage was having on Seth and Brian. Even though she desired to be with her husband at church, she felt comfortable at her old church and hated the idea of leaving. When Linda finally worked up the nerve to talk about the issue with her pastor, she was told gently, "You need to be with your husband."

For Linda, the move was uncomfortable. She had heard the labels placed on people who went to Heritage. They couldn't be expected to march to the traditional church beat. At the same time, however, Linda intuitively understood she and Seth needed more than church as usual. At Heritage she sensed a commitment to authenticity, a slow and painful growth leading to a deeper kind of joy. While she and Seth worked on their marriage, they also each pursued ministry in the context of meaningful community. Over and over they heard the mantra: every member in ministry. As the focus began to move outward, away from self, paradoxically, their joy increased.

Through Heritage, the Berls' lives have changed. The things they both hold dear have altered dramatically. They understand the vitality of prayer, the necessity for honesty and love, and the need for an ongoing commitment to each other. Their marriage is far from perfect, they say, but they can now share feelings and be heard at deep levels. Seth doesn't run as often. Linda doesn't cry as often. They laugh and pray together. They call each other best friends.

✠

After Linda was diagnosed with breast cancer, a loving community prayed over her before the surgery. Holding hands with the friends God had used to help transform his family's life, Seth understood a new reality: *God possesses the ability to transform life.* It is a reality that has sustained him through Linda's recovery.

Chiyomi Takeuchi

In the gap between two worlds, Chiyomi Takeuchi felt trapped. No matter which way she turned, she seemed to run into a wall. One month after moving into a home near Vancouver, British Columbia, she often found herself walking the dark hallways alone, searching for a way out of the pain. Her husband of five years had just moved out. The memories of her baby, who had died so young, haunted her. In every sense, she was an alien—a stranger in her own house and a wanderer in a strange land. She doubted she would ever find a place to call home.

Chiyomi knew she needed to find something to hold on to. Without a sustaining purpose, she knew she could fall a long way. Already, a strange illness—an inflammation caused by an autoimmune response—was taking its toll physically. Emotionally, she was racked with guilt and fear. Spiritually, she sensed bankruptcy. Having been raised a Buddhist, she searched for a temple, but the only one she could find nearby was Chinese. For Chiyomi, it wasn't the religion that mattered as much as the cultural identity. If Japan was home, Buddhism was the fire burning in the hearth. Just after she learned there were no Japanese temples in the area, a friend and coworker—also Japanese—invited her to a gospel music festival. Chiyomi had to ask what a gospel music festival was.

Mostly it was music. And it touched something deep inside her. For a few minutes, a man by the name of Ken Shigematsu gave a short speech. He talked about God and invited everyone to the upcoming Easter service at a church called Tenth Avenue. Chiyomi decided to attend. During the service, Ken spoke about forgiveness. Chiyomi longed for it. During the next few months, Chiyomi returned again and again—sitting in a back pew and slipping out the door, hoping no one would try to put pressure on her to convert to Christianity. She simply wanted to explore, absorb, and contemplate. Eventually she warmed up to the people surrounding her—many of them, like her, representing an ethnic minority yet uncommonly focused together on a common worship. Over time, she became involved in small groups, where she found a safe place to continue to explore the gospel and a warm community of people who began to melt the numb places of her heart. For the first time in her life since leaving Japan, she felt as if she had found a home. When Ken spoke of God, Chiyomi resonated. She felt it was the same God she had been lifting her prayers to.

But Jesus troubled Chiyomi.

Her Japanese heritage made her keep Him at a distance. When she heard that Jesus was the only means of salvation, she hesitated. Accepting this claim would necessitate a betrayal—of her family, her culture, and all that it meant to be Japanese. A conversion to Christianity for Chiyomi would mean the loss of a precious and connecting heritage.

For three years, her faith lived and suffered between two worlds. Her church—and her deepening community—gave her freedom to wrestle. It was their unconditional love, the sharing of lives, that formed a conduit for the Holy Spirit.

Her conversion came unexpectedly. A friend of Chiyomi's was having a difficult time. An ongoing e-mail conversation revealed a series of catastrophes in this friend's life: Her husband left her for another woman; her child was diagnosed with leukemia; her mother passed away; and she herself suffered injuries in an auto accident. In a response to an e-mail labeled "The good thing is, it can't get any worse," Chiyomi struggled for words of comfort. What could she say to her friend—a Christian most of her life—that would help? Suddenly and forcibly, a verse came to her from the gospel of John, which Chiyomi had been studying in a small group.

"I am the true vine, and my Father is the gardener. He cuts off every branch in me that bears no fruit, while every branch that does bear fruit he prunes so that it will be even more fruitful" (John 15:1–2).

She is not sure where the words came from, or if they did her friend any particular good. She is certain, however, that the words rose up powerfully within her own being, and the Spirit resided within her. She says there was a sense of joy she had never experienced before—one that has stayed with her, even during difficult times. She marks the moment as when she came to believe in the person and work of Jesus Christ.

Although Chiyomi says life has a deeper purpose and she has found a place to belong, she still struggles with her health and faith. She still moves between two opposing worlds. It took her two years to decide to be baptized. After settling on a date for a baptism, she backed out. Unsettling dreams of her family and images of betrayal haunted her. Would her new home in Christ and at Tenth Avenue mock her old home—the family ancestry and tradition? Was she willing to pay the cost?

Finally, she had a chance to talk with her father, uncle, and brother about religion. She asked them what religion the family was. They replied, "Buddhist." That was the way they were raised. She confessed, "But I go to church." After a long, silent pause, her father answered, "You are an adult. That is your choice."

In a way, the conversation freed Chiyomi. With her church family surrounding her, she was baptized. But on a deeper level, Chiyomi had hoped her father might protest. That would have given her an easier chance to tell him the difference Jesus had made in her life.

Putting It All Together

Kevin, Evelyn, Barb, Seth and Linda, and Chiyomi all represent lives transformed by faith. And they were transformed because five churches worked diligently to become healthy in order to share the gospel more effectively. They were transformed because, with God's help, each church moved along the continuum:

From consumerism to community. Community Church of Joy looked beyond its apparent success—the numbers, the huge campus, the large staff—and realized it had created a congregation of consumers, not disciples. By focusing on connected community and on people rather than on programs, Community Church of Joy grew healthier, deeper, and more effective at what it wanted to do: transform lives.

From incongruence to code. Heritage Church, out of space in its warehouse and on the verge of an expensive building program, realized something was wrong: Spending so much money on a beautiful new building went against the church's code. By reaffirming its foundational identity—that people are more important than programs or buildings—Heritage Church held on to what made it so unique and effective at reaching out to others.

From autocracy to shared leadership. When Pastor Ken Shigematsu arrived at the declining Tenth Avenue Church, he encountered significant resistance to change. But with careful leadership—by engaging the adaptive issues at a deliberate pace, raising competing values, mobilizing others for ministry, and building rapport—the church became a place that champions social justice and where ministry to the needy is thriving.

From cloister to missional. From the moment of its founding, The Garden's mission has been to share God's love with others. Being missional has allowed this church to reach groups of people in their neighborhood who would likely not attend a more traditional church, and it has also paved the way for compelling wider outreaches such as the AIDS documentary *The Power of One.*

From inertia to reinvention. Fairfax Community Church was stuck in a literal and figurative dead end. But after reevaluating their mission, the congregation came away with a stronger sense of identity and figured out new ways to fulfill the church's unique code. They discovered healthy methods of dealing with change, and as a result, Fairfax Community Church is now a flourishing ministry with a significant impact on its expanding community.

Each of these congregations has learned that becoming a transforming church is not a quick process. They've found that, although dealing with the root problems rather than the symptoms can be difficult and painful, the results are well worth the effort.

✠

Is your church ready for a change? Are there problems that need to be addressed? If you have the courage to face the adaptive issues, the tenacity to deal with inevitable resistance, and the humility to ask for God's help, then be assured: Your church can and will be transformed into the image of Christ—one step at a time.

13

PARTNERING TOGETHER

I thank my God every time I remember you. In all my prayers for all of you, I always pray with joy because of your partnership in the gospel from the first day until now, being confident of this, that he who began a good work in you will carry it on to completion until the day of Christ Jesus.
—Philippians 1:3–6

I am a realist; I know that many who started this book have quit reading before they arrived here. But, you didn't. The fact that you are still reading is a yardstick of your seriousness and intentionality.

But now that you're nearing the end of the book, you might be thinking, *Now what? Where do I go from here?*

You and I have something in common. As the respective author and reader of *Transforming Church*, we both know that this book, by itself, will not produce a transformed or transforming church.

We're both committed to going beyond the book.

So, how can we achieve a true partnership—the kind the apostle Paul addressed with his Philippian readers?

The answer is found where it has always been discovered: in relationship. God has created all of us as incomplete by ourselves. As Paul explained it to his readers in Corinth, the abundance of resources in one supplies the needs of others; in other times, the roles reverse. That reveals an equality of strengths (2 Cor. 8:14), which releases true partnership.

A Kansas sheriff told one of my colleagues a remarkable little story that shines a light on the path ahead—for you and for me.

You Are Not Alone

When the small-town sheriff was first elected, he suddenly realized that, despite his years as a deputy, he really knew very little about being a sheriff. So he asked his two living predecessors and the neighboring county sheriffs about how to acquire the skills and tools necessary for the job. Most told him it was a lonely job and that he should get used to it, and that he should be very suspicious of other agencies.

However, this new sheriff could not accept that attitude. He reached out—and what he learned astonished him. He found that the nearest big-city law enforcement officers were willing and eager to help him. All he had to do was ask and their personnel and resources would show up the next morning in his county. Furthermore, state and federal agencies—FEMA, the Center for Missing and Exploited Children, the Department of Justice, and even the Secret Service—were not only willing to help, but were very generous with computers and other equipment.

He also forged relationships with the American Red Cross, the Salvation Army, and other private sector organizations. Years later, when he was given a crucial role in the aftermath of a tornado in a neighboring county, he asked for a mobile law enforcement center from FEMA. They delivered the high-tech, state-of-the-art command center on-site in a matter of days.

He said that the main thing he learned was, "We are never alone."

Sadly, the entrenched territorialism of the former leaders had kept their own leadership realms isolated and impoverished. Their pride and possessiveness kept great treasures unknown and unlocked.

All it took to unlock them was the humility of asking.

Is it any wonder that this sheriff has run unopposed for the last two elections?

We Want to Help

Many of you are like that sheriff. You want to acquire the proper skills and tools to do the job right—if only you knew where to find them. Let me assure you, the lesson the Kansas sheriff learned applies to you: You are never alone.

God has placed a burden in my heart for churches, pastors, church leaders, and each church's unique mission field. My colleagues at TAG Consulting and I really do care about you, your church, and God's people. We want to help.

Over the past several years we have been developing resources and services that, as you align with where God is already at work, will get you well on your way to transforming your church. Together with our publisher, David C. Cook, we are working to get those necessary resources into your hands and into your church.

Let me describe some of the options that are available to you in your places of service.

Transforming Church Field Guide and DVD

Some things do not become clear or real until we see and hear them delivered by a real, live human. That is the reason I spent hours teaching the material of this book in DVD format. The result is a two-disc, four-hour guide through the transformation process. We like to think of this product as "TAG in a box."

As always happens in live presentations, I go beyond the material and concepts that are captured in this book. You and your team will benefit from those spontaneous insights that happened in the instructional sessions. While part of the DVD summarizes the principles in this book, the real value is the introduction of a process and a series of exercises that will help your leadership team apply the principles in the book.

In addition, we have designed a detailed "Field Guide" in support of the book and the DVD. So, this bundled product of DVD and written guide will take serious leaders deeper into the ideas and stories found in the book. The package is perfect for taking leadership teams through an interactive process of getting the concepts off the page and into action. For more information on the Field Guide and DVD, visit www.transformingchurch.net.

Transforming Church Index

TAG Consulting developed the Transforming Church Index (TCIndex), a sophisticated and comprehensive survey for local churches in North America. It is based on feedback from over 25,000 respondents who answered over 100 questions in over 500 answer choices.

The TCIndex database includes churches of all sizes and of many ethnicities, from all parts of the United States and representing a wide variety of theological perspectives and denominational and nondenominational affiliations.

This survey tool is a veritable listening device that will help you hear the previously unheard sounds rising from your congregation. I've seen hundreds of leaders sit in astonishment when they read the completed survey; for the first time they could hear their congregation.

In the Transforming Church Index process, the survey is administered online (paper is also available) over the course of several weeks and is open to everyone in your congregation. Your congregation's responses are then combined into a single fifty-four-page report. The final report would contain scores for the same fifteen scales and the Composite Score, along with more detailed information about each score, how your congregation compares to a national norm, and how various groups within your congregation differ in their perspectives.

This could be the most important tool to getting you well on the highway through transformation. (Note: The TCIndex is described in chapter 1 of this book.)

Transforming Church Snapshot—A Free, Quick Evaluation of Your Church*

We developed the Transforming Church Snapshot as an "appetizer" for the Transforming Church Index. As such, it gives a quick view of your church's overall health and potential. It was designed for individuals to complete the survey to reveal their church's general strengths and weaknesses and give leaders the tools to consider decisions. Please understand, it does not offer the depth and detail of the TCIndex, but it is a valuable tool for considering and approaching the whole subject and task of change.

The Transforming Church Snapshot measures fifteen significant scales and a Composite Score that provide a view of your church based on the principles in this book. Your responses to the survey are scored on those measures, providing a quick snapshot of your church. As you read your results, keep in mind that your responses are simply your opinion and are not necessarily the same opinion of others in your church. A reliable analysis of your congregation would require your church to participate in the full Transforming Church Index (a survey for the entire congregation). The full Transforming Church Index report also contains information about many survey questions that are not included in your Snapshot report.

To take this survey, go to www.transformingchurch.net and enter this product key: **ncptff6lkl.**

*Normally there is a charge for the Snapshot, but we have made it free to those who have purchased this book.

TAG Consulting Services

And, finally, if you need real, live people to stand with you in the work, we will be there on-site. Think of this service as what FEMA was to the small-town Kansas sheriff. You call and we will deliver the people and the tools you need to guide you on your journey. For more information on this service, go to www.transformingchurch.net.

Transforming Church Association

As a membership organization, the TCA has been designed to provide an environment for transformation. The TCA provides downloadable resources, monthly conference calls, and an annual TC Summit to its members. We see our clients as members of our family. All are committed to networking in a wide reach of partnership with others who have experienced similar dynamics, crises, and great opportunities.

Transforming Church Institute

We designed the Transforming Church Institute as a contemporary reflection of Ephesians 4:12: "to prepare God's people for works of service, so that the body of Christ may be built up." It is more intensive than the TCA. Partners in the Institute may build their own process to regular coaching, on-site consultations from our Transforming Church team, an annual TC Summit, and participate in small peer groups of like-minded pastors. For more information, visit www.transformingchurch.net.

☩

On May 4, 2006, a film crew showed up in my backyard. The show *I Want That! Tech Toys*, which airs on the Home & Garden Television network, was looking for a great backyard to feature outdoor stereo speakers that look like rocks. The episode aired on HGTV on September 6, 2006. After several years of effort, my lawn finally looked pretty good. I will never weed out all of the crabgrass or dandelions, but I can safely say my yard is healthier than it was. Progress is always the goal. I am finally seeing the fruits of my labor.

It takes years to grow a healthy lawn. It can take much longer to grow a healthy church. But when lives are transformed, you will be thankful for every roadblock you overcame, with God's help, on the journey of change.

Just last week I stood at the edge of my backyard, admiring the expanse of lush green grass all around me. But when I looked more closely, I realized that, in spite of all my efforts, the crabgrass had returned. (Fortunately, I saved the HGTV episode showing that I used to have a perfect lawn!) Growing a healthier lawn, like growing a healthier church, is an ongoing process. When problems recur, don't give up—just keep working on the root problems and trust that transformation will come. As for me and my lawn? Oh, well … time for more topdressing and aeration.

AFTERWORD

In a day and age when style so often trumps substance, it is especially refreshing to read a book of true substance—which is why I found the book you are holding so revitalizing. I underlined and underlined; I asterisked and asterisked; I uttered amen and amen. As you probably know from your own experience, forming, building, and leading a church is hard work ... really hard work. Anyone who says otherwise is either deceived or lying. In fact, it's warfare—of the spiritual kind. There are no easy answers or quick solutions. And as for simple formulas or copycat strategies, forget about it.

Complicating the challenge is that formal pastoral education and training includes very little in the way of organizational leadership training. Leading and managing change, for example, involves great understanding and skill—tools that we pastors are generally forced to learn in the school of hard knocks. I know from personal experience that that school carries a high price for the pastor who enrolls.

This helps explain why I find Kevin Ford's book so refreshing and of such substance. In it, he offers godly wisdom forged from real-world experience. It is obvious that he understands the basis of being a good consultant: Ask the right questions. It's also obvious that he possesses a biblically defined perspective as he focuses on quality (health), not quantity (numbers). If you're like me, you heard the "ring of truth" over and over again as you read.

Now the question before you is, What will I do with what I have read? This is the million-dollar question, as Kevin has challenged his reader to undergo honest and reflective evaluation and then face the prospect of change. Perhaps you feel a bit overwhelmed by the very thought of such evaluation, not to mention the implications of potential change. Such a response is understandable. Honest evaluation is never easy, and change can be downright frightening.

Having said that, what options do you have? Ignorance is not really bliss, is it? And which of us went into the ministry because of the comfort and ease of life that it offered? You want fruit—much fruit for the glory of God—right? God does too. So go after it! You never need to fear that which God is in. Stating the obvious: God's desire to see health and abundant fruit in His church far exceeds the same desire of all His children combined.

So let me encourage you to heed the words of James (1:22 NASB), "But prove yourselves doers of the word, and not merely hearers who delude themselves" with regard to *Transforming Church*. Kevin has laid out a much-needed road-map for change. He's asking the right questions and pointing us to God-honoring answers. So I strongly urge you to read this book … again. Take your time and read it as an instruction manual. Assemble your thinking and your practices one step at a time. I believe that by the time you make your way to the book's conclusion for a second time, you will be very pleased by what God has built … in you and through you.

—Don Cousins,
author of *Experiencing LeaderShift* and
coauthor of the curriculum study *Network*

RESEARCH METHODOLOGY FOR THE TRANSFORMING CHURCH INDEX

About the Transforming Church Index

On September 12, 2006, *USA Today* published a cover story about a national survey on religion in America. "Believers just don't see themselves the way the media and politicians—or even their pastors—do, according to the national survey of 1,721 Americans, by far the most comprehensive national religion survey to date. Written and analyzed by sociologists from Baylor University's Institute for Studies of Religion in Waco, Texas, and conducted by Gallup, the survey asked 77 questions with nearly 400 answer choices that burrowed deeply into beliefs."[24]

As a frame of reference, this book was based on a database of more than 7,000 records in the Transforming Church Index with 110 questions and over 600 answer choices. Both the TCIndex and the survey mentioned in *USA Today* are intended to "map the domain," as I'll explain later in this appendix. The TCIndex was designed initially by TAG Consulting, our consulting firm, based on a survey we developed for companies (the Healthy Business Index). That survey was developed in conjunction with a leading management professor from the McDonough School of Business at Georgetown University. The TCIndex is built around 110 questions plus 20 adjectives used to describe the church. The TCIndex is primarily conducted online through TAG Consulting's Web site, but paper surveys are generally made available to people who don't use the Internet. Visit www.transformingchurch.net to review the questions.

TCIndex Participating Congregations

The research for this book is based on data collected through the TCIndex database. Churches generally choose to use the survey for a variety of reasons: to get a snapshot of how healthy they are, to prepare for a building project or a capital campaign, to measure progress over time, to test the waters before making a change, or to help identify the factors that are hindering the church's effectiveness. Initially, data was collected from churches who chose to participate. Some churches paid to participate; others participated under grant funding from several sources. Since we have completed the research project for this book, all churches pay to participate in the TCIndex. The church's results are compared to national norms.

Our database includes churches from a variety of theological perspectives and denominational and nondenominational affiliations. We have churches of all sizes and styles. A variety of ethnicities are represented.

Some quick facts about the database used for this book:

Geographical distribution
- 10 percent of the churches are in the South/Southeast
- 14 percent are from the Mid-Atlantic and New England
- 11 percent are from the Southwest (including Texas)
- 11 percent are from the West Coast
- 54 percent are from the central part of the country

Denominations (or affiliations) represented include
- Advent Christian
- American Baptist
- Anglican Communion
- Assemblies of God
- Bible Church
- Christian and Missionary Alliance
- Christian Reformed Church
- Church of Christ
- Church of God
- Disciples of Christ
- Episcopal Church USA

- Evangelical Lutheran Church in America
- Independent Baptist
- Independent Christian
- Lutheran Church—Missouri Synod
- Nazarene Church
- Presbyterian Church (USA)
- Presbyterian Church in America
- Progressive Baptist
- Reformed Church in America
- Southern Baptist
- United Church of Christ
- United Methodist Church
- Wesleyan Church

We also have a solid representation of nondenominational churches.

The Research Methodology

Our primary research scientist, Mark Brekke, provides the following explanation of our current approach to research:

When the American public considers results of a survey, it most often thinks of "polls" that consist of just a few questions ("items"), asked of a carefully selected sample of people. We are used to hearing the results of political polls, Gallup polls on a variety of issues, and exit polls during elections that report the percent answering a question a certain way (often yes or no, or identifying which candidate they voted for), with a margin of error of, usually, 3 to 4 percent.

While those types of surveys are very useful, they are also very limited. They answer single questions but do not capture either the breadth of context and reasoning of the respondents or the depth of meaning that underlies the respondents' answers. They are also unable to reveal anything about the way people structure their thinking on the issue. That is, typical polls do not capture the "cognitive constructs" (dimensions, compartments, facets, areas of concern, etc.) that often subconsciously underlie the answers.

The ongoing research through the Transforming Church Index is designed to do what the typical poll does not: map a large, complex domain of interest. There are several advantages to this kind of research. The primary one is that past research has shown that, once the domain is mapped, the boundaries and landmarks (the "conceptual structure") remain consistent both for a broad group of people (in this case, congregations across many church bodies) and over a long period of time (often twenty years or more). For example, when Merton Strommen carried out trend analyses on the structure identified in his book *Five Cries of Youth*, he found no change after fifteen years in four of the five constructs, and only slight change in the fifth.[25] This kind of consistency and persistence of structure allows researchers to study trends over long periods of time; make decisions with lasting impact; and develop tools, materials, and curricula that have broad and continuing value.

One key feature of this more expansive and persistent research is the identification of what we call "item clusters." An item cluster is a set of interrelated items in which each item asks a slightly different question having to do with the same topic, issue, or cognitive construct, but asks it from a different angle or in a different way. A good item cluster is one that is internally consistent, which is a measure of reliability. That is, people who give a high rating to one item in a scattered set of perhaps five or six items tend to give a high rating to *all* of the items in the set. Simultaneously, those who give a low rating to one item also tend to give a low rating to the other items of the set.

A second feature of this research is that the item clusters are identified *by the respondents themselves* by the way they answer the full questionnaire, not by the researchers beforehand. Item clusters are developed using the data collected with the questionnaire. The researchers do not presuppose that certain items are related to certain others. True, they developed the questionnaire with questions they think are probably related, but even more, they hoped to include items that covered the entire domain of study. The respondents' answers to the items are analyzed using techniques that identify which items are tightly interrelated. (We will discuss the techniques below.) The analysis is done blind to the content of the items: When interrelated sets of items are identified, they are formed without any attention to the content of the questions. Only the consistency of the respondents' answers is taken into account. After each item set is found, the researchers then look at the content of the items in each set and identify the larger concept that each item set describes. What results are item "clusters," each describing a discrete concept more accurately than any single item can and together providing a map of the field of study.

For example, say that a researcher is interested in people's food preferences. The researcher develops a questionnaire that asks how much a person likes or dislikes different foods. The researcher puts items into the questionnaire regarding virtually every type of food he or she can think of. After surveying a few thousand people, the researcher applies the techniques to search for the structure of food likes and dislikes that underlies people's answers. Many interrelated item sets are identified, but let's examine one that contains brownies, Hershey's bars, Fudgsicles, Cocoa Puffs, and Nesquik. The researcher examines this set and quickly realizes that the concept being described is "preference for chocolate." That is, people who like one type of chocolate-flavored food tend to like others, and vice versa. By using this set of items to measure how much people like chocolate-flavored foods, the researcher gets a much more reliable answer than if only one of the items were used. The researcher also has the advantage of being able to study a smaller, but more thoroughly defined and manageable set of concepts, as opposed to studying each individual item. Finally, since the researcher has identified a conceptual area with each item cluster—in this case, preference for chocolate—he or she can use the information to develop new materials that will meet the needs of a group of people.

Using our example, suppose the researcher found that people tend to like chocolate-flavored foods more than lime-flavored foods. The researcher could then reasonably predict that, all else being equal, a new chocolate dessert would sell better than a new lime dessert.

Item clusters based on the original questionnaire items are often called "first-order" clusters. It is also possible to search for structure among the first-order clusters, using the same process as described above. This, then, yields a "second-order" structure, or "cluster families," that further defines the domain of study.

One way of thinking about all of this is to consider a map of the world. The whole map is the "domain of study." To know more about the domain, one might study individual people as "items." Those people group into cities, or first-order clusters. Finally, the cities group into countries, or second-order cluster families. Now one can begin to make sense of the domain because the map now has delineated areas and landmarks.

When doing this type of research, it is important to understand that though the *structure* is generally stable and persistent over time, the *level* of each conceptual construct in the structure can vary dramatically between groups and over time. In our example above, the degree of liking chocolate-flavored foods might differ significantly between men and women, children and adults, different ethnic groups, or regions of the country. Or it might change in one group over time (if, say, chocolate was found to be a carcinogen). The beauty of highly reliable item clusters is that one can be much more confident that observed differences or changes are real, because a cluster measures the construct more precisely and consistently than does a single item.[26]

We have conducted two scientific studies on the data for this book. The first study represents the primary organization of concepts for this book, conducted by QED Consulting. The second study was conducted by Brekke Associates, Inc., after the manuscript was completed. We were pleased that the five key indicators provided an organizing framework for the final fifteen item clusters that were identified in the second study.

Study #1

In August 2004, we contracted with Don Smith, a statistician from QED Consulting in Arlington, Virginia, for the first study. Don ran the data through a series of statistical analyses, using SPSS (Statistical Package for the Social Sciences), version 12.0. He initially:

1. Ran frequencies of all variables to detect out-of-range values. (None were detected.)
2. Identified unusable data.

The resulting database contained 7,773 records. We then went through the process of data reduction. Don conducted reliability analysis on all scales using computed mean values on each question for each church. Data was then formatted into two separate files, one file with churches as the unit of analysis and one file with questions as the unit of analysis.

Following the data reduction, we conducted a cluster analysis to determine how questions cluster. The cluster algorithm first assigns questions to initial clusters and then iteratively adjusts cluster membership to maximize homogeneity of the clusters (i.e., clusters of items that are most similar to one another and at the same time most different from other items).

The net result was that we initially discovered five clusters that provided the basis for this book. Once cluster membership and cluster centers were determined, the cluster values for each church were analyzed to determine the median. We then compared each church to the cluster medians.

Study #2

Since research is an ongoing process, we will continue to learn more about the data as the database increases. By April 2006, the database had over

15,000 records, and this more robust database demanded a more scientifically rigorous study. We developed a strategic partnership with Brekke Associates, Inc., for the purposes of continued research in the Transforming Church Index. The following is a summary of the second Transforming Church Index study, the first conducted by Brekke Associates, Inc.

Identification of item clusters. First-order item clusters were identified from the TCIndex CI using a process developed originally for *A Study of Generations,*[27] used on several large subsequent studies including *Ministry in America,*[28] *Youth Ministry That Transforms,*[29] and *The Study of Exemplary Congregations in Youth Ministry.*[30] The process has been automated and refined by Brekke Associates, Inc., over the past twenty years. The method, as applied to this study, was as follows:

Three mathematical methods—each blind to content, not informed by any preconceived categories, and designed to identify distinct, interrelated sets of items—were used to analyze the survey items:

- Principal component (factor) analysis, with varimax rotation (using PROC FACTOR in SAS, version 9).[31]
- Principal factor analysis, with varimax rotation (using PROC FACTOR in SAS, version 9).
- Homogeneous keying (using software developed by Brekke Associates, Inc., based upon the work of Loevinger, et al.).[32]

All nondemographic items were entered simultaneously into analysis by each of the three methods. In addition, each of the three analyses was run on three TCIndex datasets:

- The full file of TCIndex respondents ($n = 13,588$), with mainline denominations and nonmainline denominations given equal weight.
- Small congregations (TCIndex $n <= 60$), with each congregation given equal weight.

- Large congregations (TCIndex I $n > 60$), with each congregation given equal weight.

The combination of three methods and three datasets yielded nine analyses. The results of the nine analyses were compared using software written by Brekke Associates, Inc. The software identified item sets that met the following criteria:

- At least three items.
- For each item, the factor load for each method is the highest factor load found for the item, or if not the highest load, it is either 0.35 or greater or it is 0.30 or greater and within 0.1 of the highest load.
- One method's factor load could be less than the highest load for any given item.
- For at least one item in the set, the factor load for each of the three methods is the highest factor load found for the item.

Item sets containing a large number of items (approximately fifteen or more) were analyzed again to see if item subsets existed within the set.

For each item set meeting these criteria, the software created a table that included the internal consistency reliability of the set (Cronbach's alpha) and, for each item, the exact text, the factor load by each method, item to total correlation, reliability with item removed, and a list of other identified item sets that include the item. Each set was then examined by the research director, who identified the item sets with the strongest combination of high factor loads; high reliability; and meaningful, identifiable content. By examining the content of all the items in the resulting "cluster," the research director identified the concept that served to "skewer" the set, and gave the cluster a short description. The research director also evaluated the fit of "borderline items" (items with relatively low factor loads) to the rest of the cluster; generally, such items were discarded. Items that fell into multiple item sets were retained in a single cluster only if they contributed substantially to the cluster's reliability and if the item content was conceptually consistent with the overall cluster content. An item could finally be used in only one cluster, resulting in "discrete" clusters. This process of analyzing the survey items yielded fifteen discrete first-order item clusters having to do with church health (see below).

Computation of cluster scores. For each respondent, a score for each cluster was assigned by computing the mean of the respondent's answers to the cluster items. The respondent must have answered at least two-thirds of the cluster's items to be given a valid score. If not, the score was set to a missing value that excluded the score, but not the respondent, from statistical analyses.

Identification of second-order cluster families. The first-order discrete cluster scores were analyzed to determine whether a second-order structure existed. The same process was used as for the identification of first-order clusters, this time treating the first-order cluster scores as if they were items. The analysis indicated that there is not a second-order structure; i.e., all of the first-order clusters were determined to belong to a single second-order cluster.

Based on Brekke's research, we found that all but one of the first-order item clusters aligned with our five key indicators. Below, I have organized the various clusters around the five key indicators. I have included the actual questions for the survey so you can see how the data relates to each indicator. In some cases, respondents are asked to indicate which of certain adjectives describe their church; relevant adjectives are included in the lists below.

Key Indicator #1: Consumerism/Community

A healthy community is one in which people experience casual relationships, deep relationships, and feel personally connected to the church's purpose. These scales help identify whether people are "consumers" or "partners in ministry." They help to identify whether the church has a strong sense of social connections or fellowship. They also identify whether a church fosters caring relationships, which go deeper than the more casual relationships associated with social connections.

1. Personal Connection to Church's Purpose

I count around here.

I am cooperative around here.

I am taken seriously around here.

I am important around here.

I am trusted around here.

There is faith in me around here.

I can make a difference around here.

I am valuable around here.

I am helpful around here.

I am efficient around here.

I have a clearly defined role in the church.

I have a clear understanding of my role in fulfilling the church's mission.

My actions influence the church.

2. Social Connections

Adjectives chosen included:

Fellowship

Relational

Friendly

Close-knit

Warm

Family

Loving

Our church enjoys a healthy sense of fellowship and community.

3. Caring Relationships

I feel cared for by a leader within this church.

This church addresses the practical needs of its members.

If I need counseling or advice, I know whom to go to in the church.

The church cares as much about its members as it does about its programs.

When one person is hurting around here, we effectively minister to that person.

Key Indicator #2: Incongruence/Code

A church's code is its identity, or personality. While the survey doesn't tell us what the church's code is, it does tell us whether or not people have a deep personal connection to what the church is all about. These scales measure respondents' general sense of excitement and enthusiasm about the church, the unique focus of the church, their personal growth through the church, and whether or not they think the church is meeting the needs of its members.

1. Excitement about the Church

   I believe our church is heading in the right direction.

   I am excited about where our church is headed in the next few years.

   I love telling my friends about my church.

   I am satisfied with our church's worship services.

   Overall, I am satisfied with the way that the leadership of this church is performing its job.

2. Unique Focus

   This church has a clearly defined vision of the future.

   This church has clearly differentiated itself from other churches in effective ways.

   Our church has a clearly defined group(s) of people that we are trying to reach and serve.

3. Personal Growth

   This church has helped me grow spiritually.

   This church has helped me be more effective in my everyday life.

   As a result of attending this church, I feel more prepared to minister to others than I would have otherwise.

This church stressed the importance of personal growth and spiritual maturity.

Key Indicator #3: Autocracy/Shared Leadership

Leadership is too narrowly defined in many circles. In our research, leadership that mobilizes people for ministry is a combination of several factors. Effective leaders raise important and difficult issues with the people. Various points of view are respected and people are free to speak their minds. Members need to trust that leaders have the best interest of the church in mind. They need to know that the church's resources are effectively managed. And they need a sense that the church has clear objectives that are well communicated and executed.

1. Raising Issues

    When unpopular changes occur, people who disagree are still cared for in this church.

    All members are encouraged to discuss their opinions about change.

    When people decide to leave the church, they are cared for in the process.

    Everyone is free to speak his or her mind here.

    Great efforts are made to understand various points of view.

    In most conversations in this church, people are treated with respect.

    Difficult issues or subjects are addressed in helpful ways.

    Conflicts are handled well by leadership.

2. Trust in Leadership

    Messages from the leadership of this church can be taken at face value.

    Our leaders practice what they expect others to do.

    When our leaders tell us where we are heading, I can confidently trust in what they have said.

    In my church involvement, I know that I can count on full support from the leaders.

The leaders of the church have the best interest of the church in mind at all times.

3. Financial Leadership

Our church effectively manages its financial resources.

Our leaders publicly discuss financial issues about the right amount of time (not too much, not too little).

I am aware of our church's financial condition.

Our church discusses financial issues in an appropriate manner.

4. Effective Management

Our church takes time to celebrate achievements and accomplishments.

Our pastors and leaders do an excellent job of communicating expectations to members.

The church promotes a healthy balance between work, home, and church responsibilities.

Lines of authority and responsibility are clear in this church.

Our church effectively meets goals (deadlines, results, and budgets).

New information is effectively communicated to a large number of church members.

This church makes effective use of various communication methods (bulletins, newsletters, telephone, e-mail).

Our leaders effectively establish the church's direction, purpose, and objectives.

Our leaders effectively mentor other people in leadership roles.

Our committees or task forces effectively contribute to the overall success of this church.

Key Indicator #4: Cloister/Missional

Being missional starts with a clear sense of vision: We know who we are trying to reach. But being missional is also measured by a church's sense of contribution to its local community. The impact on the local community is first perceived at the level of programming. Do we meet the needs of various people groups? Then it moves to broader questions of how the church relates to the local community. Do we keep up with the changes in our community? Are we a good citizen? Does the local community know what we do? These questions are critical in determining a church's effectiveness in proclaiming and demonstrating the gospel in their unique context.

1. Meets Needs

This church effectively meets the needs of children.

This church effectively meets the needs of its teenage youth.

Our church effectively meets the needs of its single adults.

This church effectively meets the needs of its families.

This church effectively meets the needs of senior citizens.

I am satisfied with the church's programs and services outside of our regular worship service.

2. Local Impact

Adjective chosen included:

Outreaching

Our ministries and programs reflect the felt needs of our community.

Our church keeps up with the changing needs of our community.

Our church's programs and ministries are effectively promoted in our community.

Our local community (or neighborhood) knows what our church stands for.

Our church strives to make a difference in people's lives outside of our own church.

If our church were to close down, our contribution to the community would be sorely missed.

Our church has a reputation as a "good citizen" in our community.

I have been encouraged by this church to reach out to my neighbors.

Our church is as interested in "making a difference" in our community as we are in growing our own membership.

We set the standard for other churches to follow when it comes to community involvement.

Key Indicator #5: Inertia/Reinvention

A church must be able to reinvent itself. Change is inevitable, and how a church handles change is critical. The first cluster below overlaps, to some extent, with leadership clusters. How leadership handles the communication process is critical in managing change effectively.

The other clusters examine whether or not the church embraces change and how innovative the church is in its approach to ministry.

1. Communication about Change

    When concerns are voiced to leadership, those concerns are taken seriously.

    When big decisions are made, many people are included in the decision-making process.

    Our leaders accept constructive feedback.

    Leaders keep me informed about new things that concern me at the church.

2. Embracing Change

    This church retains its members.

    Our church effectively closes down programs or ministries that are no longer effective.

    Changes are readily embraced by our congregation.

    Visitors quickly experience what our church is all about.

    Each individual member feels connected to the big picture of what the church is trying to accomplish.

    Everyone is motivated by the church's vision for the future.

3. Innovation and Creativity

    Adjectives chosen included:

    Creative

    Cutting-edge

    Innovative

    Contemporary

    Upbeat

Refining the Data

Research is an ongoing and iterative process. As long as our database expands, our research will continue. TAG Consulting plans to research additional questions and topics in the future. As the landscape of the American church continues to evolve, our research results may change as well. The research for this book is an accurate snapshot of the American church early in the twenty-first century. Because of the close correlation to biblical principles of ecclesiology, we feel confident that the principles in this book are, to some extent, universally applicable. Any changes or differences in the future will most likely be contextually driven.

To God be the glory!

NOTES

1. Heifetz and Linsky presented these ideas at the TAG Consulting Roundtable 2004 and 2005, where they were the featured speakers. Their principles are also outlined in their book *Leadership on the Line* (Boston: Harvard Business School, 2002) and Heifetz's book *Leadership Without Easy Answers* (Cambridge, MA: Belknap, 1998).

2. The Lord of the Rings trilogy: *The Fellowship of the Ring, The Two Towers, The Return of the King*, DVDs, directed by Peter Jackson, novels by J. R. R. Tolkien (2001–2003; Los Angeles: New Line, 2004).

3. Geoffrey Colvin, "'Co-Creation' Is Your Latest Invention," *Washington Post*, http://washingtonpost. com, May 6, 2008, D03 (accessed August 22, 2007).

4. The Barna Research Group, "Awareness of Spiritual Gifts Is Changing," The Barna Update, February 5, 2001.

5. "Polls from 2003," BuildingChurchLeaders.com, www.christianitytoday.com/bcl/features/pol-larchive.html (accessed August 22, 2007).

6. "The Good to Great Pastor: An Interview with Jim Collins," *Leadership* (Spring 2006): 48.

7. As I was analyzing the research from the Transforming Church Index, I struggled to find the best term to describe what we were discovering. Evangelistic? Evangelical? Missionary? Mission-oriented? Outreaching? All of those terms, however, mean too many different things to various Christians. I arrived on "outward focused." Then people read the manuscript. They all said, "Boring!" In the postmodern world, the choice of words is absolutely critical because one word can mean so many different things to so many different people.

   Toward the end of working on this book, I began consulting with an organization called Presbyterians for Renewal. They hired me to help them clarify their focus and purpose. The word *missional* kept popping up in our discussions. I interviewed Darrell Guder, a professor from Princeton, as part of the process. He evidently coined the term, which the Presbyterians for Renewal adopted as part of their mission statement. It resonated with me because it says that a church doesn't just do evangelism, missions, or outreach. A church should *be* missional. It's a state of being rather than simply an activity. Our research was much more about the church's state of being than it was about the church's activities. So, *missional* was the word.

   The Lausanne Conference on World Evangelization (2004), which my father used to chair, defines missional this way: "those communities of Christ-followers who see the church as the people of God who are sent on a mission." In his article "The Missional Church," Jim Thomas says, "This word implies at least two theological and ecclesiological course corrections. On the one hand, *missional* hints at moving from church as a 'club' for Christians, to church as Christ's body, sent by God to reconcile the world to Himself. On the other hand, *missional* means moving from missions as an activity in which a few Christians are sent to foreign countries to convert unbelievers, to *mission* as God's most basic purpose, intended for all believers." (See www.urbana.org/_articles. cfm?RecordId=993.)

8. See www.christianitytoday.com/bcl/features/polls.html (accessed August 22, 2007).

9. Heifetz, *Leadership Without Easy Answers.*

10. Neil Postman, *Amusing Ourselves to Death* (New York: Penguin, 1985), 3.

11. Robert Putnam, *Bowling Alone* (New York: Simon & Schuster, 2000).

12. J. R. R. Tolkien, *The Fellowship of the Ring* (Norwalk, CT: Easton Press, 1954), 64.

13. Quoted in G. Jeffrey MacDonald, "The Message: God Is Cool," *USA Today,* August 22, 2005, D4.

14. PBS, "Interview: Clotaire Rapaille," *Frontline,* see www.pbs.org/wgbh/pages/frontline/shows/per-suaders/interviews/rapaille.html.

15. G. Clotaire Rapaille, *7 Secrets of Marketing in a Multi-Cultural World* (Provo, UT: Executive Excellence, 2004), 97.

16. Heifetz, *Leadership Without Easy Answers* and Heifetz and Linsky, *Leadership on the Line.*

17. William C. Taylor, "The Leader of the Future," an interview with Ronald Heifetz, *Fast Company* (June 1999), 130.

18. Ibid.

19. Ibid.

20. Heifetz, *Leadership Without Easy Answers.*

21. Ibid.

22. *American Heritage Dictionary,* 4th ed., s.v. "Cloister."

23. John P. Kotter, *Leading Change* (Boston: Harvard Business School, 1996), 5.

24. Cathy Lynn Grossman, "View of God Can Reveal Your Values and Politics," *USA Today,* September 12, 2006.

25. Merton P. Strommen, *Five Cries of Youth* (New York: Harper & Row, 1974).

26. M. J. Brekke and M. L. Brekke, "How the Study Was Conducted," in *Youth Ministry That Transforms: A Comprehensive Analysis of the Hopes, Frustrations, and Effectiveness of Today's Youth Workers,* ed., M. P. Strommen, K. Jones, and D. Rahn (Grand Rapids, MI: Zondervan, 2001), 341–60.

27. M. P. Strommen, *A Study of Generations: Report of a Two-Year Study of 5,000 Lutherans between the Ages of 15–65, Their Beliefs, Values, Attitudes, and Behavior* (Minneapolis: Augsburg, 1972).

28. D. S. Schuller, M. P. Strommen, M. Brekke, Association of Theological Schools in the United States and Canada, Search Institute, *Ministry in America: A Report and Analysis, Based on an In-depth Survey of Forty-seven Denominations in the United States and Canada, with Interpretation by 18 Experts* (San Francisco: Harper & Row, 1980).

29. M. P. Strommen, K. E. Jones, D. Rahn, *Youth Ministry That Transforms: A Comprehensive Analysis of the Hopes, Frustrations, and Effectiveness of Today's Youth Workers.*

30. Luther Seminary, *The Study of Exemplary Congregations in Youth Ministry,* available at www.exemplarym.com.

31. SAS, version 9.1 (Cary, NC: SAS Institute Inc., 2002–2003).

32. J. A. Loevinger, et al., "A Systematic Approach to the Construction and Evaluation of Tests of

Ability," *Psychological Monograph* 61, no. 4 (1947): iii–49; J. Loevinger, "The Technique of Homogeneous Tests Compared with Some Aspects of Scale Analysis and Factor Analysis," *Psychological Bulletin* 45 (1948): 507–529; and P. DuBois, J. Loevinger, and G. Gleser, *The Construction of Homogeneous Keys for a Biographical Inventory* (San Antonio: U.S.A.F. Human Resources Center, Lackland Air Force Base, 1952).

ABOUT THE AUTHOR

Kevin Ford is the chief visionary officer and managing partner of TAG Consulting. Kevin's expertise includes strategic planning, organizational development, market research, and leadership development. Kevin has facilitated the development of more than four hundred strategic plans throughout North America. He was the senior consultant for the redesign of the U.S. Army staff—the largest employer in the nation. He works with large organizations such as the Federal Aviation Administration and the Salvation Army, as well as small businesses, churches, and nonprofits. As a researcher, Kevin has provided tools, surveys, and software systems that are in use throughout North America.

Kevin has been quoted extensively in the press and has appeared on dozens of business-related television and radio programs. Interviews and quotes have included the *Los Angeles Times, Entrepreneur, Management Review, Employment Review, BusinessWeek, Financial Services Marketing, Wall Street Journal, Human Resource Executive,* and *HR Today.* Kevin earned a bachelor's degree from the University of North Carolina and his master's of divinity from Regent College in Vancouver, British Columbia.

Kevin has spoken publicly to thousands of people around the world and is in constant demand as a facilitator and speaker for various corporations and organizations. He has led CEO roundtables with Jim Collins, Ron Heifetz, and Margaret Wheatley, and was a speaker at the 2002 YPO Aspen gathering with Southwest Airlines executive chairman Herb Kelleher, *Time* editor-in-chief John Huey, and former United Airlines CEO Jerry Greenwald. Kevin was one of ten featured speakers at the 2002 Organizational Development Summit with Peter Senge and Phil Harkins.

In addition to his business experience, Kevin has a background in full-time Christian work. He has worked in local church settings and in parachurch organizations. His father is Leighton Ford, and his uncle is Billy

Graham. Kevin and his wife, Caroline, live in northern Virginia with their daughters, Anabel and Leighton.

ABOUT TAG CONSULTING

TAG Consulting does work with five distinct organizations. In our work with credit unions, businesses, government, nonprofit organizations, and churches, we specialize in strategic planning, leadership development, conflict resolution, marketing, and organizational development. TAG Consulting also conducts employee surveys and reviews, as well as leadership coaching. For more information about TAG Consulting corporate services, please visit www.tagconsulting.org. For church consulting information, please visit www.transformingchurch.net.

WANT MORE?

Log on to www.transformingchurch.net
for more resources.

And for your free church evaluation tool, the Transforming
Church Snapshot, visit the Transforming Church Web site
and enter the product key **ncptff6lkl**.